Suzy Gershman's

BORN TO SHOP

LONDON

*The Ultimate Guide for
People Who Love to Shop*

13th Edition

Wiley Publishing, Inc.

For Meredith & Elizabeth, with big hugs and kisses—
Love, Mom

Published by:

Wiley Publishing, Inc.
111 River St.
Hoboken, NJ 07030-5774

ISBN 978-0-470-14665-1
Editor: Jennifer Polland
Production Editor: Katie Robinson
Cartographer: Guy Ruggiero
Photo Editor: Richard Fox
Production by Wiley Indianapolis Composition Services

This revision reported by Sarah Lahey; written by Suzy Gershman and Sarah Lahey.

For information on our other products and services or to obtain technical support, please contact our Customer Care Department within the U.S. at 800/762-2974, outside the U.S. at 317/572-3993 or fax 317/572-4002.

Wiley also publishes its books in a variety of electronic formats. Some content that appears in print may not be available in electronic formats.

Manufactured in the United States of America

5 4 3 2 1

CONTENTS

MAP LIST

ABOUT THE AUTHORS

Suzy Gershman is a journalist, author, and global shopping goddess who has worked in the fashion and fiber industry for more than 25 years. Her essays on retailing have been used by the Harvard School of Business; her reportage on travel and retail has appeared in *Travel + Leisure, Travel Holiday, Travel Weekly,* and most of the major women's magazines. The *Born to Shop* series, now over 25 years old, is translated into eight languages.

Suzy's *Where to Buy the Best of Everything: The Outspoken Guide for World Travelers and Online Shoppers,* a guide to the best brands, stores and shopping destinations worldwide, will be published in March 2008.

Gershman is also the author of *C'est La Vie* (Viking and Penguin Paperback), the story of her first year as a widow living in Paris. She divides her time between her homes in San Antonio, San Diego, Provence, and the airport.

Suzy also leads shop and spa tours; contact borntoshoptours@yahoo.com for details or go to www.suzygershman.com.

Sarah Lahey is the Editorial Director of the *Born to Shop* series. She spends several weeks each year buying antiques and collectibles in London and nearby U.K. villages. Sarah lives in Tiburon, California with her husband, Tom when not traveling for *Born to Shop.*

TO START WITH

This is a totally different edition of *Born to Shop* and one in which for the first time in many, many years, I've had help—a lot of help. Sarah Lahey, the Born to Shop Editorial Director, did a lot of the travel to the U.K. and the research and reporting for this book. I joined her for some trips but she did all the dirty work on her own. For me, London is fun for a few days, but the prices make me nuts.

Both Sarah and I wanted this revision to have as much survival information as possible. We've taken out some of the fanciest hotels and added some less expensive hotels. We've done a lot of reporting on bus fares and shopping at Superdrug.

There's no place like London, and if you can afford to go, it's always time to go to London, if only for a few days. You may even get to the point where the prices don't bother you too much, as you just figure this is a one-off opportunity and you'll cut back elsewhere. Tomorrow is another day . . . and all that.

I have also added opinions from my young staff. Two twentysomethings, one American and one British (for the insider's view), have contributed to this edition. I thank them for including stores I didn't know of or that didn't interest me, and hope they provide another layer of context for you.

Thanks also to turbo-shopper Alison Wheatley at The Athenaeum, Roy Simes at the Hilton Green Park, Tim Marsden, Jennifer Lloyd, Scott Donnelly, the team at the Langham, and all the old friends of mine from Hong Kong who have relocated to London and strive to help you beat the shopping blues.

If you want to shop London and the area with Sarah and me, please join us on a Born to Shop London tour, which usually takes place in the early spring. Write to us at borntoshoptours@yahoo.com, or check my website, www.suzygershman.com, for details.

STICKER SHOCK

Despite the ever shrinking dollar, there are *still* plenty of great buys in London. Sarah's friend, Scott, found one of the best. He had considered buying a coat at the **Hugo Boss** shop in New York, but couldn't justify spending $895; a week later, he found the same coat at Hugo Boss on London's Regent Street for £325 ($650), full retail price. Scott not only saved $245 by buying in London, but he also collected the $60 VAT refund.

Chapter One

....

THE BEST OF LONDON AT A GLANCE

NO MONEY PLEASE; WE'RE BRITISH

Prices in London and the U.K. are downright obscene. But wait—it's not as bad as you first think it will be. There's bad and then there's seriously bad.

There are some buys and even some bargains, and there *is* value for money—things that are pricey but worth it, or expensive but still lower priced in the United Kingdom than in the United States.

If you are in a hurry, or can afford to be in London for only 24 hours (I feel your pain), this quickie chapter is meant to give you an overview of the best buys. As we go to press, the pound is at an all-time high against the dollar. At two American dollars ($) per British pound (£), you'll want to weigh each purchase and think twice before dropping pounds on impulse buys.

Remember, bargains in Britain are often hidden, and those on a flash dash don't always get the best buy. If finding the bargains doesn't matter, then London has fabulous airport shopping—Terminal 5 at Heathrow should be open in time for your next trip.

Okay, 'nuff said. Let's go shopping, mates!

You Have Only 1 Hour to Shop

Obviously, what to do depends on where you are. If I have a heavy day ahead of me, I try to get people to come to my hotel or to keep my meetings in the Mayfair area so that I can at least get some fresh air—even though a walk along Regent Street or Oxford Street gives me more than a breath of fresh air . . . it gives me credit card debt!

If you find yourself in Mayfair with an hour to shop, and you want to go into just one place, your best bets are **Liberty** and **Asprey,** if only to look around. But once you're here, you'll want to shop until you drop, too. If you don't care about the glitz and the glimmer, then maybe your 1 hour should be spent in a practical fashion at the flagship **Marks & Spencer** at Marble Arch.

What I generally do with my hour (and what I suggest for any die-hard shopper) is the following, and this of course assumes that I can easily get to Marble Arch at the corner of Park Lane and Oxford Street:

- For the best value in low-priced off-the-runway fashion, head straight to the new **Primark** on Oxford Street. *Note:* Be there when the store opens and grab as much as you can quickly; the fitting-room queue grows longer as the day goes on. Blue bloods need not apply; this is down-market shopping.
- Then bus it toward Oxford Circus to **Topshop**—and be sure to go downstairs to find more women's things and browse the cheap copies of hot fashions.
- Dash into **Superdrug** (across the street from Topshop, on Oxford toward Tottenham Court Rd.) for everything you need and don't need, and for loading up on stuff from Original Source.
- Saunter along Regent Street, smelling the air and taking it all in; pop into **Liberty;** then turn left at the sign for Carnaby Street. Race for the **Lush** shop (no. 40) and buy all the gifts you've ever wanted or needed—and a few goodies for yourself, too.

You Have Only 1 Hour to Shop in Knightsbridge

If you're in Knightsbridge and want to spend your hour here, I suggest a trip to **Harvey Nicks** and then a quick whiz through the food halls at **Harrods** for souvenirs and some Krispy Kremes for tomorrow's breakfast. Or just exit Harvey Nicks— if you can drag yourself away from one of the best department stores in London—by way of Sloane Street. Be dazzled at **Shanghai Tang,** where clothes and gifts and fabrics from China offer a dizzying array of colors and energy. Then make your way toward Sloane Square, popping into **Jo Malone** (no. 150) for scents and bath or beauty treatments that cost two-thirds their U.S. prices. When you get to the department store Peter Jones, turn right and head into **General Trading Company,** a small department store of high style and gift items for the home, with a Zen/colonial-Indian flavor.

You Have No Real Shopping Goals but Want a Quick Spree That's Very London

- Head for **Covent Garden.** (Yes, there is a branch of **Lush.**)
- Explore Covent Garden's entire marketplace, but don't forget that if you need a few gifts, there's a tiny branch of **Hamleys** (great gifts for kids) and a **Culpeper the Herbalist** (wonderful bed and bath products, including aromatherapy) here as well.
- Walk away from Covent Garden out the front end and go to **Neal Street** for an eyeful of cutting-edge British street fashion and shoes you just can't believe, as well as branches of stores such as **Mango,** a Spanish chain that makes inexpensive copies of the latest fashions.
- Check out the minimall **Thomas Neal's** by popping into tenant **Space.NK,** a beauty store specializing in cult brands of makeup. (Don't buy the American brands, as they are very expensive.) If you enjoy vintage clothes, there's a small shop in the mall that has some nice things.

BEST OF LONDON

....

Best Department Store

SELFRIDGES
400 Oxford St., W1 (Tube: Bond St.).

If you remember a dowdy old British department store targeted to little old ladies, think again: Selfridges has totally re-created itself. This department store is now the talk of the town for all the young and hip designers' clothes, the grocery store, the designer boutiques (check out the new Wonder Room— an arcade of big-ticket mini-boutiques), the clothes made especially for the store, and the largest makeup and beauty department in Europe. I also like the newspaper/magazine section in the rear of the ground floor. © 870/837-7377. www. selfridges.com.

Best Specialty Store

HARVEY NICHOLS
109–125 Knightsbridge (at Sloane St.), SW1 (Tube: Knightsbridge).

Harvey Nicks sells style by the yard and is the specialty store of choice for Sloane Rangers—it was the favorite department store of Diana, Princess of Wales. It's known for its blend of designers, home style, gourmet market, and good eats. Note that there is a branch of Wagamama, the noodle shop, in the basement. © 207/235-5000. www.harveynichols.com.

Best Chemist (Drugstore)

Eeeek, I'm having a tough moment here and must declare a tie, as I am now torn between my teeny-bopper heart and my conservative traditionalist heart.

Traditional choice: **Boots** (multiple branches).
Teeny-bopper choice: **Superdrug** (multiple branches).

Open-late-and-on-Sunday choice: **Bliss Chemist**, 5–6 Marble Arch, W1 (Tube: Marble Arch).

Best British Multiple (Chain)

LUSH
123 King's Rd., SW3 (Tube: Sloane Sq.); 11 The Piazza, Covent Garden, WC2 (Tube: Covent Garden); 40 Carnaby St., W1 (Tube: Oxford Circus); 80–82 Regent St. (Tube: Piccadilly Circus); 96 Kensington High St., W8 (Tube: High St. Kensington).

Now that Lush has stores dotted around the U.S. as well as a strong international presence, it might not offer the novelty you seek. And, heaven knows, the prices are frightening. But if you don't know the gimmick, it's still worth delighting in. Despite myself, I am still a huge fan. Each store is set up like a deli, with beauty treatments in tubs, and soaps in giant cheeselike wheels. The bath bomb is the biggest draw, but there are also products with silly names, a newsletter that clues you in on the latest, and enough razzle-dazzle to make you forget that you would never, in your right mind, let a five-dollar bill float down the bathtub drain if you weren't on holiday. www. lush.com.

Best Multiple You May Not Know

MUJI
41 Carnaby St., W1 (Tube: Oxford Circus); 157 Kensington High St., N8 (Tube: South Kensington); 118 King's Rd., SW3 (Tube: Sloane Sq.); 187 Oxford St., W1 (Tube: Oxford Circus).

The Japanese-minimalist multiple named Muji has stores all over the world, with many, many locations in London. Muji specializes in clean lines, great nonbranded merchandise, and fair prices. Some stores are larger than others; there are also Muji stores or boutiques within most London department stores and malls. www.muji.co.uk.

Best Places for Dishes

- Affordable: **Harrods,** 87–135 Brompton Rd., SW1 (Tube: Knightsbridge; © 207/730-1234; www.harrods.com).
- Dream on: **Thomas Goode,** 19 S. Audley St., W1 (Tube: Green Park or Hyde Park Corner, but really, no one takes the Tube to a store such as this; © 207/499-2823; www. thomasgoode.co.uk).
- Discount, but with a limited selection: **Portobello China & Woollens,** 89 Portobello Rd., W11 (Tube: Notting Hill Gate; © 207/727-3857; www.portobello-ltd.com).

Best Mad Hatter

PHILIP TREACY
69 Elizabeth St., SW1 (Tube: Sloane Sq.).

Ascot, anyone? A wedding, perhaps? The king of British toppers has some sublime pieces and many that are wild, wacky, wonderful, and way out there. Be prepared to pay—and have photographers standing by. © 207/824-8787. www.philip treacy.co.uk. (See "Best Hidden Shopping Street" in chapter 4, p. 91.)

Best Designer Resale Shop

PANDORA
16–22 Cheval Place, SW7 (Tube: Knightsbridge).

How can you beat £35 ($70) for a YSL blouse? Enough said. The location right near Harrods makes this easy to check out. © 207/589-5289.

Best Flea Markets

- Saturday: **Portobello Road** (Tube: Notting Hill Gate).
- Sunday: **Camden Lock** (Tube: Camden Town), and the car-park sales in **Brighton** and **Lewes.** (See chapter 10 for details.)

Best Market Experience

COLUMBIA ROAD FLOWER MARKET
Columbia Rd., E2 (Nearest Tube: Old St.; or bus no. 26, 48, or 55).

Don't fret, it's not just flowers. Although the streets are filled with cut flowers, plants, herbs in pots, and small trees, there are also shops selling antiques and fun home furnishings, tiny outdoor markets with heaps of olives, and so on. Several shops and bistros sell coffee, bagels, and other goodies. It's crowded by 8:30am; most of the stores open at 9am. They're open only on Sundays, so don't think you can come back during the week for a less-crowded stroll. www.columbia-flower-market. freewebspace.com.

Best Addition to Regent Street

APPLE STORE
235 Regent St., W1 (Tube: Piccadilly).

Surely you are no stranger to Apple's retail business, but this large branch store has brought some really nice energy to a street that was drowning in the boredom of one multiple after the next. You can play with Apple toys and even check your e-mail for free here. *Note:* If you're visiting in the summer and traveling with kids, there are free workshops and even a summer camp program held at the store. © 207/153-9000. www. apple.com.

Best Shopper's Lunches

THE CADOGAN
75 Sloane St., SW1 (Tube: Knightsbridge).

Nestled right into the shopping district, The Cadogan (say *kuh-duh-gun*) was once owned by Lillie Langtry and was home to Oscar Wilde. Now it's a member of Leading Small Hotels of the World and a swank place to stay. The insider's tip? There's a three-course gourmet lunch for £22 ($44). © 207/235-7141. www.lhw.com/cadoganuk.

THE FOUNTAIN RESTAURANT
Fortnum & Mason, 181 Piccadilly, W1 (Tube: Green Park).

The store has reopened with fab new interiors throughout; accordingly, The Fountain Restaurant is newly coifed and better than ever for a quick traditional lunch. Do share a table if asked; I've met some amazing local folks over a plate of Welsh Rarebit. © 207/734-8040.

WAGAMAMA
Lower floor, Harvey Nichols, 109–125 Knightsbridge, SW1 (Tube: Knightsbridge).

There are more than 20 of these noodle bars around town, but I always refuel here when shopping Sloane Street. It's quick, delicious and easy on the wallet. www.wagamama.com.

Best Vintage Clothing

STEINBERG & TOLKIEN
193 King's Rd., SW3 (Tube: Sloane Sq.).

An Ali Baba cave of vintage, much of it designer caliber and very expensive. Don't miss a trip downstairs. The specialties are from the '30s and the '60s. © 207/376-3660.

Best Outlets

BICESTER VILLAGE
50 Pringle Dr., Bicester, Oxfordshire.

Created along the same lines as an American outlet village, complete with pedestrian-only main street and cutie-pie storefronts, this place is about a 70-minute drive from London. You can get here by train or tour bus; see p. 278 for details. And for heaven's sake take pity on one of the most embarrassing moments of my professional career when I called this place Bi-Chester. It's "Bista."

The mix is all very upscale, with mostly international brands and some British lines, so you should know your labels. For British specialty brands, check out **Molton Brown, The White Company,** and **Ken Turner,** among others. Okay, okay, there's also **Ozwald Boateng,** a Savile Row bespoke tailor who makes rock-'n'-roll clothes for guys. ✆ **1869/323-200.** www.bicester village.com.

Best Source for Postcards

VICTORIA & ALBERT MUSEUM
Cromwell Rd., SW7 (Tube: South Kensington).

The gift shop has changed but the postcards are still good; you can see the art if you want to. ✆ **207/942-2000.** www.vam. ac.uk.

Best Place for Royal Souvenirs

BUCKINGHAM PALACE GIFT SHOP
Sorry, open only Aug–Sept. At the end of the Mall, on the road running from Trafalgar Sq. (Tube: St. James's Park).

HISTORIC ROYAL PALACES (INCLUDES TOWER OF LONDON)
Palaces have banded together to form a marketing confederation (how American!) and have redone their gift shops, offering replicas of the crown jewels at the Tower of London gift shop.

Best Bookstore

HATCHARDS
187 Piccadilly, W1 (Tube: Piccadilly Circus).

Some bookstores are larger, but none are more fun. There are floors and floors of books here, plus a staff that knows and reads everything. ✆ **207/439-9921.** www.hatchards.co.uk.

Best Toy Store

HAMLEYS
188–196 Regent St., W1 (Tube: Oxford Circus).

A veritable theater of retail, worth a visit even if you don't have kids. © 0870/333-2455. www.hamleys.com.

Best Teenage Hangouts

NEW LOOK
500–502 Oxford St., W1 (Tube: Marble Arch).

The bad news: This store isn't nearly as good as Topshop. The good news? It's less expensive. There are two huge locations on Oxford Street, convenient for all shoppers. The Marble Arch store is the flagship. There's another branch at 175 Oxford St. (Tube: Oxford Circus). The looks are here and the prices are low. © 207/290-7860. www.newlook.co.uk.

PRIMARK
499–517 Oxford St., W1 (Tube: Marble Arch).

This is the place for £3 ($6) T-shirts and the latest off-the-runway knockoffs for teens and 'tweens. Sure, they may fall apart after a few trips through the washer/dryer, but at these prices, who cares? © 207/495-0420. www.primark.co.uk.

TOPSHOP
36–38 Great Castle St. (at Oxford and Regent sts.), W1 (Tube: Oxford Circus).

The flagship Topshop is a mecca for boys and girls. Now there's even a branch of Miss Selfridge inside the Oxford Circus store. © 207/636-7700. www.topshop.co.uk.

Best Gift for Your Best Friend

Boots No. 7 Protect and Perfect Beauty Serum, £17 ($34), available at all Boots' stores. The bad news? You'll need to be there when the shop opens as they usually sell out within 15 or 20 minutes. The word on the high street is that it's better than Botox. *Tip:* If you can't snag a bottle in the U.K., stop by your neighborhood Target; you might get lucky.

Best Wedding, Bar Mitzvah, or Christening Gift

ABRAS GALLERY
292 Westbourne Grove, just off Portobello Rd., W11 (Tube: Notting Hill Gate).

Beautiful hallmarked silver frames in all styles and sizes are available in this tiny basement shop. Prices are about half what you'd pay in the U.S.; a 4-inch by 6-inch frame with blue velvet back is under £50 ($100). *Note to Bridezillas:* The silver flatware is heavy, huge, and drop-dead gorgeous. There are about a dozen patterns to choose from and you'll be amazed at the prices. The more place settings you buy, the bigger the discount.

Gifts for Not Many £

- **Anything from Lush**—one of my faves is the Ballistic Barrel (three bath bombs in a container). I just bought some baby bath bombs in pale blue for a novelty baby gift. Not every product is brilliant, so you'll need to experiment; the good ones are so good that you'll go back to buy more the next day—and rue the day you didn't bring home more.
- **Cashmere liquid washing soap from N.Peal.** Okay, so this is a novelty gift, but it goes a long way for the person who has everything.
- **Duchy Originals,** organic biscuits (cookies) from Prince Charles, available at all fancy food shops and food halls in department stores. *Note:* These have almost no sodium, making them a great gift for anyone on a salt-free diet.
- **Tea, coffee, or cookies from Fortnum & Mason,** the famed purveyor of gourmet foods. The teas and coffees have such fabulous packaging that they make exciting gifts based on their looks alone.

- **Thornton's Toffee,** by far the best toffee in the world. There are branches all over London and there's almost always a sale underway.
- **Aromatherapy fan from Culpeper the Herbalist,** £15 ($30); with the scent of your choice, an additional £3 to £5 ($6–$10).
- **Silk-knot cuff links from Thomas Pink,** £5 ($10).
- **Filofax planners and inserts.** Prices vary, but you'll pay basically half the U.S. retail cost.

Best Gifts Under $15

- **Crisps,** available at any supermarket or cafeteria, about £1 ($2) per small package. I buy the oddball flavors of potato chips and hand them out as gifts. Some of the flavors are so bizarre (steak and kidney pie?) that you can only laugh.
- **Bath bomb** (£3/$6) or **Red Rooster soap** (prices depend on size, but £3/$6 will usually do it) from Lush.
- A **tabloid newspaper,** with at least one tacky headline and news of yet another royal scandal, 20p (40¢).
- **Original Source** shower gel, shaving cream, or moisture mousse. I'm nuts for Orange & Grapefruit as well as Tea Tree & Mint, which I use for shaving my legs because it smells great and leaves a tingle afterward. The mousse is a light-weight foam that serves as a body oil post-shower. Available at all drugstores, for under £3 ($6) per product.

Unusual Gifts for the Person Who Has Everything

- **Desk accessories from Smythson of Bond Street.** There are all sorts of doodads and gadgets here. I buy the tiny magnifying glass as a 50th-birthday gift for loved ones, £25 ($50); with an engraved case, £35 ($70).
- **Asprey's unique silk scarf belt with leather buckle.** You buy the scarf and the leather buckle separately, which means you can buy the buckle and attach it to your own scarf collection. The buckle costs about £50 ($100).
- **Columbia Road Flower Market original gray plastic tote,** only at the Columbia Road Flower Market, £3 ($6).

- **Gift certificates for afternoon tea at the Dorchester Hotel.** These come wrapped in an elegant box that is perfect for presentation. Full tea costs about £20 ($40). If you would like the vouchers sent to you or directly to your gift recipient, call © 207/629-8888 and ask for the Promenade.
- **A dog portrait from the Stephanie Hoppen Gallery,** on Walton Street.
- **Aroma Cushion,** available at many department stores. These small pillows come with a variety of treatments—there's everything from Deep Sleep to Animal Spirit. Oh yes, don't forget Monthly Moon. Prices range from £15 to £20 ($30–$40).
- **Anything from Basia Zarzycka,** 52 Sloane Sq., SW1 (Tube: Sloane Sq.), where whimsy floats in the air and gift items range from decorated lampshades to fashion accessories. Prices soar on the wings of doves; see below.

Ten Best Shops in London

I hate lists like this because they don't really evaluate a store; they take into account the entire city and its retail scenario and are balanced to make a whole. On the whole, I like this whole, which includes shops that happen to be close together so you can walk from one to the next; with the exception of two of the stores on this list, they are all either on King's Road (or nearby Sloane Sq.) or in Mayfair.

Note that I have left out shopping experiences, alternative retail, and entire events, such as Covent Garden, Greenwich on a Sunday, walking from Ledbury Street to Portobello Road along Westbourne Grove, and so on. My choices are based on thrills or chills.

ASPREY
167 New Bond St., W1 (Tube: Bond St. or Green Park).

For years, Asprey was a traditional, stuffy, noncreative place to shop: okay for the Royals but not very sexy. All that has changed; it's now young and fun and jazzy and very sophisticated. While it may have once been simply a jewelry store, it now sells a lifestyle. The interior has been created as the courtyard of a very fancy British neighborhood, with brick walls running in a half-circle, welcoming you into your own private village. If you buy nothing, it's worth it just to stand and gawk. Note that everything here is so expensive (handbags begin at £1,000/$2,000) that you know this is the kind of place where money is not discussed. www.asprey.co.uk.

BASIA ZARZYCKA
52 Sloane Sq., SW1 (Tube: Sloane Sq.).

This store is not for everyone, and it is unlikely that you will actually buy anything here unless you cashed out your tech stocks before the crash. But you must come here to simply gawk at the creativity, energy, high style, and whimsy in picture frames, accessories for fashion and home, lampshades, shawls, handbags, and so on. The prices are very, very high; the attitude is equally elevated—but it's still one of the best stores in London. © 207/730-1660. www.basia-zarzycka.co.uk.

BOOTS WELL-BEING CENTRE
128 Kensington High St., W8 (Tube: Kensington High St.).

The Boots Well-Being Centre is nothing short of astonishing—perhaps the most exciting store in London. It looks so average from the front that you will wonder if I am daft, so give me a break here. The space is very deep, gets wider in the rear, and has an upstairs with spa, herbal meds, and more. Many brands of makeup, health, beauty, bath, hair, and sun products are sold on the ground floor. (Arrive early to buy the Boots No. 7 Protect and Perfect Beauty Serum.) You can call ahead (© 0845/121-9001) to book spa appointments, which is a good idea since they do book up. Spa hours are Monday through Saturday from 9am to 7pm, Sunday from 11am to 5pm. www. boots.com.

GENERAL TRADING COMPANY
2–4 Symons St., Sloane Sq., SW3 (Tube: Sloane Sq.).

This is a totally new cup of tea for those of you who haven't stumbled onto the changeover on your own—the General Trading Company as Princess Di knew it ain't no more. The icon store fancies itself as GTC with a modern logo and a cool, Calvin Klein kind of environment. This mini–department store has a lot of good gift and novelty items. © 207/730-0411. www.general-trading.co.uk.

LIBERTY
Great Marlborough St., W1 (Tube: Oxford Circus).

Give me Liberty or give me death. This fabulous department store has great architecture on the outside and the inside, lots of charm, good clothing, good William Morris prints, good needlework department, good everything.

They recently lost the lease on their Regent Street wing, so all departments are now located in the Tudor-style building on Great Marlborough Street. The store entrance is located on Great Marlborough, just around the corner from Regent Street. © 207/734-1234. www.liberty.co.uk.

LUSH
123 King's Rd., SW3 (Tube: Sloane Sq.); additional locations around town.

Lush is set up like a deli, with bath and skin-care items sold by the chunk or in a salad container. It's home of the bath bomb, Red Rooster soap, and many yummy and silly gift items for everyone you know. Original, creative, and exactly what you travel the world to find. © 207/376-8348. www.lush.com.

PICKETT
32–33 Burlington Arcade, W1 (Tube: Piccadilly Circus); 149 Sloane St., SW1 (Tube: Sloane Sq.); 6 Royal Exchange, EC3 (Tube: Liverpool St.).

One of the reasons I think Trevor Pickett is so clever is that these stores have been able to reinvent themselves each year, pivoting from purveyor of pashmina (so *last year*) to ethnic jewelry and a look that is sublime and special. There are a handful of shops all over town. © 207/493-8939. www.pickett.co.uk.

TABIO
94 Kings Rd., SW3 (Tube: Sloane Sq.); 66 Neal St., WC2 (Tube: Leicester Sq.).

Okay, so this is an expensive source for fancy socks from Japan (prices begin at £10/$20), and you think I am nuts. Hang on a second. These socks are so unique, imaginative, and inventive that even if you never wear socks, you should pop in for a look-see. Make it a point to look at men's and women's socks, tights, footies, toeless socks, and other oddball inventions. There's a new store in the Covent Garden area (Neal St.); the brand is also sold at major London department stores—but you want to see the whole range, so go to the store. © 207/591-1960, King's Road; © 207/836-3713, Neal St. www.tabio.com.

THOMAS GOODE
19 S. Audley St., W1 (Tube: Green Park or Hyde Park Corner).

This is the fanciest china shop in the world with room after room of dishes, and even some antiques. *Insider's tip:* Don't miss the bomb in the rear room—they unearthed it after World War II and put it on display. Talk about a bull in a china shop. © 207/499-2823. www.thomasgoode.co.uk.

VV ROULEAUX
102 Marylebone Lane, W1 (Tube: Baker St. or Bond St.).

A few years ago, VV Rouleaux was a fancy ribbons-and-trimming store at Sloane Square. While it still has a shop there

(54 Sloane Sq., at Cliveden Place), the best location to visit is the new shop on Marylebone Lane, where two levels of ribbons and stuff just knock you out with their colors, textures, and possibilities. Buy trims, artificial flowers, home style, and more. © 207/224-5179. www.vvrouleaux.com.

Chapter Two

·····················

LONDON DETAILS

WELCOME TO LONDON

···

Every time I visit London, I try to come up with a new way of surviving without despairing over the high cost of everything. I used to pretend that the dollar and the pound were equivalent, that something cost the same in sterling as it would in dollars. This game is getting harder and harder to play, although it will save your sanity—until the bills come.

If you're into reality TV or reality banking, ugh, it's not pretty. Last time I looked, the dollar was not trading at two to one as we've been thinking painfully, but actually at £1 = $2.09. That is enough to scare Harry Potter right back into the train station. If you do lie to yourself, make sure you settle up mentally before the bills arrive. Meanwhile, try a spoonful of sugar in the Mary Poppins tradition. Consider

- going for a shorter stay
- booking an apartment or less expensive hotel
- getting out of the city on day trips

No matter what, don't let the high prices stop you from a visit to London. As pricey as it might be, London is still a treat for the eye and the soul. Shop with care, look right, and mind the gap.

OH, GROW UP

To make your bucks go as far as possible, home in on what you can't find in the United States or have never seen elsewhere. Spend time in grocery stores and street markets, buy vintage clothes and not wines, do the sales and shop off-season, hit the outlet malls and off-price shops, and snoop around museum stores.

I get enormous joy from stores such as **Topshop** and **Superdrug,** which offer cheapie fun items at bargain-basement prices. I sometimes take a taxi to the **Tesco** supermarket on Cromwell Road, where I do a lot of gift shopping from the foodstuffs shelves. Tesco also carries bestseller books at discount prices and its own line of designer makeup.

Marks & Spencer has reinvented itself and added some new lines that can compete with the best of High Street; what's more, there's always a sale underway—Born to Shop Editorial Director Sarah Lahey just got a knockout pair of £9 ($18) jeans. Despite it all, there are deals!

I gave up the luxury of room service when I discovered my fancy-dan hotel charged extra for room service, tray service, and room delivery. With a few of these research trips under the belt (literally), Sarah and I are now regulars at **Tesco, Sainsbury's,** and **Marks & Spencer's** food halls. And now that **Whole Foods** has opened on Kensington High Street, the choices for takeout are endless.

As for clothing, remember that America does bargain-basement very well. However, the British do knockoffs of cutting-edge catwalk fashions that the U.S. isn't quite tuned in to yet. Strolling down Oxford Street, I couldn't help but notice the number of multicolored shopping bags from **Topshop, Primark,** and other value-priced stores dangling from the arms of young fashionistas.

The British have also refined Power Shopping, which entails heading out of town on a day trip to do big-haul purchases at lower prices. The most popular of such destinations is **Bicester Village,** a factory-outlet mall, but there are others. Suburbs have their own **TJ Maxx** stores, which is called **TK Maxx** in the U.K.

Britain really wants your business—here are some deals to look for:

- Airfares (both transatlantic and, in some cases, from London to other European points) have held steady for the past few years, even with the devaluation of the dollar. Even peak summer fares average $600 or $700 round-trip; off-season seats go for less than $300 round-trip from the East Coast. There's often an airfare war in progress, even in peak season.
- British Airways frequently has deals with low fares or with add-ons to other cities in Europe—through London, of course. Some special offers include a 3-night hotel stay.
- Hotels have rebates, promotional rates, deals in dollars, and all sorts of enticements to get you to come visit and spend a few of your hard-earned dollars.
- London and the surrounding area are home to low-cost airlines that serve continental Europe. If a week in London is too expensive for you, consider adding on 3 or 4 days at another destination. I have friends who often fly Ryanair (www.ryanair.com) from the U.K. to destinations all over Europe—sometimes for £10 ($20) per flight.
- Internet sites are the dumping ground for airlines and hotels; they often advertise shockingly low deals that will free up many of your precious shopping dollars. Spend time online and use assorted sites to research the bargains. One section of **www.travelbritain.org** has special deals that include luxury hotels. Another good bet is **www.londontown.com**.

GUIDES TO LONDON

The number of guidebooks to London is staggering, and the prices can quickly add up. Because more and more information is available online (often for free), I suggest that you do a good bit of your investigation through websites, which also have the ability to be updated immediately.

Don't, however, miss *London A to Z* (say "A to Zed"), the map guide that everyone, absolutely everyone, uses—locals and tourists alike. It's an in-depth street finder that will even tell you which Tube stop to use. Buy it at news kiosks on the street or in bookstores; most hotel gift shops also sell these guides.

Note that the **British Tourist Authority (BTA)** has a few offices scattered around the United States that give away tons of free brochures. The maps and other goodies are totally free in the States, but you must pay for these items if you pick them up at tourist centers in Britain. BTA has an excellent bookstore as well.

GETTING THERE

From the United States

There are a number of ways to get to England from the United States, but since there isn't yet a tunnel that connects Boston with Britain, you'll probably be best off in an airplane.

The *QE2* quit its transatlantic crossings to make way for a new sister ship. The *QM2 (Queen Mary 2)* makes the crossing in 6 luxurious days at a variety of prices, depending on size and location of your cabin.

You'll find that airfare prices from New York to London are particularly competitive because so many carriers want a piece of the action. You may also discover price breaks from new gateway cities that are launching service, so New York is not your only way to London. Ask, depending on where you're coming from.

All airlines offer similar seasonal promotions. These deals change from week to week, so you need to do your homework.

If you find that all prices are the same, what should you base your choice on? I'd consider the airport itself, safety, convenience, ability to change your ticket and the cost for doing so, frequent-flier mileage, overweight costs (I do a lot of shopping, remember?), and perks.

LHR (London Heathrow) has always been a zoo, but with the scheduled opening of the new Terminal 5 in March 2008, all that is set to change. Five times larger than the current long-haul hub (Terminal 4), T5 promises no queues, no strikes, and only 15 minutes to the departure lounge upon arrival at the airport, or 10 minutes to clear immigration after arriving from overseas.

And shopping . . . well, duh. T5 promises an airport mall like no other. It will be home to luxury brand shops including **Mulberry** and **Smythson,** high street labels including **Ted Baker,** and Paul Smith's latest store, **Globe.**

You might also consider flying into Dublin. Aer Lingus offers nonstop value flights from seven U.S. cities, including Orlando and San Francisco, and there are several low-fare airlines offering connections on to London and E.U. cities. Allow 2 to 3 hours for a Dublin connecting flight.

Be prepared to spend a lot of time online for comparison's sake. There's lots of information out there and some of it is conflicting.

BRITISH CARRIERS

BRITISH AIRWAYS   I make it simple by pretty much sticking with one carrier for the New York–London run: British Airways (BA). Every trip finds new improvements onboard, and a huge number of promotions and deals are offered. In-flight amenities are extended to economy, which is not true on all other airlines. You'll get a free toothbrush and overnight kit, even in the "back" of the plane.

British Air also offers complete package tours with hotel rooms—in and out of London—and many specials. My best secret: BA doesn't always advertise its rates. Watch for an American Airlines or United airfare war, and then call BA, which will match the current lowest fares. Don't forget to look for special deals online, directly through the airline and through discounters as well. In the U.S., call © **800/AIRWAYS** or go to www.britishairways.com.

BMI (BRITISH MIDLAND)   This airline has been expanding and now has two divisions, a low-cost carrier that serves continental Europe and a long-haul service with flights to U.S. cities such as Chicago, Las Vegas, and Washington, D.C., with service to Manchester. BMI is a member of the Star Alliance, so you can earn United Mileage Plus points, all of which qualify for elite status. The airline has modern everything, including an in-flight chef who cooks for business-class passengers. You can, of course, connect to LHR or elsewhere. In the U.S., call © **800/788-0555** or go to www.flybmi.com.

VIRGIN ATLANTIC   Virgin is a strange creature that many consumers love and others simply find amusing. It has three classes of service—sometimes four—so what you get varies; but the Upper Class is amazingly creative and comfortable. Virgin has slots at LHR and Gatwick. In the U.S., call © **800/ 821-5438** or go to www.virgin-atlantic.com.

U.S. CARRIERS

AMERICAN AIRLINES   I sometimes book American Airlines, especially when I am in and out of Paris and London and will connect one-way via the Chunnel. Born to Shop Editorial Director Sarah uses her American miles for free and upgraded tickets from San Francisco to London. She can upgrade from their lowest fare for 25,000 miles plus $300 each way if space is available. And since she's an AAdvantage Platinum member, she gets priority upgrades.

AA has weekend deals that are offered at the last minute: You get to stay for only a weekend (but it's a long weekend), and you book directly through the website. The special deals listed on this site sometimes include London; you can often find an off-season round-trip fare from an East Coast city to London for under $300. Call © **800/433-7300** or go to www. aa.com.

CONTINENTAL   Continental has service from Newark to Gatwick; I found a round-trip flight in high season (mid-October) for $353, less than half the rate of the flights from JFK. Continental is also one of the airlines that offers business-first, a far more comfortable option than on planes that still have three classes of service. Call © 800/231-0856 or go to www.continental.com.

DELTA AIR LINES   Delta has regular London Gatwick service from New York, Cincinnati, and Atlanta, and they also offer business-first, which provides far more value than regular old business class on those airlines that have three classes. Call © 800/241-4141 or go to www.delta.com.

UNITED   Prices on United are competitive with the other big-name carriers and they often run a promotion offering Mileage Plus bonus miles to the U.K. To grab these extra miles, log on and register before booking your ticket online. If it's important to you, note that United and US Air are both members of Star Alliance—and US Air sometimes has better prices. Call © 800/864-8331 or go to www.united.com.

US AIRWAYS   I recently made my first transatlantic flight on US Air from London to Philadelphia and was amazed by how few of the passengers were actually going to Philly, the home base for this carrier. The airport is gorgeous, it works very well for connections between international arrivals and onward-bound domestic U.S. travel, and fares can be quite good. This airline's website is also one of the easiest to navigate. And not only does US Air offer service to London, but it also has flights to Manchester as well as Scotland. It also operates nonstop service between Charlotte, North Carolina, and Gatwick. Depending on the time of year and the flight load, you may find a round-trip ticket for $368.

I just found a deal on US Airways where they'll discount a business-class ticket by 20% plus give you 20,000 bonus miles or a 10% discount off an economy ticket with 10,000 bonus miles; this deal is good only if you use your MasterCard and fly September through November. www.usairways.com.

Web Warnings

I tried to do various bookings on prominent travel websites—especially the ones that offer deals—and always found myself thrilled by the initial offerings. Then when I got to actually booking the fare, I was furious that I was traded up and could never get the low fares I had been teased with. These sites often list fares without taxes added, so when the total price comes up, you end up paying lots more—sometimes to the tune of $200 per ticket.

CONSOLIDATORS & DISCOUNT WEBSITES

I don't fly on consolidator tickets because I'm always collecting mileage, but if cash is short and you don't qualify for one of the cheap winter rates, perhaps you'll want to try one of those brokers that specialize in tickets on major scheduled airlines. Note that rates are usually for peak travel or last-minute travel, when you won't usually qualify for a low-cost ticket.

Numerous websites offer bargains and discounts, some at the last minute. Just to give it a shot, I put in the same dates of travel in all of the major airline sites and then ran the prices against **www.cheaptickets.com**. The route was from Chicago to LHR. For the most part, the online broker gave me the best prices; it also provided a chart showing all the carriers, offered the choice of nonstop vs. stops, and told me the airfare *and* the total price of the ticket once all taxes and fees were applied. The site was easy to use and clearly showed that one airline had a better deal than all the others.

STUDENT FARES

You need not be in school to qualify for a student fare; you just need to be under 26 years old. And you often need an ID card to prove it.

From Continental Europe

BY TRAIN Remember that tickets and passes bought in advance in the U.S. through **Rail Europe** (© 866/BRITRAIL) often offer the best deal.

Eurostar, the train that travels through the Chunnel (which connects France, Belgium, and Britain), makes it a breeze to get to London from the Continent; as we go to press, the Brits have finally gotten it together for their portion of the high-speed track through Britain that connects to the new Eurostar terminal in London's St. Pancras International station—cutting travel time to 2 hours, 15 minutes. Set your stopwatch.

There are promotional fares available, also senior fares. You can buy the tickets in the U.S. through **Rail Europe** or **BritRail** or while you are actually in London, although if time is short, you do not want to wait in line for an hour. Rail Europe often has promotional deals, such as train tickets packaged with a rental car. Go to www.raileurope.com.

Note the various quirks in pricing, especially if you're buying train tickets from Europe. Go online and do some homework so you're prepared for all the choices and all the different price possibilities. I just found a round-trip, second-class seat on the Eurostar for £74 ($148), by booking in advance. I priced several options and it didn't seem to matter if I stayed over a weekend or just a couple of days midweek. Youth and senior fares are also available—if you qualify (you must be 60 or have valid student ID).

BY AIR There's a new air war going on from continental Europe into London (and vice versa), partly because the train has cut travel time and prices. If you're flying, you can choose not only from **British Airways** and other international carriers, but also from more and more new regional airlines that are getting into the fray. These offer competitive prices and often serve alternative airports, which may not be as far away from London as Heathrow. Here's a trick: Price one-way as well as round-trip tickets even if you need only a one-way leg; often

Low-Cost Carriers

Many of the new small airlines that serve continental Europe do not have offices in the U.S. Often their flights can be booked only online, through a travel agent, or by making a long-distance call to London (most offer discounts if you book online). Note that most of these carriers do not have transatlantic routes, but rather specialize in travel within the U.K. or continental Europe. And remember, these carriers usually use alternative airports and not Heathrow. Some serve airports at Southampton or Birmingham.

Try the following (local U.K. phone numbers are listed):

- **BE:** ✆ 0871/522-6100; www.flybe.com.
- **BMI:** ✆ 0870/6070-555 (short haul) or ✆ 0870/6070-222 (long haul); www.flybmi.com.
- **EasyJet:** ✆ 0870/600-0000; www.easyjet.com.
- **Monarch:** ✆ 0870/040-5040; www.flymonarch.com.
- **Ryanair:** ✆ 541/569-569; www.ryanair.ie.

the round-trip ticket costs less than a one-way. Simply throw away the unused portion.

Also ask the airlines about promotional deals: **Air France** had a fabulous deal whereby two family members traveling together got tickets at half-price. Remember to work every angle; there's competition for your business, so fight for the best rates possible.

Alternative Airports

Almost all of the new small airlines use alternative airports such as Standsted, Luton, or City Airport. City Airport is very close to Canary Wharf and is attracting more and more of the business visitors; Standsted and Luton are both north of the city. EasyJet serves London's Luton and Gatwick. Before you jump on the Tube or dash to the airport, *know which one you're headed to!* Also try to get a brief understanding of transportation options into town.

Airport Transfers

If you take a taxi from LHR into central London, expect to pay up to £100 ($200). A taxi from Gatwick into town will be a prohibitive £150 ($300). You will do much better by taking the train or the bus.

The Heathrow Express (£30/$60 for a return ticket), www.heathrowexpress.com, offers 15- to 20-minute train service every 15 minutes right to Paddington Station; the Gatwick Express (£28–£45/$56–$90 return), www.gatwickexpress.com, will take you to Victoria station; and you can take the Stansted Express (£24–£40/$48–$80 return), www.stanstedexpress.com, to Liverpool Station.

Shopper Beware: The Heathrow Express is scheduled to change its service in March 2008 to include the new Terminal 5, but bypass T4. You'll no doubt be flying into T5 anyway. A less expensive option to and from Heathrow is called Heathrow Connect, www.heathrowconnect.com. At £13 ($26) for a return ticket, the journey is 15 minutes longer and stops at stations along the way, but you can snooze on the train and use the £18 ($36) you saved to buy lunch. All train tickets may be booked online with a 10% discount.

There is also shuttle-bus service via the **Airbus** (© 208/ 400-6656).

Electronically Yours

Aside from all the travel information you could ever need and all the deal-surfing you might want to do, please note that most London stores now have websites and even online shopping capabilities, so you don't even have to go on a trip in order to shop abroad. This doesn't beat a trip to London, but it's something to think about.

Here's a basic trick for finding a British something-or-other online. Okay, so you know that if you're taking a wild guess at a website, your tendency is to go for the business name and simply add a ".com" to the end, right? Right. If it's a British source, instead add ".co.uk"—international companies tend to be registered with a ".com," but often regional stores or regional branches of big-name stores use the more local handle.

There are far too many websites for tourist information to list here, but whether you need train schedules or theater listings, it's all on the Internet. I've listed some of my favorite sites and some of the most unusual.

www.excite.co.uk: A good search engine and general reference site.

www.londontown.com: Tourist site that specializes in bargains and promotions.

www.timeout.co.uk: Site for the weekly entertainment-listings guide *Time Out.*

www.royal.gov.uk: Buckingham Palace website.

www.squaremeal.co.uk: Restaurants by area, price, and cuisine (and even by gastropub).

www.tatler.co.uk: It's *Tatler,* the monthly glossy magazine, and I can't live without it.

www.vogue.co.uk: Not to be outdone by *Tatler,* it's the website for *British Vogue.*

www.officiallondontheatre.co.uk: Official half-price and discount theater-ticket booth.

www.londona2z.co.uk: Tourist site that is updated daily with tips on shopping, eating, hotels, and entertainment.

GETTING AROUND LONDON

- Buy an *A to Z*—(say Zed not Zee)—it's a detailed street map in book form. It's essential for knowing where you are going and how to get there.

- Get free maps to the Tube and bus system in major Tube stations. If you've always depended on the Tube, reconsider buses and begin to learn the major bus routes from your hotel.
- Walk whenever possible.

By Tube

The Tube—London's famous Underground system—is the personification of the good news and the bad news. When it's working, it gets you just about everywhere you need to go; it serves 275 stations in six zones, including all the airports. Trains run until 12:30am. But something goes wrong down there just about every day of the week, and you can waste a lot of time waiting for a train that's not coming or diverting yourself through stations and lines you had no interest in visiting in an attempt to get somewhere while your precious hours in London are wastin' away.

Note: I am not talking terrorism here. Long before the bombings of July 2005, I was forced to stop using the Tube simply because the system doesn't work that well. There are endless repairs being made to the system and trains can be delayed or lines shut down for hours.

The good news: There's usually a sign posted in the station giving you the status of any delays. This information is written on a memo board propped up near the turnstiles, so you can see what's happening before you pay to enter the station. Pay attention before you insert your ticket!

A single trip usually costs £4 ($8) (yeah, I'm serious); if you wait until after 9:30am, you can buy an all-day pass for £5 ($10), which is a good deal. Since shops don't open until 10am, you probably won't need to travel during rush hour anyway. And this ticket will take you all the way to the theater after the stores close. A few guidelines to keep in mind:

- You can get information online at www.theTube.com.
- If you can't figure out how to use the automated machine, pay for the least expensive ticket and be prepared to pay up as you exit—or stand in line at the ticket window.
- If you are on and off the Tube more than once in a day, or if you're going to Greenwich, buy a 1-day Travelcard that includes more than zones 1 and 2.
- If you're spending a week in London and plan to explore it from dawn until dusk and don't really know what you're doing—except that you want to do it all—purchase the **Oyster** (see below). You can get information on all the prices and choices at www.transportforlondon.gov.uk.

THE TRAVELCARD

If you're in London for 3 days or less, and plan to travel early in the morning and take at least 3 trips a day, it might be worth getting a **Travelcard** (for use on the bus, Underground, and British Rail in Greater London). This can be added to the **Oyster,** or purchased separately. There are various types of Travelcards. A 3-day card begins at £19 ($38); children traveling with you either ride free (under age 4) or get their own card to accompany you for £1 ($2).

You can buy Travelcards before you get to London—they're available in the U.S. through Rail Europe, through various London hotel promotions, and online. In Paris, you can get Travelcards in the Gare du Nord. Sometimes promotional airfare packages include a Travelcard.

THE OYSTER

If you travel to London often, or plan to use public transportation for more than 3 days, you'll want to purchase an Oyster Card for Visitors. It's a smartcard that can store up to £90 ($180) of pay-as-you-go credit, and can be used on Tubes, buses, and some national rail services in London.

There's real value in using the Oyster system, as prices are always less than those for tickets bought at the station. For example, a single day trip using Oyster is £1.50 ($3) as opposed to a £4 ($8) ticket purchased from the machine. Oyster credit can be used as you need it and never expires. What's more, the automated daily pricing calculates the cheapest fare for your journey.

The cards cost £3 ($6) each and are sold with an initial £10 ($20) or £15 ($30) balance on them to pay as you go (that is, a card with a £10/$20 balance will be £13/$26). They can be topped with additional money at Tube Stations, Oyster Ticket Stops, and London Information Centres. If you have a balance of under £5 ($10) left when you're ready to leave the U.K., you can get a refund at a Tube station ticket office and they will cancel the card.

You can buy an Oyster card at most Tube station ticket offices, at some National Rail ticket offices, or online at www. tfl.gov.uk/oyster.

By Bus

Several of the tourist travel passes cover both the Tube and the bus; the best sales pitch I have seen anywhere, however, is published by London buses, which remind you that the price of Tube passes goes up every year, whereas the price of a bus ticket has not increased. What's more, bus tickets cost half the price of Tube tickets, so they're a bargain.

While Sarah prefers the Tube, I have switched over to bus use; the bus is slower, but I enjoy the sights along the way. The old-fashioned double-decker is dying out; new buses have TV sets in them and all sorts of new technology.

Please note that you can no longer pay your fare when on the bus. There are now little yellow machines that allow you to buy a single ticket at the bus stop before you board.

I buy a booklet of six bus coupons, available at newsstands and cigarette stores. I call these the Tab Tix because they are small hexagonal pull tabs that come in a booklet; you pull one off for each ride. They cannot be used on the Tube. A single bus ticket costs £2 ($4), but if you buy the coupon book, you'll pay £1 ($2) per ride, the same price as using your Oyster card.

You can buy a bus map in any bookstore, or pick up a free neighborhood bus map in your local Tube station.

Tip: If I can't find a bus to where I want to go, I hop any bus headed to Oxford Circus or Piccadilly. Then I Tube or cab it to my final destination from there or even connect to another bus once I get oriented.

By Taxi

Taxis are plentiful because they are so darn expensive. No wonder Mary Poppins liked to fly. The flag drops at £2.20 ($4.40) and escalates quickly. I find that a taxi always costs me a tenner or more (about £10/$20), no matter where I am going.

CLIMATE CONTROL

To book an environmentally friendly ride, consider calling **Climatcars** (© 208/968-0440). This new carbon-neutral London taxi service has a fleet of Toyota Prius petro-electric cars to provide karmic rides around town and beyond. It costs less than rival cab companies, and you'll have a posh ride, to boot. All taxis have leather seats, minifridges stocked with complimentary bottled water, glossy magazines, and newspapers.

CALLING AROUND

To call London from the United States, dial © **011** (the international code), **44** (Britain's country code), and the phone number, which includes the local area code automatically.

Note that every single phone number in Britain changed in 2000, and many mobile phone numbers changed in 2001. Anything you may have in your Blackberry that begins with a "181" or "171" is the wrong number, but it can be easily updated.

The modern British phone number begins with 207 or 208, but is sometimes written as 020, with the 7 or 8 attached to the seven-digit number, making it an eight-digit number (duh). Numbers listed solely as eight-digit numbers take 020 before them.

If you are calling the U.S. from the U.K., remember:

- As in all E.U. countries, you dial 00, then 1, then the area code and number.
- Phone lines, especially from the United States and the United Kingdom, are inexpensive these days if you have an international calling plan. Rates should be no more than 12¢ a minute. Ask your carrier before you leave home; it may pay to call home and then have them call you right back.
- Be aware of the actual charges incurred each time you use one of these newfangled access codes that have been marketed as bargain phone rates. Yes, you get U.S. phone rates, which may be less expensive than those offered by British Telecom (BT), but you pay a per-call surcharge—so if you talk for only a minute, or get the answering machine of the party you're calling, you're paying a very hefty price for those airwaves. Also, varying rates mean that if you aren't on a promotional deal—12¢ a minute—then you may be paying $1.18 a minute. You can have several rates depending on which branch of these services you use at the time.
- Local phone cards offer the best deal. I buy mine at a kiosk and get 200 minutes for £5 ($10) (See there? Another bargain!) Any news agent will sell you one; just be sure to ask for a card that is good for calls placed anywhere in the world. *Tip:* The post office does vigorous advertising of its phone cards, but these are very expensive compared to what you can buy at any newsstand.
- *Warning:* If your hotel charges you for local calls, you will be charged for minutes on the phone line even while using your phone card. I once paid £100 ($200) for using my phone card to call the U.S. A hotel that includes local calls as an amenity becomes important if you speak on the phone a lot.

GETTING ONLINE

Although many hotels have business centers where you can get online, London also has scads of Internet cafes—there are even some inside the big department stores on Oxford Street, as well as a branch of **EasyEverything,** 358 Oxford St., W1 (Tube: Bond St.), where access costs £1 ($2) per 20 minutes. (This is the best buy in town.) *Tip:* Go to the **Apple Store,** 235 Regent St., W1 (Tube: Piccadilly), to check your e-mail for free.

If you want to use your laptop to get online from your hotel room, you will usually be charged for a local call. Your service provider may also charge you for international use. The low point of one of my hotel bills was discovering that I paid £50 ($100) for Internet use.

SHOPPING HOURS

Shopping hours are downright unorganized in London. Tuesday seems to have later store openings in the morning, while Wednesday, Thursday, and Friday have slightly later closings in the evening. Note that some stores may stick to such hours three of these days per week, while others observe only one or two of them. Some guidelines:

- If the store normally opens at 10am, on Tuesday it probably opens at 10:30am.
- Very few stores in London open at 9am. Almost all of the big department stores and multiples open at 10am. *Note:* If you have an early beauty-parlor appointment at a department-store salon, do not panic. One of the store doors will open at 9am with direct access to the salon.
- Canary Wharf stores do open early, as they want to attract people coming to and from work.
- Covent Garden stores may not open until 11am.
- Very few stores close for lunch.

- All stores close early in London. They do not know the meaning of late. To a British store, a *late night* means it's open until 7 or possibly 8pm.
- Sunday retail hours are limited, usually from noon to 5pm. Some establishments, usually grocery stores or tourist traps, open at 11am on Sunday. *Tip:* Harrods does not open on Sundays except right before Christmas.

Holiday Hours

The change in Sunday retail has created a huge wave of uncertainty about the rigid laws regarding holidays as well. Used to be, stores were closed on holidays. These days, no one really knows who will do what.

I am usually in London on Easter weekend because stores are sometimes open for Easter Sunday and Monday shopping—and this includes Harrods. Yep, **Harrods** was open on Easter Monday, but not Sunday. Also note that some branches of a store may be open while others will be closed, as was the case with **Boots.**

Many an unhappy shopper has written to ask me to warn readers about Christmas hours: Stores are closed for as many as 3 days in a row right at the Christmas season—they observe Christmas Eve, Christmas Day, and Boxing Day (the day after Christmas). Stores close again for New Year's Day.

Bank holidays are celebrated at regular intervals in the British calendar; they seem to fall around the same time as the feasts of the Virgin, but ever since Henry VIII split from Rome, no one in England is big on Feasts of the Assumption. Bank holidays affect retail but in an odd way: The banks and smaller stores close, but the big stores and multiples are usually open.

Chemists' Hours

If you need an emergency prescription filled, or just have a late-night personal need, there is always a chemist (drugstore) open somewhere in London on a later-than-usual basis. The **Boots** at Piccadilly Circus stays open until 10pm and is also open on Sundays; **Bliss Chemist** at Marble Arch is open on Sundays. The only 24-hour pharmacy in London is **Zafash** at 233–235 Old Brompton Rd. (Tube: Earls Court).

There's often a pharmacy or chemist at the train station. Condoms are sold in vending machines in most restaurants and in hotel gift shops.

ROYAL MAIL: SHOPPING & SENDING

News agents sell books of royal stamps in cute little red packages. When you purchase a book, you must specify whether you want international stamps. Stamps do not have denominations printed on them.

If you decide to mail items home, you can buy Jiffy bags in the stationery department of any department store or at an office-supply store. Then head for any post office or ask your concierge to do the deed. Mark your package "Unsolicited Gift" and place its value at, say, $25 (unless it's even less, of course). You may legally send one package per day home to the U.S. if its value is under $50.

Tip: If you plan to ship anything large or are considering reserving a container, see chapter 7, "Home Furnishings & Design Resources," for detailed information on shipping.

MONEY MATTERS

I recommend using a credit card for your purchases while in Britain. Plastic is the safest, and it provides you with a record of your purchases (for Customs as well as for your books). It also makes returns much easier. Credit card companies, because they are often associated with banks, also give the best exchange rates.

The bad news: Many banks and cards now add a fee for international transactions. On a recent visit to London, I had an additional $45 in fees just for using my Visa card. Ouch!

To avoid paying credit card fees, check out the Capital One card. It has no annual fees and imposes no fee for foreign purchases. Capital One's mileage program requires more miles for free tickets and you can't use CO miles for upgrades. American Express imposes a 2% fee, while Visa and MasterCard tack on 3%.

Traveler's checks are good—especially if you buy them in sterling and lock in a good rate—if you can cash them. But few stores in London will accept traveler's checks these days, even when they are in sterling. Try to cash them at your hotel.

Best plan: Stop at an ATM and take money directly in sterling as needed, although your bank in the United States will charge you a flat fee (usually $5) for each hit. Some people have the kind of MasterCard that does not charge a fee for international withdrawals. Check your card's rules before you leave home.

Currency Exchange

Currency exchange rates vary tremendously. The rate announced in the paper (it's posted in the *Herald Tribune* every day) is the official bank exchange rate and does not particularly apply to tourists. Even by trading your money at a bank or an ATM, you will not necessarily get the same rate of exchange that's announced in the papers. Here are some tips for your monetary transactions:

- You will get a better rate of exchange for a traveler's check than you will for cash, because there is less paperwork involved for banks, hotels, and so on.
- The rate of exchange can be fixed if you buy traveler's checks in the U.S. in sterling. There will be no fee for cashing them in Britain, and shopkeepers are happier to take checks in sterling, whereas they rarely know what to do with checks in U.S. dollars—or simply won't touch them.
- Expect a bank to give you a better rate than your hotel, although it may not. I've found the best rate of exchange at the American Express office. Usually it gives an exchange

that's close to the bank rate, and it does not charge for changing traveler's checks or personal checks.

- Don't change money (or a lot of it, anyway) with airport vendors, who will have the worst rates in town—yes, even higher than your hotel's.

- I like to have some foreign currency on hand for arrivals. After a lengthy transatlantic flight, I don't want to stand in line at some London airport booth to get my cab fare. Your home bank or local currency-exchange office can sell you small amounts of foreign currency so that, when you arrive in London, you have enough change to take care of immediate needs. Do keep this money readily available on landing—you don't want to have to undress in the taxi to reach your money belt, nor do you want the money packed in a suitcase.

- If you're arriving at London Heathrow and plan to take a taxi into "town," have at least £100 ($200) on hand. If you're arriving at Gatwick and plan to take a taxi into London, have a minimum of £150 ($300) handy. If you're taking the bus, the train, or the Tube, £25 ($50) will be sufficient.

- Have your bank card with you; this is by far the easiest way to get money and to control how much foreign currency you have left over. All of the London airports have ATMs outside their arrivals areas, and there's rarely a line. Find out how much your bank charges for each international withdrawal.

- Do not exchange money with friends or take/make loans in dollars to sterling (or vice versa), as you will not only lose money but possibly lose friends; one side of such a negotiation always loses out.

- Make mental comparisons for quick price reactions. I figured $2 (ouch!) to £1 for this edition. Know the conversion rate for $50 (£25) and $100 (£50) so that you can make a judgment in an instant.

- Expect to pay a commission (often hidden) each time you change money—even at banks. That commission is commonly

£3 ($6) but can be as much as £5 ($10) per transaction! Compare the cost of the commission (if you have to pay one) with your hotel's rate; sometimes convenience is the lesser of two evils. There is no commission at American Express or Barclays for their respective cardholders.

- If you want to change money back to dollars when you leave a country, remember that you will pay a higher rate for them. You are now "buying" dollars rather than "selling" them.

Tipping

When you travel, it works better if you plug into the local rules and denominations for tipping, because the amounts are pegged to local coins. If you normally tip $1 per suitcase at a hotel, you are not going to stand there with your calculator and tip 50p in London. You need to go with the local standards. And yep, it's £1 ($2) per suitcase. Some useful tips:

- If you don't have sterling for tips, U.S. dollars are preferred to euros.
- In restaurants, ask if VAT and service are included (in most cases, it is clearly stated on the bill). Note that in the U.K., this matter is not as flat and dry a rule as in continental Europe—in most cases in London, you add a tip. But I once had a dreadful experience whereby I made an expensive miscalculation and lost £20 ($40) because the tip was already included.
- Check to see what the deal is with room service; you might add a tip to the bill only to find that a service charge and a tip have already been included.
- If the hotel doorman gets a taxi for you, tip him 50p.
- At the hairdresser, tip a total of 15% on the whole—that usually means £2 ($4) for the shampoo person and £4 to £5 ($8–$10) for the stylist.
- In taxis, round up the bill to the nearest number that is somewhere around 10%. If the driver has been particularly helpful, round up a bit more.

- If the concierge staff has been helpful, tip £10 ($20) on checkout—more if they have been incredibly helpful.
- At the airport, there is a fixed price of £10 ($20) for sky-caps, which to me includes the basic tip. Since carts are free at London airports, use them.

The Export Tax Scheme (VAT)

When you bring an item to a cash register in the United States, sales tax is added to the sticker price of your purchase. In Europe, the tax is added before the item is stickered, so the price on the sticker is the total amount you are charged.

If you are not a British subject and if you take the goods out of Britain, you are entitled to a refund on the VAT (value-added tax). You may also get a refund on the VAT for hotel rooms and car rentals, but that's another subject.

The VAT is 17.5%. You may think you should be getting a 17.5% refund on your purchases; however, that is a major oversimplification of the system. You will most likely get back 15% or even 13%, and you may pay a fee to get this rate back.

The basic value-added tax system works like this:

- You are shopping in a store with prices marked on the merchandise. This is the true price of the item, which any tourist or any national must pay. (I'm assuming you're in a department store with fixed prices, not at a flea market.) If you're a national, you pay the price without thinking twice. If you're a tourist who plans to leave the country within 6 months, you ask a salesperson, "What is the minimum expenditure in this store for the export refund?" before shopping.
- The rate varies from shop to shop—usually touristy neighborhoods and drop-dead-chichi stores have a higher quota. The law states that a refund can come your way with a minimum expenditure of £50 ($100). However, in some shops you may be asked to spend £75 to £100 ($150–$200) before you qualify.

- More and more stores, especially the fancy ones, charge a commission for issuing the VAT refund. Expect to lose $10 of the refund.

- Check out the size of the refund before you see stars (or discounts) in your eyes, especially if you are going to many cities in the E.U. and are expected to show the goods at Customs at the point of departure.

- Judge for yourself whether you are certain the store that you are about to do business with will actually give you the refund after the paperwork is done. If you're dealing with a famous department store or a reputable boutique, there should never be a problem. However, I have had considerable problems with several big-name boutiques in both London and the countryside. Most stores have switched to Tax-Free Europe, a firm that does the tax-back for them. This is a reliable firm with a desk at the airport to give you an instant cash refund. It's also a very rich firm because they get a big hunk of your money.

- Sometimes the only savings you get when shopping abroad is the VAT discount. Don't knock it if you can afford it.

- If you go for the VAT, budget your time to allow for the paperwork before you leave the country. It takes about 5 minutes to fill out each form, and you must have the forms completed when you present them upon exiting the country. There can be long lines.

- Along with the VAT forms, you will be given an envelope. Sometimes the envelope has a stamp on it; sometimes it is blank (and you must provide the postage stamp before you leave the country). Sometimes it has a special government frank that serves as a stamp. If you don't understand what's on your envelope, ask.

- When you are leaving the country, go to the Customs official who serves the VAT papers. Do this before you clear regular Customs or send off your luggage. The Customs officer has the right to ask you to show him or her the merchandise you bought and are taking out of the country. The law requires you to have the goods with you, and the

Customs officers at Heathrow are especially vigilant (read, tough).

- If you have too much stuff to carry onboard, you must allow plenty of extra time, as you'll have to exit immigration with your baggage while a security guard stands by, and then get rid of your checked luggage. I dare say 17.5% for a £50 ($100) purchase just isn't worth this kind of aggravation.
- Right after you've done passport control in Heathrow, go to the VAT desk (to your right if passport control is to your back) to show your goods and get your paperwork taken care of. All of the paperwork takes some preparation (filling in your name, address, passport number, and so on), which you are expected to have completed before you stand in the VAT line. It really gums up the works for everyone else if the officer has to explain to you that you should have already done the fill-in-the-blanks part and would you please step over to one side.
- Whether the officer sees your purchases or not, he or she will stamp the papers, keep a set (which will be processed), and give you another set in the envelope. You then mail the envelope (which usually is preprinted with the shop's name and address or has been addressed for you by the shop). There is a mailbox next to the officer's desk. Or use the Tax-Free Europe desk for an instant refund.
- When the papers get back to the shop and the government has notified the shop that its set of papers has been registered, the shop will then grant you the discount through a refund. This can be done by issuing a credit on your credit card or by cutting you a check, which will come to you in the mail, usually 3 months later. (It will be in a foreign currency. Please note that your bank may charge you to change it into dollars.) If you're smart, you will indicate that the refund should be credited to a bank card or American Express so that you end up with a refund in dollars.
- If you opted for a Tax-Free Europe voucher, after it is stamped you can go to the Tax-Free Europe desk in the airport and get your money. You can ask for it in a variety of

currencies, but the conversion rate will not be very favorable. You'd do best to take the cash in sterling and save it for your next trip—or spend it at the news agents on wonderful British magazines.

SAILING AWAY

If you are on a ship that departs from Southampton and are worried about your VAT, fret not. Have everything prepared and ready and watch carefully for the VAT post box, which is on a wall somewhere near the gangplank and after immigration. There is usually no Customs agent and no inspection, so just put the papers in the box, and you're off.

U.S. Customs & Duties

To make your reentry into the United States as smooth as possible, follow these tips:

- Know the rules and stick to them!
- Don't try to smuggle anything.
- Be polite and cooperative (up until the point when they ask you to strip, anyway . . .).

Remember:

- You are currently allowed to bring in $800 worth of merchandise per person, duty-free. Before you leave the U.S., verify this amount with one of the Customs officers. Each member of the family is entitled to the deduction; this includes infants. You may pool within a family.
- You pay a flat 10% duty on the next $1,000 worth of merchandise.
- Duties thereafter are based on a product-type basis. They vary tremendously per item, so think about each purchase and ask storekeepers about U.S. duties. They will know, especially in specialty stores like furriers or china shops.

- The head of the family (who need not be male, by the way) can make a joint declaration for all family members. Whoever is the head of the family should take the responsibility for answering any questions the Customs officers may ask. Answer questions honestly, firmly, and politely. Have receipts ready, and make sure they match the information on your landing card. Don't be forced into a story that won't wash under questioning. If they catch you in a little lie, you'll be labeled as a fibber, and they'll tear your luggage apart.
- Have the Customs registration slips for your personally owned goods in your wallet or easily available. If you wear a Cartier watch, be able to produce the registration slip. If you cannot prove that you took a foreign-made item out of the country with you, you may be forced to pay duty on it.
- Remember the duty on ready-to-wear and stay within the $1,800 U.S. Customs limit, on which you will pay only $100 duty. After that, you'll get into higher duties on clothes, and your bargains may be tarnished. Generally speaking, you can save on U.S. prices if you buy British when it's on sale or if you get the VAT refund.
- The unsolicited gifts you mailed from abroad do not count in the $800-per-person rate. If the value of the gift is more than $50, you pay duty when the package comes into the country. Remember, it's only one unsolicited gift per person for each mailing. Don't mail to yourself.
- Do not attempt to bring in any illegal food items—dairy products, meats, fruits, or vegetables (coffee is okay). Generally speaking, if it's alive, it's *verboten*. I don't need to tell you that it's tacky to bring in drugs and narcotics.
- Antiques must be 100 years old to be duty-free. Provenance papers will help (and so will permission to export the antiquity, since it could be an item of national cultural significance). Any bona fide work of art is duty-free whether it was painted 50 years ago or just yesterday; the artist need not be famous.
- Dress for success. People who look like "hippies" get stopped at Customs more than average folks. Women who

look like a million dollars, who are dragging their fur coats and carrying Gucci handbags and have first-class baggage tags on their luggage—but declare they have bought nothing—are equally suspicious.

- Laws regarding ivory are new and improved—for elephants, anyway. You may not import any ivory into the U.S. Not to worry, as there is little new ivory for sale in London. Antique ivory should have provenance or papers to be legally imported. But wait, Sarah tried to send a set of antique silver and ivory cutlery to the U.S. with a shipment of other antiques. The fish forks had silver hallmarks with proof of age, but there was no arguing with the shipper. He refused to send the goods.

- *Warning:* If you arrive in the U.S. by ship, note that the store personnel onboard all ships report to U.S. Customs who their big customers were and what they bought onboard! Don't try to run anything in—they are waiting for you with your name on a list. Let the buyer beware.

SAVINGS STRATEGIES

English-made ready-to-wear should be less expensive in England, but don't get caught assuming anything. Especially if the dollar has been dancing.

- European designer fashions can work to your advantage, mostly depending on the dollar. There is a strange rule of retailing that generally applies only at sale times, but you can still score on European designer fashions at the end of the season and at big clearance sales. That's because everybody in Britain, if not still broke, is being very, very careful about purchases or is buying *used* designer clothing.

- If you are investing a few hundred pounds, you may want to seriously think about a conversation piece that travels. Whether you buy clothes or accessories, anything from the

Bad Buys in London

With prices as high as they are, and the tendency to mentally go to parity, watch out for some of these items, which only on examination and reflection can turn out to be bad buys. Things to look out for:

- **"Moderately priced" clothes.** These are not moderately priced in England—they are downright expensive. If you expect to find both fashion and quality for less than £25 ($50) or so, forget it. Note that they seem inexpensive when they cost £10 or £25, but in fact that's a $20 T-shirt and a $50 skirt—prices you can find in the U.S. However, if you're willing to give up quality, you can find some great trendy items; head straight to the new **Primark** on Oxford Street to wallow in the bins.
- **Origin and quality.** The adorable £17 ($34) handbag I once bought in a middle-class department store lasted exactly a week before the shoulder strap pulled out and snapped. Before that, I was prepared to tell readers to rush into this store and snap up all the cheap bags. Junk wears like junk. Don't waste your money.
- **Sweaters (or jumpers).** Although these may be pushed at you from every direction, think twice. Unless you buy from an outlet, get seconds or discontinued styles, or snag a big markdown, you may not find the savings you expected on lamb's wool or cashmere. Brits come to America to buy cashmere. British sale prices on a cashmere jumper are rarely below £100 ($200).
- **American brand names.** Clothes from the Gap have their American price code on the tag, and the price in dollars is merely translated into pounds sterling. Honest, I'm not making this up. Something on the sale rack for "19.99" means it's £19.99, or about $40.

cutting-edge kids will give you something to brag about once you get home.

- Even with the cost of shipping to the U.S., you will save money on china and crystal if you buy it on sale or in outlet stores. Sarah bought a cheap day return train ticket to Stoke-on-Trent, bought service for 16-plus serving pieces at an outlet, and had it shipped to California; total spent: $600. Plain old retail can offer savings if you don't ship.

- More specifically on the home-decor front: fabrics. If you crave the cabbage roses or the toile, locally made fabrics cost less in London. Know your yardage and allow for the repeat. Few dealers will ship your order because they don't want to compete with their U.S. showrooms. I found great buys on designer closeout bolts at Peter Jones. Prices were slashed 70% off retail and most remnants were large enough to upholster a small chair or ottoman.

- Basically, shoes are a bad buy in Britain. That is, regular high-fashion shoes or even moderately priced high-fashion shoes are a bad buy. In Britain, they sell cheap shoes at high prices.

- Savings on big brands? Forget it. Luxury brands purchased in the U.K. are a bargain only when the dollar is strong against the pound. When times are tough, even British brands can be less expensive in the U.S.

Chapter Three

....

SLEEPING & EATING IN LONDON

LONDON OR BUST

....

London is one of the most expensive destinations in Europe these days, but smart shoppers who take care with their trip planning can still get lots of value from their travel funds.

I stayed in an apartment on my last trip and loved it. While it's great being pampered in fabulous hotels, I found that the conveniences and value of the apartment far outweighed the extravagance of a hotel room. The space alone was a luxury. I was able to pick up dinners to go, and make my own morning coffee, and—the best part—a maid cleaned it all up every day.

If you normally stay in luxury hotels, check out the amenities or special offers available if you upgrade to a club floor. I downgraded from the club floor on a recent stay, thinking I would save money since I didn't like the breakfast buffet and didn't think the club floor was worth it. Was I ever wrong! I ended up spending much more, including $9 per cup of coffee each morning and over $200 for local phone calls over a 3-day period (I was online)—and local calls were free for club-floor guests.

Moral of the story: Analyze your needs before you book accommodations, and then see how to make the hotel or apartment stay work on your behalf.

SLEEPING IN LONDON

Under Covers

Airline prices may be low, but *baaaaaby,* it's cold outside if you don't have a hotel room—and hotel prices are usually high, unless you are very clever.

It's not hard to find a fabulous hotel in Mayfair—or anywhere else in London—but you may want to give some serious thought as to what combination of location, price, and ease of making reservations suits your budget and sensibilities. Hotel rates are sky-high, so without a deal or a secret find, you may find that a weekend in London is all you can afford.

I've found that my accommodations are the single greatest factor in ensuring whether my trip has been a dream or a nightmare. I believe in luxury hotels, but I also believe in getting the most for my money, which is one of the reasons I like London in the winter so much. Luxury hotels have deals!

Please keep in mind the following:

- Rates for London accommodations are fairly uniform and are based on the rank of the hotel—all five-star hotels cost almost the same amount per night; the same holds for all four-star hotels, and so on. In other words, you may actually be able to afford a hotel that you thought was out of reach.
- Promotions are not uniform. You can better your life with a hotel you didn't even know you could afford if you get the right promotion, or you can be miserable. Many hotels have special deals, especially in winter. Almost every hotel discounts rooms from January to March, when business is down, but they'll sometimes discount during other time periods as well. When hotel rooms are empty, management gets creative. Use this fact to your benefit, and don't be shy about places with hoity-toity reputations. Note that it behooves you to spring for an international call to negotiate directly

with the hotel of your choice; it's unlikely that a toll-free international reservation service will have as much flexibility as a real live local person smelling a deal.

- Watch out for parity deals—these used to be fairly commonplace but they're getting more and more difficult to find. They do appear as limited promotions, usually on the hotels' own websites. By parity, I mean that they trade the sterling price for an equal dollar price, saving you half!
- If you are a regular at a specific hotel but want a break, don't be afraid to write to the general manager of the property and request what you want.
- Look to the chains for promotions for which you may qualify. **Hilton, InterContinental, Thistle,** and **Le Meridien** all run specials, even in the summer season. Often, you can prepay for a room in U.S. dollars. Also, as hotel groups merge, there may be hotel members that you are not familiar with; again, ask. Even the **Four Seasons** has deals.
- Always check the hotel's website before booking on an online discount site. It could save you hundreds of dollars.
- Look for oddball locations or special events, such as luxury hotels that have just been opened, bought, sold, or are rumored to be in financial trouble—frequently, they have deals just to bring in cash or to gain new clients.
- Check out chains and/or hotels in a chain that you have never heard of so that you know for next time. Take a break from shopping to research hotels for your future trips.
- To thine own self be true: If you're the type of person who really doesn't care where you stay or if you're someone who spends little time in your hotel room, book a dump—or at least a less-than-well-known hotel. I know plenty of people who have traded down from five-star hotels to three-star properties in order to keep coming to London.
- Check out concierge floors or executive deals at hotels that offer "free" breakfast and possibly drinks or tea; breakfast can be downright expensive these days. You may pay more, but you'll also get a lot more. If you talk on the phone—this

Pea in a Pod

Flying the dreaded red-eye to London has always meant spending hours upon arrival with bed-head and rumpled clothes, as you wait for your hotel room to be ready. Travelers arriving at Gatwick can now rent small inexpensive compartments for anything from a 4-hour nap to an overnight stay. Designed by genius Paul Priestman, who configured Virgin Atlantic's posh first-class cabins, the accommodations resemble Japanese capsule hotel rooms. The 46 pods at Yotel (www.yotel.com), as it's called, feature private bathrooms with rain shower heads, foldout desks, free Wi-Fi, and 20-inch flatscreen TVs. Prices start at £25 ($50) for 4 hours in a standard cabin (75 sq. ft.); a deluxe version with a bigger bed begins at £40 ($80). As we go to press, another Yotel is scheduled to open at Heathrow.

includes going online or using a phone card—you may want a plan that includes free local calls.

- Consider sharing a luxury room with a friend or bulking up the number of people in the room so that you can giggle together in style.

Newfangled Hotels

If you really are the kind who considers the room just a place to sleep, you may be interested in some of the new, low-cost hotels in London—some of which are either in test markets or simply the first of their kind to be offered to the public.

The easyJet people, who have expanded their concept into a variety of easy options, now run the first low-cost **easy-Hotel**, 14 Lexham Gardens, Kensington, W8 (www.easyhotel. com), where a tiny room starts at just £25 ($50) per night.

Luxury Lowdown

If you're going to be in London for only a couple of nights and can't bear the thought of anything less than a luxury hotel, you may be able to grab a promotional rate. Certain luxury hotels, including the ones with the most famous names, can be more affordable than you might think.

Resist the little voice inside that says you shouldn't even try to stay at "a place like that." Don't be afraid to call around, use toll-free numbers, fax the general manager of a fancy hotel, or ask for a deal from all of your resources. You just may be pleasantly surprised. Don't be intimidated!

A few tips to remember:

- Big chains may have gem hotels that you've never heard of—check them out on a reconnaissance trip, then book for your next stay. Think about the many hotels that are members of the Hilton family but may not be well known, such as the **Hilton Mews,** a true gem (although the rooms are very small), and the **Hilton Green Park** (where you'll find large rooms in a prime location).
- Check out business-oriented hotels such as those clustered around Canary Wharf. These offer a very non-London environment, great shopping, few tourists, and a location only 12 minutes from the heart of town—and you can get fabulous weekend deals.
- Weekend package deals are popular. Usually called "weekend breaks" in Britain, they are meant to generate business when businesspeople and their expense accounts have not filled the ranks. You'll often find a 3-nights-for-the-price-of-2 offer.
- Single rooms in fancy hotels sometimes cost a lot less than you would expect. These rooms may be tiny, but they are luxe; and if it's truly just you and your shopping bags, you may get one of London's poshest hotels for a song.
- Combination city/country deals are sometimes offered. If you are traveling around Great Britain, consider arranging

your schedule so that you spend the first weekend in London at one hotel, travel during the week (rates are lower in the countryside and in Edinburgh), and then return to London for the second weekend—maybe even to a different hotel, depending on the deal. Also check out Birmingham and Manchester, which are big cities with big international airports but also interesting shopping ops and many air and hotel deals.

Apples & Oranges

When you begin to gather information and make price comparisons, be sure that you are comparing apples with apples. I just had a terrible experience wherein I stayed at two so-called luxury hotels with rooms at about the same price. One of the hotels was a dream come true; the other had two tour groups, lost my luggage, gave me a room so bad that I rejected it on first sight, and took 24 hours to change a light bulb. Niceties such as turndown service and plush towels were not to be found.

Warning

As you research and compare hotel prices, make sure you check to see if the tax has been added in. Usually rates are quoted without tax. And with the tax at a whopping 17.5%, you will wince when you see the total tax and room rate together.

The Big Splurge

All hotels in London are expensive. Luxury hotels can easily cost £250 to £350 ($500–$700) per night for a double room; some of them cost a lot more than that. I once asked a London hotelier friend why people would pay £250 ($500) a night. He explained that the room you'd get for £125 ($250) is frequently in such a bad hotel that you'll be delighted to pay twice as much to get exactly what you want. Because London is so expensive, you are the only one who can decide where there is real value and where there is psychic value . . . and which one you care most about.

THE BERKELEY
Wilton Place, SW1 (Tube: Knightsbridge or Hyde Park Corner).

First off, be sure that you pronounce this properly—it's *Barkley*. Now you're ready to be converted. This hotel is the secret find of a secret sect of fine shoppers and businesspeople who settle into the rather plain-looking building that hides a world of comfort, including one of the most famous spas in town (with rooftop pool and retractable roof) and a new bar, called the Blue Bar, which is not only chic but also the hangout of many movie stars.

The hotel is so dedicated to shopping that it gives guests a shopper's map and directions to hidden and nearby shops that aren't your ordinary chain or multiple. You'll be within walking distance of all the best shopping in town—just a block from Harvey Nicks and Sloane Street. Also note that, as well situated as the hotel is for well-known shopping areas, it prides itself on guiding visitors to the little-known spots hidden in Belgravia. Until I stayed here, I'd never had a way to connect the dots before, and always got lost roaming around the little streets off Sloane. Now I am found.

There's always special promotions listed on the hotel website. One of the best deals for U.S. visitors is the Great London Weekend, where you get 3 nights for the price of 2; you must check in on Friday. ✆ **800/637-2869** in the U.S. Local phone ✆ **207/235-6000**. www.the-berkeley.co.uk.

THE CADOGAN
75 Sloane St., just off Sloane Sq., SW1 (Tube: Sloane Sq.).

Within the walls of this Knightsbridge charmer, some of London society's most colorful figures made controversial history. In 1895, Oscar Wilde sipped hock in room no. 118 as he awaited arrest on charges of committing offenses against young men, and Lillie Langtry cavorted here with Edward, the future king of England.

Today, the hotel is still the epitome of refined discretion (we spotted a former presidential mistress in the lobby during our visit). The draw is obvious: A recent refit has brought luxurious contemporary style to the guest rooms and suites, while maintaining a sense of history, elegance, and (assumed) privacy in the public areas.

The location is perfect for Sloane shopping; check out the "Shopping in Knightsbridge" package, which includes 2 nights, dinner with champagne, late checkout, and a £50 ($100) gift certificate to Harvey Nicks. © 207/235-7141.

THE INTERCONTINENTAL LONDON PARK LANE
One Hamilton Place, Park Lane, W1 (Tube: Hyde Park Corner).

The InterContinental's glamorous location, with straight-on views of Buckingham Palace, is now matched by its fab new interiors. The hotel was just refurbished to the tune of $113 million, with a knockout lobby by London design firm J2 and all new damask- and linen-swathed rooms. The new Elemis Spa is the size of a McMansion and provides individually tailored treatments, whether you have only minutes between shopping excursions or hours to indulge.

This is a hotel where it's worth the extra pounds to splurge for access to the Club InterContinental Lounge. You'll be treated to complimentary buffet breakfast, lunch snacks, and evening cocktails with enough hors d'oeuvres to consider it dinner. The lounge also has free Wi-Fi, along with computers to check your e-mail while you sip a cocktail. This is value!

Food lovers and aspiring chefs can arrange an "Insider Experience" whereby resident renowned chef Theo Randall will take them on a taxi tour of London's food shops followed by lunch specially prepared by him in his kitchen. © 207/409-3131. www.intercontinental.com.

THE LANGHAM
1C Portland Place, Regent St., W1 (Tube: Oxford Circus).

A member of Leading Hotels of the World, the Langham is in a perfect shopping location—a block from the junction of Oxford Circus and Regent Street. The hotel was built in Victorian times and has been renovated to its old-fashioned splendor. Rooms vary enormously, ranging from ho-hum to drop-dead gorgeous. A spa has been added; there are also a club floor with the usual amenities and a business center in the lobby, where you can buy a computer card and use the Internet for less than it will cost to use your laptop in your room. © 207/636-1000. www.langhamhotels.com.

THE MILESTONE HOTEL AND APARTMENTS
1 Kensington Court, W8 (Tube: High St. Kensington).

It was Pierce Brosnan who first told me about this hotel, which is a secret hidden in plain sight. A member of Leading Hotels of the World, it's in a fabulous shopping location, at the edge of Kensington High Street, and is as British and cabbage rose as you can imagine. There are also six two-bedroom apartments, which rent by the week.

The usual old-fashioned British amenities are mixed with modern ones—library, billiard room, butler, business center, and spa with small indoor pool. While rates are often over $600 a night, in the off season, there may be special promotions for less, or packages worth the extra pounds. In September, they offer a special deal including room plus admission to London Fashion Week events. © 800/223-6800 in the U.S. Local phone © 207/917-1000. www.milestonehotel.com.

Fabulous Finds

THE ATHENAEUM HOTEL AND APARTMENTS
116 Piccadilly, W1 (Tube: Green Park or Hyde Park Corner).

I thought about listing this property under Apartment Living, but I was afraid you might miss it and that would be a big mistake. It could also go in the splurge category, but most of all, it's one of my best finds. Ever.

On our last trip to London, my husband and I stayed in a flat adjacent to and owned by the Athenaeum Hotel. Not only were we based in a fab Mayfair apartment, but we also had all the services and luxuries of a deluxe hotel. Our flat had a large living/dining room with a fireplace, and a full kitchen with washer/dryer, oven, full-size fridge, and microwave. I didn't see a dishwasher, but the twice-daily maid service included dish duty. There were two huge windowed bays, one with a desk full of computer and power plugs, and the other in the bedroom with a beautiful antique dressing table. The marble bathroom was huge, and Tom loved the power shower. I can't tell you how nice it was to come back to our London home at the end of the day, pop dinner from Marks & Spencer's food hall into the oven, and relax in front of the big flatscreen TV. —S.R.L.

Occupying a row of Edwardian town houses connected to the hotel, the one- and two-bedroom apartments are individually designed and decorated. Some are classic British, some are contemporary, and all are family, couple, and girlfriend-weekend friendly. Each apartment has a sofa bed in the living room, so lots of friends and family could camp out comfortably. With only two apartments per floor in each town house, privacy is assured, and there's a Long Stay Guest Programme in place if you really can't bear to leave. ✆ 207/499-3464. www. athenaeumhotel.com.

The Hilton Green Park
Half Moon St., Mayfair, W1 (Tube: Green Park).

Over the years, I have been a loyal and consistent Hilton customer. They have a lot of properties in London; the hotels are varied in terms of style, location, and price. The Mayfair location couldn't be more convenient; this hidden Hilton couldn't be a better find. Within a 5-minute walk are the Green Park Tube station, Piccadilly restaurants and shopping, two food halls (Marks & Spencer and the fab new Fortnum & Mason), plus a Sainsbury's for in-room snacks. Shepherd Market with great restaurants and Michaeljohn Salon are a quick stroll away.

The hotel is based in a series of 14 Georgian town houses dating back to 1730. Recently refurbished, all 162 bedrooms now have a modern minimalist design with state-of-the-art equipment including PlayStation and phones with dataports.

On one visit, I had a small but charming deluxe double with king-size bed and private patio accessible through French doors. My last stay was in a much larger room in the same category—more space, no patio. Curious, I asked to see some other rooms, and even the smallest single was more than adequate with a twin bed, wall of windows, and huge bathroom. —S.R.L.

You can easily book this hotel on the Hilton website. If you can plan ahead, their advance-purchase rates beat all the competition. © 800/HILTONS in the U.S. Local phone © 207/629-7522. www.hilton.com.

MILLENNIUM MAYFAIR
44 Grosvenor Sq., W1 (Tube: Green Park).

The Millennium Mayfair is tucked into Grosvenor Square in Mayfair and equidistant to Bond Street, Oxford Street, and Piccadilly. This hotel recently completed a top-to-bottom redo and now boasts some of the best rooms in London, most of which are good size with huge bathrooms. While special deals are always available on the hotel's website, I usually book on London.com, which continually offers the best price.

Out of season, you can get a standard room for under £150 ($300) but the price goes up in high season. Sarah has stayed at this hotel for years and always requests room no. 429; it's really a junior suite, but sold as a deluxe double. Celebrity chef Brian Turner has opened his latest restaurant in the hotel, which is a member of the Millennium/Copthorne group mentioned below. ✆ 800/465-6486 in the U.S. Local phone ✆ 207/629-9400. www.millenniumhotels.com.

THE ROYAL GARDEN HOTEL
2–24 Kensington High St., SW (Tube: Kensington High St.).

Location! Location! Location! That's what real estate is all about and this deluxe property occupies one of the prime sites in London. Overlooking Kensington gardens at the top of Kensington High Street, the Royal Garden Hotel is convenient to the shopping neighborhoods of Kensington, Notting Hill, and Knightsbridge. The Tube is a 5-minute walk away, and there are plenty of restaurants nearby. Whole Foods has opened across the street, and Starbucks is within view; it doesn't get much better than this.

Not only is the location great, but you'll get good value for your money. This is a five-star property with all the bells and whistles, and (get out the highlighter) you can often book a weekend break for under £150 ($300) a night including VAT and full English breakfast. Book early and use the hotel website. ✆ 207/937-8000. www.royalgardenhotel.co.uk.

Value Visits

CORUS HOTEL HYDE PARK
Lancaster Gate W2 (Tube: Lancaster Gate).

Sarah found this hotel online when planning a last-minute trip with some girlfriends, and has since recommended it to others who also love the location and, especially, the price. Located on Hyde Park, the hotel has recently been completely refurbished, and if you book or upgrade to a deluxe room, you'll be over the moon, as they say here.

Basic rooms are very small but have just about everything you need, including good hair dryers and irons. There are no chests for storage, only built-in shelving, but we found plenty of room for a week's worth of gear plus everything we bought. ✆ 844/736-8601; www.corushotels.com.

LINCOLN HOUSE HOTEL
33 Gloucester Place, W1 (Tube: Marble Arch).

We received a letter from this B&B hotel asking to be considered for *Born to Shop London,* and although we haven't stayed there, we love the location and, best of all, the deals. Not only are their rates reasonable (most rooms are under £100/$200), but they will sometimes offer an additional 10% discount to U.S. and Canadian visitors coping with disastrous exchange rates.

The small Georgian hotel is located between Oxford and Marylebone streets, a 5-minute walk from Marble Arch. A full English or vegetarian breakfast is available for an additional £3.50 ($7) per person. This is not the Dorchester, but if you are looking to save money, give it a try and write to tell us what you think. ✆ 207/486-0166.

The Chain Game

Below I've listed my favorites among the many chain properties represented in London:

CROWNE PLAZA   This chain is a more upmarket division of Holiday Inns; note that its prices are usually quoted per person (not per room). There are three London branches, geared mostly toward businesspeople—one in the Docklands, one in the City of London, and one at Heathrow airport. ✆ 877/227-6963 in the U.S. www.crowneplaza.co.uk.

HILTON   Hilton is not the big-box hotel of your childhood. Take a look at the **Hilton Trafalgar**—the first boutique hotel in the chain. There are plenty of other Hiltons in London, too, in all sizes, shapes, and flavors; they differ enormously but do offer some advantages. If you're into wow, the recently rehabbed **Hilton Paddington** is a Victorian railroad hotel done in Art Deco glitz, somewhat like the new Hilton in Paris. The location right above Paddington Station also has some obvious transportation benefits. Sarah has fallen for London's **The Hilton Green Park** (p. 58).

HOLIDAY INN   Holiday Inn advertises some great promotional deals and has hotels not just in London and the U.K., but all over the world. There are always promotional deals on its website. © **800/282-0244** in the U.S. www.holiday-inn.co.uk.

MARRIOTT   Marriott's hotel near the American Embassy in Mayfair has been well known for years, but there is now a newer property right near the London Eye, across the bridge from Big Ben, overlooking the River Thames and not too far from Waterloo International or the City. You can often use frequent-flier miles to book. © **888/236-2427** in the U.S. www.marriott.com.

MILLENNIUM/COPTHORNE   See above (p. 59) for information on the Millennium Mayfair; there's another Millennium located in Knightsbridge, right on Sloane Street. This chain is known for its excellent promotional deals. © **800/465-6486** in the U.S. www.millenniumhotels.com.

RADISSON EDWARDIAN   With a half-dozen hotels in London and one at the airport, Radisson Edwardian offers excellent value for the money in its four-star hotels. In the past couple years, it has taken over several new properties in good locations, renovated them, and elevated the quality of the product. Furthermore, you can often find Radisson rooms online at great prices. Locations tend to be in the Covent Garden area, which is convenient for museums, theater, and browsing. © **800/333-3333** in the U.S. www.radissonedwardian.com.

THISTLE   Thistle often runs a "Shop 'til you Drop" promotion to coincide with the January sales. This is not the high end of the scale, but do you care? www.thistlehotels.com.

Apartment Living

If you don't want to be anyone's guest at all, you may want to consider renting a flat, which not only works out cheaper on a nightly basis, but also gives you the option of cooking some of your meals. An apartment also makes the most sense if you're looking for value and are facing the need to rent two hotel rooms.

Although prices vary tremendously, you can get a nice flat with two bedrooms and two bathrooms in a slightly suburban London neighborhood in the range of £500 ($1,000) per week. Expect to pay £650 ($1,300) minimum—or a lot more— for a small luxe flat with a fine location.

When renting a flat, ask if the quoted price includes the VAT and if maid service is included. June and July are the most popular months and should be booked well in advance. There are usually special offers or deals for winter and off-season months, just as with hotels.

If you do not want to rent through an agency, you may want to go directly through proprietors who have listed their homes through a website like **www.vrbo.com**. The letters stand for "vacation rentals by owner," which tells you everything.

The **Barclay International Group** (© 800/845-6636 in the U.S.; www.barclayweb.com) is an American firm that will book you into any of its apartments in London.

The **Apartment Company** (© 207/835-1144) is a British firm that seems to work much like Barclay, with similar properties. Depending on the size of the flat, you're looking at £750 to £2,000 ($1,500–$4,000) per week, plus VAT.

Craigslist (www.craigslist.com) has become a consistent good resource for holiday apartments—both rental and trades. Craigslist is a good bet for last-minute rentals, which is just what you need when you grab that promotional weekend airfare.

The **Athenaeum Hotel and Apartments** (© 207/499-3464). See p. 57, earlier in this chapter, for information on these luxe apartments.

Airport Hotels

If you are connecting through LHR and need an airport hotel, you won't have trouble finding one. Many airlines have links with a specific hotel that will offer you a price break or other amenities and privileges. I once stayed at a Holiday Inn at the airport and was lent a Virgin Atlantic bathing suit! Indeed, I often pick my hotel based on the spa and pool services—that way I can go for a swim and get a massage.

The $250-million **Sofitel London Heathrow** at Terminal 5 is scheduled to open in late March 2008 with more than 600 rooms. It will connect directly to the airport via a link bridge into one of the new terminal's atriums.

Note that many airport properties provide shuttle service into London for free or a small cost. Airport hotels usually charge less than London hotels, so they may be a worthwhile alternative if you have only half a day to explore London before you connect elsewhere.

And speaking of shuttles, the airport system for the hotels in the immediate area is called the **Hotel Hoppa.** (Hey, don't shoot the messenger.) You do not call your hotel directly on arrival, but instead buy a shuttle ticket, find the proper zone (color-coded) for your hotel, and go outside to await the next shuttle. Round-trip tickets are discounted.

Beyond the Airport

What you may not realize is that Heathrow is very close to the town of Windsor, and isn't that far from a few English country-house mansion-style hotels; so if you want luxury and convenience (or charm and convenience), you don't have to stay at the airport to be close to it. Many of these nearby hotels will include airport transfer in the price, just ask.

EATING IN LONDON

More, please. Since Oliver Twist had the nerve to ask for a second helping, British food has improved to the point where it is hard to get reservations at certain restaurants. What's more, the French are actually coming over from Paris just to try the cooking at a few fine kitchens that have recently earned extra Michelin stars.

If you don't want to spend all your money on food and would rather save a little for shopping, do not despair. London has more meal deals than almost any other city. Even the hotshot places have deals.

Those with small appetites or small budgets can rejoice: This is the city where the "jacket potato" (baked potato) constitutes an entire meal and can be eaten in any of the numerous potato fast-food joints, where it comes with a variety of toppings that turn it into quite a hefty meal.

I now plan most of my London meals around takeout and picnics. I usually buy prepared food at **Whole Foods, Marks & Spencer,** or the new **Fortnum & Mason** food hall for an alfresco lunch, but there are now so many grocery stores that sell prepared meals in the key shopping areas of London that you'll have no trouble finding something to please your palate and your purse. The hardest part may be selecting just the right bench or stretch of lawn on which to plop yourself.

Pizza is another of my mainstays in London; I consider it a special treat to eat at almost any branch of **PizzaExpress,** including its upmarket **Pizza on the Park.** There are almost 100 branches of this chain in the U.K., with at least 40 in the London area, so I can't list them all. The menu lists all London locations on the back.

Big-Time Meal Deals

In London, the secret to dining in style on a budget lies in knowing the two basic tricks that have been added to almost every upscale eatery's repertoire: the pre-theater meal and the fixed-price meal. A la carte prices may kill you, but a deal will enrich you.

Pre-theater meals are usually served around 6pm; note that curtain times in London vary by the production and are usually earlier than in New York. A 7:30pm curtain is generally the rule. Therefore, pre-theater dinners are available only at an early hour. If this doesn't bother you (you are American, aren't you?), you can dine like a king at some of the best tables in London for the price of a song. A little night music, anyone?

Fixed-price meals are offered in several major hotel dining rooms (dancing and/or entertainment may be included) and at the hautest of tables, including those of London's most famous Michelin-star chefs. *Note:* Many of London's fancy tables take some getting into, so the browse-and-book method will not work for you. You may want to fax ahead for a reservation, or several reservations; hold them until you can check out the situation; and then cancel once you get to town. Do give 24 hours' notice when you cancel; this is a very polite town where manners matter.

Best Spots for Ladies Who Lunch

All of the following restaurants serve dinner and are considered both hot spots and places to be seen in London. I've chosen the best ones that are also located in good shopping neighborhoods so that you can segue smoothly from store to table and back again. Note that lunch often costs less than dinner. Reservations at these places are recommended, so is proper dress.

DAPHNE'S
112 Draycott Ave., SW3 (Tube: South Kensington).

Right in the heart of the Walton Street shopping at the edge of Brompton Cross, this has been *the* place since it opened a few years ago. The food is slightly Italian; the crowd is sleek and chic. © 207/589-4257. www.daphnes-restaurant.co.uk.

NICOLE'S
158 New Bond St., W1 (Tube: Bond St.).

The place of the moment is actually inside the Nicole Farhi store. Enjoy an expensive but stylish lunch or tea here; it's the place to say you've been. Wear beige. No hat. © 207/499-8408. www.nicolefarhi.com.

SAN LORENZO
22 Beauchamp Place, SW3 (Tube: Knightsbridge).

The "in" place before Daphne's opened—and still not shabby; it was the fave of Princess you-know-who and still gets a jet-set and celeb crowd. It's right on Beauchamp Place in the middle of one of London's fine shopping streets, and within walking distance of Harrods. © 207/584-1074.

Old Faithfuls

Since I tend to do my shopping research in the same places every year, I've developed a small group of regular haunts to which I return year after year, visit after visit. They are chosen for the combination of location, style, and price.

CRITERION GRILL
224 Piccadilly, W1 (Tube: Piccadilly Circus).

Criterion Grill is what is now known as a gastropub, with set-price menus. The space is a drop-dead-gorgeous renovated theater, with tiles and Turkish/Oriental art and bold strokes. It's owned by the famous chef Marco Pierre White. © 207/930-0488. www.whitestarline.org.uk.

EAT
319 Regent St., W1 (Tube: Oxford Circus).

This is a fresh sandwich, soup, and salad bar, part of a chain, but with really high-quality tastes. I would kill for the shrimp and langoustine salad with red Thai dressing. You can also stop in just to refuel with a drink—anything from an espresso macchiato to a chai latte made with soy milk. © 207/636-8309. www.eatcafe.com.

EAT AND TWO VEG
50 Marylebone High St., W1 (Tube: Baker St.).

This is a large, contemporary diner–style vegetarian restaurant where you can get brekkie at all hours. It serves updated veg versions of comfort food (like shepherd's pie), plus untraditional diner fare (like Thai green curry). © 207/258-8595. www. eatandtwoveg.com.

In-Store Meals

Eating inside a store has become very trendy in London. **Emporio Armani** serves Italian food at a really super cafe, while **Nicole Farhi** offers her signature fare downstairs in the Bond Street flagship. **DKNY** has a snack bar that serves bagels and cream cheese, brownies, and other American-style foods. Even **Sotheby's**, the auction house, has a cafe now.

The big department stores have always had restaurants, and some have several. Nowadays, many of these store restaurants have spiffed up and are quite hip; some use big-name chefs as consultants.

The best thing for shoppers about eating in a store is the convenience factor—you're already there, so put down your bags and take a seat. Get in early if you don't have a reservation.

THE CONRAN SHOP
Michelin House, 81 Fulham Rd., SW3 (Tube: South Kensington).

Nobody combines food and shopping like Sir Terence Conran. His state-of-the-art masterpiece is still the rehabilitation of Michelin House, which features his store and its famous companion restaurant, **Bibendum.** Book way in advance and hope that someone else is paying. © 207/581-5817. www.bibendum. co.uk.

FENWICK
63 New Bond St., W1 (Tube: Bond St. or Oxford Circus).

A trendy branch of **Carluccio's** is downstairs; the Italian deli concept offers great food, many salads, and a fun crowd. You probably don't need a rez, but if you want to, call © 207/629-0699. www.carluccios.com.

FORTNUM & MASON
181 Piccadilly, W1 (Tube: Piccadilly Circus).

This firm just celebrated its 300th birthday by closing shop
for almost a year and redoing the entire store; yes, it's older
than the queen and now even more glamorous. A couple of
new restaurants have been added, and **The Fountain Restaurant,** which is very popular, has been completely refurbished.
Still my favorite, it doesn't accept lunch reservations; if you're
alone, team up with a stranger to be served more quickly. (I
do it all the time.) New store restaurants include **The Gallery**
and **1707 Wine Bar,** located in the food hall. If you feel like
ice cream and cake for lunch, try the new Parlour restaurant
on the First Floor. © **207/734-8040.** www.fortnumand
mason.co.uk.

HARRODS
*87–135 Brompton Rd., Knightsbridge, SW1 (Tube:
Knightsbridge).*

I recently had visitors to my house in Provence who came
to me via London and couldn't stop talking about the 22
restaurants inside Harrods. Although there are not actually
22 restaurants inside Harrods, London's most famous department store does have several restaurants, including the famed
food halls. In those food halls are several food bars, great for
those who are dining alone. Note that there's a charge to use
the loo at Harrods, but if you flash your receipt from a meal
there, you get to have a wee for free. A Harrods credit card
will also pay your way into the toilet. © **207/730-1234.**
www.harrods.com.

HARVEY NICHOLS
*109–125 Knightsbridge (at Sloane St.), SW1 (Tube:
Knightsbridge).*

The fifth floor of this Sloane Square institution has a gourmet
restaurant—called **Fifth Floor**—where reservations are a must.

There's also a small sushi area, **Yo! Sushi,** across from the food products. My favorite for a quick, inexpensive lunch is **Wagamama,** in the basement on Harvey Nicks—not on the Fifth Floor. Do try one of their signature freshly squeezed juices with your noodles. © 207/235-5250. www.harveynichols.com.

Picnics

Few things are more British than the picnic, and with prices so high, you may want to take some of your meals outdoors—in a park, at an outdoor event, or even in your hotel room. I usually make my picnics from supplies found at **Marks & Spencer** or other grocery stores, but several of the London food halls offer ready-packed picnic hampers. Check with **Harrods** as well as **Fortnum & Mason.** Some of these formally made picnics are not inexpensive: Fortnum & Mason offers a full picnic for two—in a container that you keep—starting at about £75 ($150).

Ethnic Eats

Because London is such a melting pot, you can dip in for any or every meal. While everyone knows the Indian food here is among the best in the world, there are plenty of other immigrant communities that offer tasty treats at fair prices. Browse some of these districts for ethnic flavors:

Brixton: West Indian

Clerkenwell: Italian

Ealing: Polish

Earl's Court: Filipino

Golborne Road: Moroccan and Portuguese

Hackney: Vietnamese

Haringey: Turkish

Highgate: Russian

Kensington: Iranian

New Malden: Korean

Soho: Chinese

Gastropubs & Bar Meals

Gastropubs are considered a new trend in British cuisine, when in fact the French have called this sort of restaurant a bistro for centuries. A gastropub has the casual atmosphere of a pub and a friendly, easygoing crowd, but boasts a decent, even well-known chef and excellent food at a fair price.

Consider taking one of your meals in a posh hotel bar, which accomplishes many things: You get to visit a swish place; it's okay to be alone; it costs less than a full sit-down, gourmet-style meal; you meet divine people; and you can stare all through your meal. The trendiest are **Claridge's Bar** (with a separate entrance from Claridge's), **Lanes Bar** (at the Four Seasons), and the **Blue Bar** (at the Berkeley).

Even if you don't drink, you can still have a bar meal—these tend toward very fancy miniature meals, such as lobster burgers, foie gras on potato pancakes, and all sorts of morsels you wouldn't have at home. You can eat for as little as £13 ($26).

Teatime

I am a longtime believer in the English custom of taking tea for two very simple reasons:

1. After you've been shopping all day, you need to plop down, drop the packages, and sip tea at 3 or 4pm.
2. If you want to save money, you can have a big tea and go light on (or skip) dinner. Conversely, if dinner isn't until 8pm or later, you'll never last without a sufficient tea break. Tea may be so expensive that dinner costs less; ask! Or buy tea a la carte.

All the big fancy hotels have tea service; you can make it your job to try a different one every day. I have discovered, however, that there are several ins and outs to getting full value from teatime, so get out your highlighter. If you're British, don't blush—I'm going to talk about money.

Generally speaking, tea comes at a set price per person and includes the tea (or coffee) of your choice and a three-round selection of sandwiches, scones, and sweets. There is also tea with sherry or tea with champagne.

Tea is usually served from 3 to 5:30 or 6pm. If sherry is served, it is called high tea. "Teatime," as a time of meeting someone or fixing your schedule, is usually meant to be 4pm; by 5pm, it is socially acceptable to start drinking. I've never heard of anyone going to tea at 6pm.

Now for the tricky part: the finances of taking tea. At grand hotels, you pay a flat fee for the total tea service, and that price is not cheap. Expect to pay an average of £13 ($26) per person, although some are £20 ($40) and prices do go higher than £25 ($50) per person at a very elegant place.

It is very unusual, especially at an elegant hotel, for tea to be served a la carte. However, at a few addresses, you may buy the full tea service for one and a second (or even third) pot of tea a la carte, thus saving about £10 ($20). Furthermore, one or two hotels allow for total a la carte tea service. Since very few people can eat all of what is provided at teatime, this is a money-saving device—don't be embarrassed to make it clear that you don't want to pay for what you won't eat.

THE BERKELEY
Wilton Place, SW1 (Tube: Knightsbridge or Hyde Park Corner).

As one of the hippest hotels in London, the Berkeley always has something new and chic happening. So it's no surprise that it has re-created teatime as a fashion statement; now, at "Prêt-à-Portea," you can get couture confections—tea cookies made and decorated like dresses, such as a chocolate cookie with pink icing made into an Oscar de la Renta dress. The price per person is £34 ($68) but you get to eat a lot of dresses. © 207/235-6000. www.the-berkeley.co.uk.

BROWN'S HOTEL
Albemarle St., W1 (Tube: Green Park).

For years, I've been sending people to Brown's Hotel for tea; now that the place has been totally renovated, you have yet another reason to visit. There's no question that it's one of the top teas in London, with scones that are among the best. You may request one setup (tea for one) and additional cups of tea, or you may ask for a platter of scones to replace the tea setup (but at the same cost) with individual pots of tea. Jackets and ties are required for the gentlemen; be prepared for a long wait if you aren't early. © 207/493-6020. www.brownshotel.com.

FOUR SEASONS
Hamilton Place, Park Lane, W1 (Tube: Hyde Park Corner or Green Park).

This is one of the best teas in London because it's different from everyone else's—and reasonably priced as well! You can do a scone-tasting tea service, or simply order a la carte at £3.50 ($7) per scone. The three kinds of scones in the tasting are peach, mango, and sultana. And I needn't tell you that, as at all Four Seasons hotels, the service is sublime and the room is in traditional English style. *Note:* Tea is not served at Four Seasons Canary Wharf, as guests tend to be there on business and do not take tea. © 207/499-0888. www.fourseasons.com.

Eats for Teens

I've made it rather clear that I don't come to Britain to do business with American brands, but if you're with teens, you may want to at least note the location of several of the big American teenage haunts that have invaded Piccadilly, such as **Planet**

Hollywood, 13 Coventry St., W1. The **Hard Rock Cafe** actually began in London; it's over near the Four Seasons, at 150 Old Park Lane. I'm fonder of **Rainforest Cafe,** 20 Shaftsbury Ave., W1, which started life in the Mall of America and now has branches all over the U.S.

Inside the **Miss Selfridge** department of the flagship Selfridges, there's a tiny cafe geared toward teens.

McDonald's and **Starbucks** can be found everywhere.

Chapter Four

....

SHOPPING NEIGHBORHOODS

YOURS IN A ZIP

Zip codes in London are called postal codes. They are made up of two sets of letter and number combinations. The first set indicates the precise part of town where the address is located, and it serves as a good pointer for shoppers who want to organize themselves by neighborhood.

If you study the map, you'll see that the metropolitan area is divided into quadrants and that these have a few subcategories, such as southwest, southeast, and so on. Then there's a central core, whose zones have the letter C in them for—you guessed it—"central." You can look up the general area of a store or shopping neighborhood just by using this map.

As you get more sophisticated at using this method, you'll learn the few overlapping places. For instance, Mayfair is W1, but Jermyn Street, at the edge of Mayfair, is in SW1. Practice, practice, practice.

LONDON BY NEIGHBORHOOD

London is one of the best cities in the world in which to pick a neighborhood and wander without specific goals. Each neighborhood is distinctive because of the way the city grew out of many individual towns. Some famous names overlap (like Chelsea and Knightsbridge); some are actually separate cities, such as the city of Westminster.

Do note that it is inappropriate to refer to London or the portion of London an American might deem to be "downtown" as "the City." In Brit-speak, the City truly means the City of London, which is a teeny-tiny 1-mile area where the financial institutions have their offices and the banking people—and the insurance people and the other suits—do their business. (Not much shopping here.)

Now then, it behooves you to know the areas of town more than ever thanks to the congestion tax, which does indeed limit noncommercial traffic but may also affect where your local friends want to meet you.

Connect the Dots by Neighborhood

If you work with a daily schedule or list of shopping goals, you'll soon see that certain neighborhoods lead directly to one another, usually by foot but often by bus. I have tried to organize this chapter by interconnecting neighborhoods related to a larger area. For me, as a person who listens to the vibes of the sidewalk, a shopping neighborhood may hold a specific mood for only 2 or 3 blocks before changing into something else. I've tried to indicate the changes and segues.

There are "new" neighborhoods popping up all the time, particularly as people get tired of moving farther out of town and begin taking over older areas and gentrifying them. We all know about Notting Hill, thanks in part to Julia Roberts, but the next Notting Hill is said to be Shepherd's Bush. Meanwhile, the East End is getting hotter and hotter and will continue to do so as gentrification arrives with the preparations for the 2012 Olympic games.

London Postal Codes

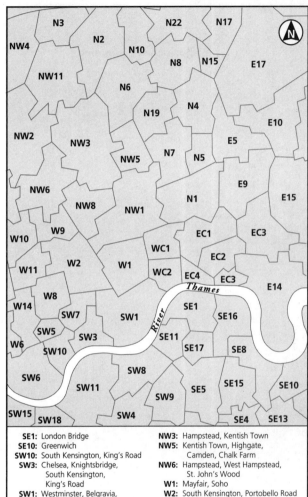

SE1: London Bridge
SE10: Greenwich
SW10: South Kensington, King's Road
SW3: Chelsea, Knightsbridge,
   South Kensington,
   King's Road
SW1: Westminster, Belgravia,
   Jermyn Street, Sloane Street
SW7: South Kensington, Knightsbridge
EC1: Islington, Angel
E 3: Tower of London, City of London
EC4: Fleet Street, Old Bailey
N1: Islington, King's Cross
NW1: Camden, Chalk Farm,
   King's Cross, Euston
NW2: West Hampstead

NW3: Hampstead, Kentish Town
NW5: Kentish Town, Highgate,
   Camden, Chalk Farm
NW6: Hampstead, West Hampstead,
   St. John's Wood
W1: Mayfair, Soho
W2: South Kensington, Portobello Road
W8: Kensington High Street, Earl's Court
W10: North Kensington, Portobello Road
W11: Portobello Road Market
WC1: Mayfair, Soho, The West End,
   Savile Row, The Strand,
   Oxford Street
WC2: Covent Garden, Trafalgar Square,
   Charing Cross Road, Piccadilly

London Neighborhoods at a Glance

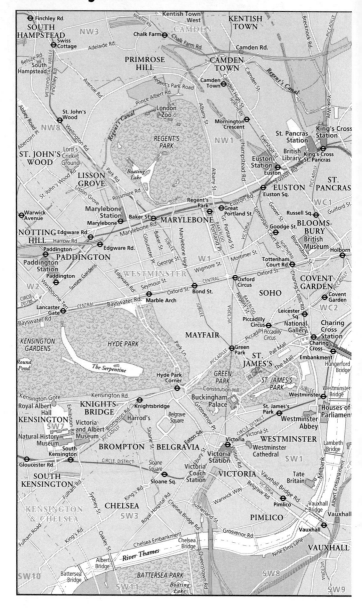

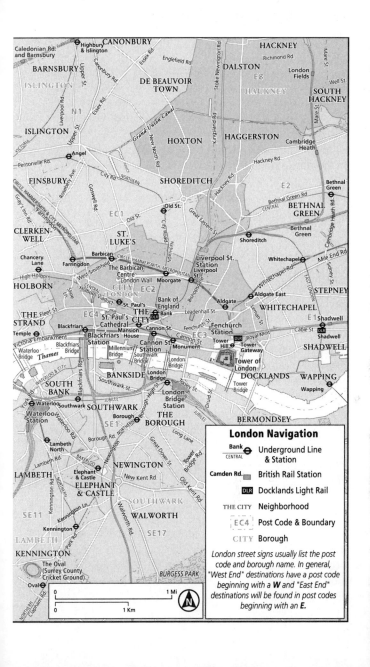

London Navigation

Symbol	Meaning
Bank / CENTRAL	Underground Line & Station
Camden Rd.	British Rail Station
DLR	Docklands Light Rail
THE CITY	Neighborhood
EC4	Post Code & Boundary
CITY	Borough

*London street signs usually list the post code and borough name. In general, "West End" destinations have a post code beginning with a **W** and "East End" destinations will be found in post codes beginning with an **E**.*

0   1 Mi
0   1 Km

THE WEST END

The West End is the name for a large portion of real estate; a W1 address is very chic—for a store or a residence. The major shopping areas in the West End are Oxford Street, Oxford Circus, Regent Street, Bond Street (Old and New), and Piccadilly. While they are well established, there are enormous changes in the vibe from time to time.

Oxford Street

To enjoy Oxford Street, you have to settle into the right frame of mind (or be 22) and begin to groove on the street vendors selling Union Jacks printed on T-shirts and underpants, the fruit and flower stands, the locals in search of a bargain, and the street fashions that pass by in hurried profusion.

The beauty of Oxford Street is the fact that most of the moderately priced big department stores are lined up in a row between Marble Arch and Regent Street. There are also a lot of teeny-bopper stores, trendy but inexpensive chains, and plenty of cheap eats; in fact, many popular stores are so popular that they have branches toward the Marble Arch end of Oxford Street and toward the Oxford Circus end as well.

The more upscale department stores are on Regent Street, just around the corner, but a million miles away. But wait, the Oxford Street department stores are reinventing themselves; the new, improved **Selfridges** is plenty upscale, and **Marks & Spencer** gets better every day.

Oxford Circus

To me, Oxford Street is the stretch from Marble Arch to Regent Street. End of story. Oxford Circus (and it *is* a circus) begins at Regent Street and continues along Oxford Street for a block or two toward Tottenham Court. In Roman-speak, a circus is a circle.

Oxford Circus has a decidedly hipper and hotter atmosphere to it than plain-old-vanilla Oxford Street. The stores are still cheap, but they sell high-fashion street looks to young people on the cutting edge of the cutting edge. My favorite? **Topshop.** A few years ago, **Niketown** moved in.

Note: Teeny-boppers may want to eventually segue over to Carnaby Street (see below) from Oxford Circus—it's just a few blocks away. Follow Regent Street toward Piccadilly until you see the sign for Carnaby Street.

Regent Street

I love to walk Regent Street from Piccadilly to Oxford Circus. It's a little less than a mile in distance and each side of the street is packed with stores, but only one side of the street appeals to me—the **Hamleys** side. (If Oxford is behind you, you're on the left-hand side of the street toward Piccadilly.) Also, the Piccadilly end is a little tacky and in need of dressing up, so it's fun to watch out for changes.

Among the big multiples are **Zara** and **Mango** (both Spanish chains that make affordable women's clothing). Regent Street still hosts the British institutions that make London retail so glorious. If there's only one store on your tour, it's got to be **Liberty.** Still occupying the same grand mock-Tudor building, Liberty has given up its Regent Street storefront, so you'll need to turn onto Great Marlborough Street to enter the store. Don't miss the fab Apple Store, where you can check your email free.

Bond Street

Bond Street has rebonded and rebounded, and everything is coming up roses, from **Dolce & Gabbana** to the flagship **Burberry** store to **Alexander McQueen.** Although Regent Street means big department stores with big names, Bond Street is small boutiques with big names. **Louis Vuitton** has a swanky store; **Donna Karan** has what looks like a museum for her fancy

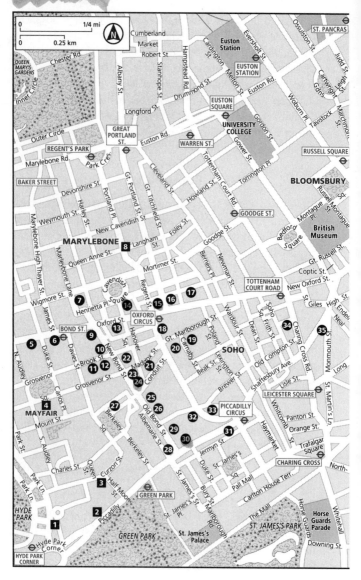

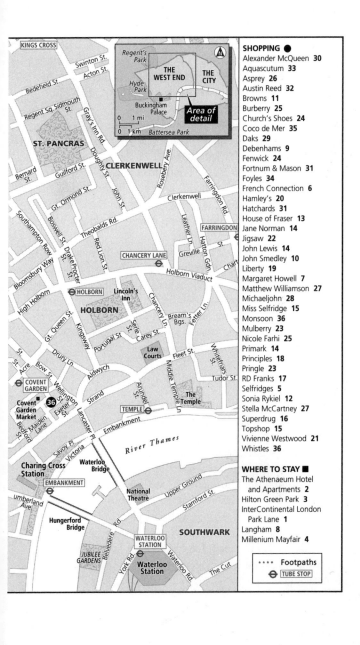

SHOPPING ●
Alexander McQueen **30**
Aquascutum **33**
Asprey **26**
Austin Reed **32**
Browns **11**
Burberry **25**
Church's Shoes **24**
Coco de Mer **35**
Daks **29**
Debenhams **9**
Fenwick **24**
Fortnum & Mason **31**
Foyles **34**
French Connection **6**
Hamley's **20**
Hatchards **31**
House of Fraser **13**
Jane Norman **14**
Jigsaw **22**
John Lewis **14**
John Smedley **10**
Liberty **19**
Margaret Howell **7**
Matthew Williamson **27**
Michaeljohn **28**
Miss Selfridge **15**
Monsoon **36**
Mulberry **23**
Nicole Farhi **25**
Primark **14**
Principles **18**
Pringle **23**
RD Franks **17**
Selfridges **5**
Sonia Rykiel **12**
Stella McCartney **27**
Superdrug **16**
Topshop **15**
Vivienne Westwood **21**
Whistles **36**

WHERE TO STAY ■
The Athenaeum Hotel
  and Apartments **2**
Hilton Green Park **3**
InterContinental London
  Park Lane **1**
Langham **8**
Millenium Mayfair **4**

· · · · Footpaths
⊖ TUBE STOP

line and another, more casual shop for the DKNY brand. **Ralph Lauren** has two shops as well, one for infants and kiddies and the other his flagship. **Bonpoint** has arrived from France; **Chanel** has totally remodeled.

You won't find any bargains in these stores (especially the American ones), but do remember that most of them have prices that will automatically qualify you for a VAT refund.

Now then, this isn't tricky, but since I frequently get mixed up, you might, too. Note that Bond Street is divided into two parts: Old Bond and New Bond. Both are chockablock with big-name designer boutiques from all over the world selling clothing, jewelry, gifts, and tabletop items—you know, your basic **Baccarat** and **Lalique** stores.

What's amazing is that many stores pick up and move from one end of Bond to the other on a regular basis. If you're a London regular but haven't been here in a while, don't convince yourself that you've been here and done that. Bond Street feels very fresh and new with a lot of new faces. The energy is contagious, and you will love coming back to see what the old neighborhood has been up to.

Piccadilly

To get to the good stuff, cut over onto Piccadilly itself and begin to walk toward the **Ritz,** where you'll find some patches of retail heaven. This is part of the Regent Street experience to me, since it is home to some special British institutions that make London such a shopping mecca. Some of my favorites include **Fortnum & Mason,** the **Burlington Arcade,** and **Hatchards,** the bookseller just a few doors from the enormous **Waterstone's** bookstore in what was once a department store. A quick detour down Albemarle Street is a must so you can drool on the windowsill of **Elizabeth Gage** jewelers. While you're there, cross the street and book a manicure or hair appointment at **Michaeljohn.**

Carnaby Street

The street itself waves artistic banners and flags to welcome you to the rebirth of this tourist trap, and there are a number of head shops selling black leather (much with studs); funny, floppy hats; T-shirts; and imports from India—with and without tie-dye. You get the picture. The teens hang out in droves. If I haven't made it clear that I loathe these shops, let me go on to explain what I do like about the neighborhood:

- The kids and the people are fabulous to stare at.
- There's a lot of energy here, and it feels like a foreign destination, which is exactly what you want from a trip to Europe.
- There are tons of postcard shops.

For my own shopping taste, there's a branch of **Boots,** there's a **Body Shop,** and there's a **Lush.** You'll also find branches of **Diesel** and Shelly's, the shoe shop for Doc Martens and hip London looks. Don't miss Newburgh Street, the tiny back street where the expensive new-wave designer shops of Soho are located.

Soho

Just past Carnaby, Soho has been a seedy neighborhood known for its porn shops. But here and there among the tattoo places and the massage parlors, there are some hip stores, and the area is somewhat transformed (but not completely). The most expensive stores are strung together in order to improve the real estate and make shopping easier for customers. Newburgh Street is such a venue; also check out Lower John Street.

Jermyn Street

These few short blocks of a shopping neighborhood run a block from Piccadilly and end at St. James's. Most of the stores here are small, with the exception of **Alfred Dunhill,** and the back of **Fortnum & Mason.** Jermyn Street represents a world that has almost ceased to exist—most of the establishments are devoted to serving the private world of the upper-crust London gent.

Press your nose against the glass of all the shops; take in the dark wood and the aroma of old money. Jermyn Street is the home of exclusive shirt shops such as **Turnbull & Asser, Hilditch & Key, Emma Willis,** and **Harvie & Hudson.** There are several places famous for toiletries, including **Czech & Speake, Floris,** and **Trumper,** and then there's **Davidoff** for the right smoke. Cuban cigars cannot legally be brought into the United States, but it is not a crime to smoke them in London. Besides these men's haunts, there are also old-fashioned suppliers such as **Paxton & Whitfield,** cheese merchants to the royal family.

22 Jermyn Street, an all suite/studio town-house hotel, is located smack in the middle of all this luxe and offers great value promotions from time to time on its website, www.22 jermyn.com.

The Jermyn Street Association publishes its own free map and directory to neighborhood shopping; it's given away at area stores.

St. James's

St. James's Street stretches from St. James's Place near Pall Mall to Piccadilly and is lined with some of London's most famous stores, many of which are 100 years old or more. It all adds to the charm of the stroll.

Most of the stores have their original storefronts or have been restored to make you think they are original. Don't miss **John Lobb** (no. 9) for custom-made shoes (you can look; you needn't plunk down a thousand bucks); **James Lock & Co.** (no. 6), a hat maker for men and women; **William Evans Gun & Rifle Makers** (no. 67); and **D. R. Harris & Co.** (no. 29), an old-fashioned chemist whose brand of toiletries is considered very chic; it's where I buy Almond Oil Skinfood and other necessities of life. **Swaine Adeney Brigg** (no. 54) has outfitted London's upper crust with leather goods for over 250 years.

Mount-Audley

There's a private part of Mayfair that you will never find unless you prowl the streets or happen to be staying at the **Mayfair Millennium** or, possibly, the **Connaught.** No, there's no Mount-Audley; these are the two fabulous shopping streets you'll want to explore. South Audley Street is the main drag of this niche to good taste and fine retail, but you will also want to wander Mount Street and end up at Berkeley Square before taking Bruton and connecting to Bond Street; or you can go across from South Audley to Davies to Oxford.

Mount Street has been known for its very fancy antiques stores in the past, but now hosts newcomers **Marc Jacobs** (nos. 24–25), and **Emperor Moth** (no. 93), where you'll find kitschy designer sportswear. **Diane von Furstenburg** (25 Bruton St.) is a neighbor, and party-wear designer **Antony Price's** studio near **Nicky Clarke** (hair stylist) should be open by the time this book is published. South Audley has a hodgepodge of delectable goods, ranging from one of London's better spy shops (honest) to **Thomas Goode,** London's most exclusive address for china and tabletop. The latter now runs a museum service so that you can bring your coat of arms out of retirement and have it painted on your next set of dishes. Yes, it's that kind of neighborhood.

This is a part of town frequented only by rich people, which is just what makes it so much fun. Don't miss **Shepherd Market,** which is closer to Curzon Street—it's a hidden medieval alley with a few shops and pubs that looks like it hasn't changed in 300 years.

KNIGHTSBRIDGE & CHELSEA

Still fashionable and "with it," Knightsbridge crosses into a few different neighborhoods and borders Chelsea to such an extent that it can be confusing for a visitor.

Once you've passed Hyde Park and are headed toward **Harrods,** you'll be on a street that is first called Knightsbridge but then changes its name to Brompton Road. This makes it especially confusing if you are watching addresses or street numbers because Knightsbridge doesn't really change its name; it just disappears into a nowhere turn. Chances are you won't realize that you've turned a corner at Sloane Street and ended up on the beginning of Brompton Road. Never mind. Pay no heed to street names, and you'll be fine.

Knightsbridge

The part around **Harvey Nichols** is decidedly different from the part that comes after **Harrods.** At the Harvey Nicks end, aside from wonderful Harvey Nicks itself, there are branches of all the multiples and a number of high-end retailers such as **Burberry.** The closer you get to Harrods, the less tony the retailers become. Once you pass Harrods, you are on your way to Beauchamp Place and then the Victoria & Albert Museum.

Harrods and Harvey Nicks are only a few blocks apart, so we're talking chockablock shopping here. Also note that Sloane Street (which has its own atmosphere and tempo; see below) leads off from Brompton at the corner where Harvey Nicks is standing. So you have to be organized and know where you're going, because there are many directions and many, many choices to make. If you head the other direction, you will end up at Beauchamp Place and maybe even Museum Row.

Sloane Street

The juicy shopping part of Sloane Street is only about 2 blocks long. Yet it is 2 blocks of cheek-by-jowl designer chic. You could glance down the street and just rattle off an international

Knightsbridge & Chelsea

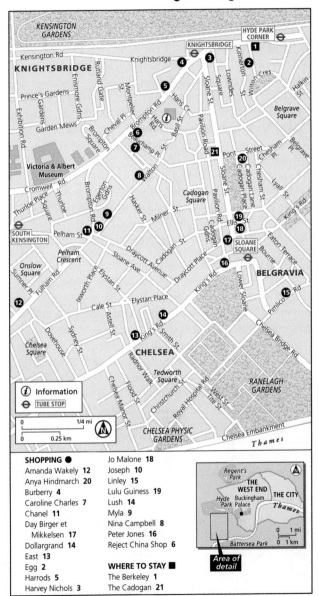

KENSINGTON GARDENS

HYDE PARK CORNER ⊖ **1**

KNIGHTSBRIDGE ⊖

Kensington Rd.

Knightsbridge **4** **3**

KNIGHTSBRIDGE

2

Kinnerton St.

Lowndes

Wilton Cres.

Halkin St.

Mitton St.

Prince's Gardens

Rutland Gate

Ensmore Gdns.

Belgrave Square

Belgrave

Exhibition Rd.

Garden Mews

Garden Gardens

Montpelier St.

Cheval Pl.

Brompton Sq.

Brompton Rd.

Hans Cr.

Hans Rd.

Basil St.

Sloane St.

Pavilion Road

5

6

ⓘ

7 Beauchamp Pl.

Victoria & Albert Museum

Cromwell Rd.

Thurloe Place

Thurloe Square

Thurloe

Brompton Rd.

Egerton Gdns.

8 Walton St.

Hasker St.

Milner St.

Cadogan Square

Cadogan Gdns.

Cadogan Lane

Cadogan Place

Pont Street

Chesham Pl.

Lyall St.

King's Rd.

21

20

Sloane St.

Pavilion St.

9

SOUTH KENSINGTON ⊖

Pelham St. **11** **10**

Pelham Crescent

Onslow Square

Sumner Pl.

Fulham Rd.

Ixworth Place

Elystan St.

Sloane Ave.

Draycott Ave.

Cadogan St.

Draycott Place

16

17

18 **19**

Ellis St.

SLOANE SQUARE ⊖

Eaton Terrace

Bourne

Lower Sloane

BELGRAVIA

Pimlico Rd. **15**

Chelsea Bridge Rd.

12

Cale St.

Elystan Place

Astell St.

King's Rd.

14

13 King's Rd. Smith St.

Chelsea Square

Dovehouse St.

Sydney St.

CHELSEA

Radnor Walk

Flood St.

Chelsea Manor St.

Tedworth Square

Christchurch St.

Royal Hospital Rd.

West St.

Tite St.

RANELAGH GARDENS

ⓘ **Information**

⊖ TUBE STOP

0 ———— 1/4 mi
0 ———— 0.25 km

Ⓝ

CHELSEA PHYSIC GARDENS

Chelsea Embankment

Thames

SHOPPING ●

Amanda Wakely **12**
Anya Hindmarch **20**
Burberry **4**
Caroline Charles **7**
Chanel **11**
Day Birger et Mikkelsen **17**
Dollargrand **14**
East **13**
Egg **2**
Harrods **5**
Harvey Nichols **3**

Jo Malone **18**
Joseph **10**
Linley **15**
Lulu Guiness **19**
Lush **14**
Myla **9**
Nina Campbell **8**
Peter Jones **16**
Reject China Shop **6**

WHERE TO STAY ■

The Berkeley **1**
The Cadogan **21**

Regent's Park

THE WEST END

THE CITY

Hyde Park

Buckingham Palace

Thames

Battersea Park

0 ———— 1 mi
0 ———— 1 km

Area of detail

who's who in big-name retailing, from **Chanel** to **Valentino**—and much, *much* more.

Jo Malone, the skin and scent queen, has a large flagship at the far end, closer to Sloane Square; David Tang has opened a branch of **Shanghai Tang. Hermès** has revamped, adding more space. Other lines with stores here include **Browns** (a branch of the South Molton St. icon), **Gucci, Oilily, YSL, Cartier, Tod's, Armani, Bonpoint, Bottega Veneta, Pink, Guideppe Zanotti, Bamford** (on Sloane Sq.) and **Louis Vuitton.** Bamford sells menswear. Don't miss **Basia Zarzycka** where you'll find whimsical gift items and accessories.

Sloane Street leads to Sloane Square, and then you're on King's Road . . . unless you want to go to Belgravia.

Belgravia

I used to call this area Sloane Street Adjacent, but now that I know it better, I'm going with the local name: Belgravia. In the old days, you moved from Sloane Street to King's Road without too much detour, but now that everyone is building and expanding and opening shops, well, the residential area here is blossoming with retail opportunities.

Pont Street, on the Beauchamp Road side of Sloane Street, is one such nook. It's always had a few stores on it, but is now home to the **Anya Hindmarch** (nos. 15–17) boutique and the Knightsbridge branch of **Agent Provocateur** (no. 16), the lingerie purveyor. **Liza Bruce** (no. 9) has one shop on Pont Street and one in Los Angeles.

Elizabeth Street, on the Victoria side of Sloane, is a 2-block stretch of independent shops selling everything from gourmet to designer fashion.

Do look at your *A to Z* for these side streets—some shops are on the west side of Sloane Street, while others are on the Belgravia-proper side. Better still, book into the Berkeley Hotel, where you'll get a map and a tour—you can even sign up for a Retail Therapy package.

Best Hidden Shopping Street

Conveniently hidden in the middle of genteel Belgravia, the 2 short blocks of **Elizabeth Street** cater to well-heeled locals as well as visitors seeking unique London finds. At pet emporium **Mungo & Maud** (no. 79), you can outfit your pooch with the latest designer doggie duds and then continue to **tomtom** (no. 63), which specializes in Havana cigars (smoke them in London, as you can't bring them into the U.S.). **Philip Treacy** (no. 69), the crown prince of British millinery, has his headquarters here, as does shoe designer Katarina Mutich (**Mootish**, no. 34). Two jewelry designers, **Kim Poor** (no. 53) and **Erickson Beamon** (no. 38), offer unusual designs in the not-too-expensive category. To assemble a picnic, visit **Mash of Belgravia** (114 Ebury St.) for gourmet groceries, French baker **Poilane** (no. 46), and, of course, the **Chocolate Society** (no. 36).

King's Road

If you continue along Sloane Street, you'll end up at Sloane Square. Here, surrounding the square, are numerous stores and many choices for your happy feet. On your way to the square, make sure you take a look at **General Trading Company**, now located right off Sloane Street on Symons Street, across from Peter Jones. Indeed, the focal point of Sloane Square itself is the medium-size department store **Peter Jones,** which has totally renovated but is still best for bed linens and fabrics.

Just as Sloane Street dead-ends and disappears, you hit Sloane Square (there's a Tube stop here) and face two options for two different retail experiences: Pimlico Road (described below) and King's Road. Totally different choices, believe me.

King's Road became famous (or is that infamous?) in the 1960s as the hot street for the bell-bottom people. Now it's mostly a congregation of multiples, but it's enjoying a renaissance as it's home to a lot of fun addresses, including the original branch of **Lush** (no. 123). **Trilogy** (no. 33, Duke of York

Sq.) is a new one-stop-shop for international denim brands including Earnest Sewn, Sass & Bide, and Paper Denim.

King's Road also possesses a few of London's best antiques arcades, as well as **Steinberg & Tolkien** (no. 193), a free-standing vintage-clothing shop that is a fashion junkie's version of paradise. Much Pucci! High prices! Who cares?!

The worst thing about King's Road is its inconvenience to the Tube. You can either go up one side and down the other and end up back at Sloane Square, or put on your hiking boots and march all the way to the 500 block, since it is kind of interesting all the way up. You can also bus it to the far end, pick and choose what interests you, and then walk back to Sloane Square.

Pimlico Road

If you were in Knightsbridge, where you did Sloane Street, and you got to Sloane Square but decided against King's Road (see above), then this is the other choice: the design- and antiques-prowler's choice. *Note:* This is not the neighborhood of Pimlico as laid out in your *A to Z*, but rather a *street* called Pimlico Road (SW1), which comes right before the real Pimlico district. To reach it by Tube, use the Sloane Square stop.

For those interested in interior design, this street is filled with shops for trimmings, fabrics, and antiques. Working designers or those with a decorating need should find some useful resources here; gawkers will simply want to stare at the goods in the incredible **David Linley** (no. 60) store.

From the Sloane Square Tube, if the station is to your back and you are facing Peter Jones, make a left on Holbein Place. This will lead you to Pimlico Road within a block; there are some shops here along the way. Just off Lower Sloane Street, on Pimlico Road, you'll find **Daylesford Organic**'s sleek new three-story deli/cafe. This is one of the best spots in London for eating in or taking out. After you do both sides of Pimlico Road, return to Sloane Square via Lower Sloane Street, which runs parallel to Holbein Place.

KENSINGTON

This neighborhood is a must if you are in the fashion business, want to see the young hip looks, or have teens and 'tweens. It's also a must for those interested in antiques, as it includes Portobello Road Market.

Kensington High Street

Like any other high street, the thoroughfare that stretches before you as you emerge from the Kensington High Street Tube station is jampacked with multiples and real-people stores. There's the architecturally interesting **Barkers of Kensington** arcade and the American chain **Urban Outfitters.** Most fun is the **Boots Well-Being Centre,** a branch of the drugstore chain Boots that offers spa treatments and myriad beauty products. Directly across the street is a **Lush** store. The **Marks & Spencer** (no. 113) branch is much less crowded than the mother ship on Oxford Street.

Kensington Church Street

Leading up the hill from the high street (therefore meeting it in a perpendicular fashion) is Kensington Church Street, not to be confused with Church Street (p. 256). It leads directly to the Notting Hill Gate Tube station. Shortly after you swing onto Kensington Church Street from Kensington High Street, there's **Lancer Square,** a sort of minimall with a branch of the famous Belgian chocolatier **Pierre Marcolini** as well as the wool and tapestry shop **Ehrman.**

Don't miss **Yacco Maricard** (no. 10), a Japanese line of sculptural clothing in hand-woven cottons, silk, and denim.

Upper Kensington Church Street is still home to several antiques shops of the high-end type, but you won't find as many as in the past. Some dealers have retired and others have closed up shop to concentrate on trade fairs and Internet sales. Survivors include **The Lacquer Chest** and **The Lacquer Chest Too**

Kensington, Notting Hill & Marylebone

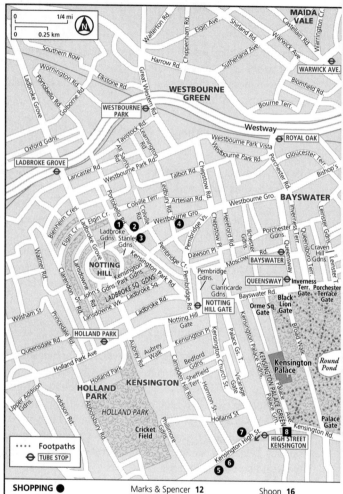

SHOPPING ●

Boots Well-Being Centre **6**
Conran Shop **17**
Dorothy Perkins **10**
Lush **7**
Marie Chantal **4**

Marks & Spencer **12**
New Look **11**
Paul Smith **1**
Portobello China & Woollens **3**
Portobello Road Market **2**
Selfridges **13**

Shoon **16**
VV Rouleaux **15**
Waterstone's **5**

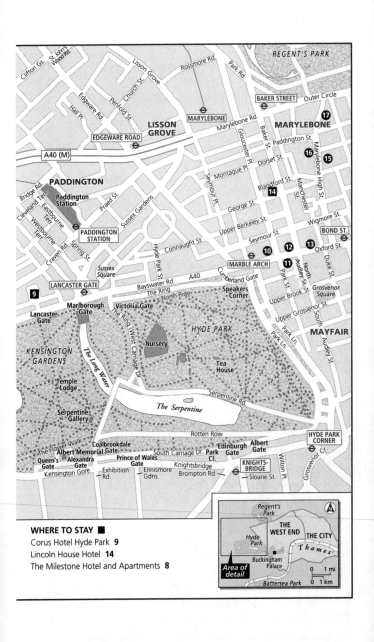

WHERE TO STAY ■

Corus Hotel Hyde Park **9**
Lincoln House Hotel **14**
The Milestone Hotel and Apartments **8**

Heeeere's Jenny:
Shopper's Tour of Kensington High Street

—by Jenny McCormick

Ladies, lace up those trainers and prepare yourself for an afternoon of trendy stores on one of London's most practical shopping streets. Packed with international names as well as local multiples, Kensington High Street is just the avenue to find the latest catwalk styles at (semi-) affordable prices. The street has so much to offer, even your fella will want to tag along!

Starting at Palace Avenue (easily landmarked by the **Royal Garden Hotel**), the main shopping area extends only .8km (½ mile) and ends at **Phillimore Gardens.** At half the size of its rival King's Road, Kensington High Street offers much the same in the way of fashion, yet is far easier on the feet. You can begin your tour after lunch and be done by high tea.

For hot looks from major European brands (these ain't your mum's jumpers), you'll find many a shop to hop. **Diesel** (no. 38A), **Miss Sixty** (no. 42), and **FCUK** (no. 168–170) all offer of-the-moment looks for those not afraid to show off their assets. These styles are great for hitting the London nightlife scene, but the price tags may be hard on your wallet.

No need to go to the ATM; just hit up the **H&M** (no. 103–111), a much more cash-conscious solution. All the now looks are available here at superlow prices. Whatever your style—from flirty to classy, punk to trendy—you'll find it without losing your mind. This particular branch has a wide selection of clothes not found in other European or U.S. locations.

Another quid-friendly option is **Zara** (no. 48–52), the Spanish brand with shops across the Continent (and in major U.S. cities, too). Zara carries a vast range of urban-chic fashions at reasonable prices.

Other multiples to check out include **Sisley** (no. 129–131) and **Muji** (no. 157), a Japanese import, which has clothing as well as modernist items for home and office.

A better bet for selection (if not price) is **Urban Outfitters** (no. 36–38). This store is a five-level mecca for knockoff runway dresses, ironic T-shirts, and funky footwear. Check out the top level for kitschy housewares (where else will you find those Che Guevara mugs?). This Urban also carries forever-hip vintage clothes for guys and gals—aptly called Urban Renewal.

After all this shopping, you need a break! With two **Starbucks**, a **Caffè Nero**, and **Crussh** (a yummy smoothie bar), there's something to satisfy everyone's taste. And now that **Whole Foods** (nos. 63–97) has moved in, you may want to stock up on picnic supplies for your hotel room. As you head back to your hotel, don't forget to stop at **Lush** (no. 96) for products to pamper yourself as you relax and rest and dream about your purchases.

(nos. 71 and 75), featuring 18th- and early-19th-century household goods; **Hope & Glory** (no. 131A), specializing in commemorative ceramics; and the "decanter lady," **Jeanette Hayhurst** (no. 32A). Sarah's husband collects antique arms and armor and is a big fan of **Michael German Antiques** (no. 38B). Many dealers do the big shows, so watch out particularly for the month of June, when there are a lot of fancy shows in town and the stores may be closed or open only at weird hours.

For a traditional British lunch (or dinner), try **Maggie Jones**, 6 Old Court Place (next to Lancer's Sq., off Kensington Church St.). **Patisserie Valerie** (no. 27) is a good choice for breakfast or a coffee break.

Notting Hill Gate

This is actually more of a residential address than a tourist-shopping district, but it is also a major segue to various areas. Right around the Tube stop are the usual suspects—fast-food joints, cash machines, **Boots**, the booksellers **WHSmith** and

Waterstone's, and so on. The area is important simply because of its location as the center of a universe.

Ledbury Grove

This is not very near the Notting Hill Gate Tube station, which is at the top of Kensington Church Street, but it's not very far, either—and is within walking distance. You may want to take a taxi to the corner of Ledbury Street and Westbourne Grove, explore this area on foot, and then end up at Notting Hill Gate. *Note:* I call this area Ledbury Grove, but there is nothing officially named Ledbury Grove.

The heart of the development is Westbourne Grove, running from Chepstow Road—try **Bill Amberg,** 10 Chepstow Rd., W2, for leather goods—to Portobello, where the market is held on Saturdays. Note that as Ledbury continues to fill and spill to Westbourne Grove and vice versa, Chepstow Road will become the last holdout for lower rents and the up-and-coming, so consider walking over the extra 2 blocks.

Ledbury Street has a couple blocks of town houses that are painted pastel colors and devoted to retail; Westbourne Grove has several blocks of cafes, antiques dealers, and boutiques including **Nanette Lepore, Smythson, and Jigsaw.** The best day of the week to visit is Saturday, because you can move on to Portobello Road Market and because **Vent** (no. 178), a leading vintage-clothing store on Westbourne Grove, is open. If Vent's hours—Friday and Saturday only, usually from 11am to 6pm—make you nuts, visit nearby **Virginia** (98 Portland Rd.).

Ledbury's row of boutiques includes a branch of **Ghost** (no. 36) as well as **Nick Ashley** (no. 57), an interesting shop for men's weekend clothes. **Marie Chantal** (no. 61A)—yeah, the princess—has opened a glamorous shop with everything for the baby who already has everything, and there's a branch of **Emma Hope** for shoes at the corner of Ledbury and Westbourne Grove (no. 207 Westbourne Grove). For a bikini, or bikini wax, stop by **Heidi Klein** (174 Westbourne Grove), and then head straight to **Myla** (no. 77 Lonsdale) for sexy lingerie and girl toys.

You can seriously browse or even hang out at **Tom Conran's Deli** (226 Westbourne Grove)—yes, *that* Conran—where you can buy groceries or sit down for a coffee or light lunch (try spinach-and-feta quiche). The area also has a few cafes and pubs, along with some specialty bookshops such as **Books for Cooks,** 4 Blenheim Crescent, and the **Travel Bookshop,** 13 Blenheim Crescent.

Note: I normally go from Westbourne Grove toward Portobello, but on a recent visit, I walked on Westbourne Grove in the other direction toward Queensway and had a ball. It's a multiethnic area where real people live, so you'll find some shops and groceries and cafes as well as a special neighborhood feel. Then you can turn onto Queensway and actually pop into the mall **Whiteleys,** if need be, although it's not a great one.

Portobello Road

There is indeed a Portobello Road, and it is the home of the Saturday market; it is also the address of many genuine antiques dealers who are open during the week. It's actually easier to enjoy the shops during the week, when the Saturday throngs, the tour buses, the German tots, and the organ grinder are not in place.

Considering how famous Portobello Road is, it's not that easy to find. *Tip:* On Saturdays, there is a chalkboard at the stairwell inside the Notting Hill Gate Tube station giving specific directions for how to get to Portobello Road. The fun starts as soon as you turn right onto Pembridge Road from Notting Hill Gate and continues as you wend your way to Portobello Road. Follow the crowd.

If indeed the market is just too much for you, work your way through part of it and then tuck into Elgin Crescent Road, which has several cute boutiques (including two branches of **Graham & Green** [nos. 2 and 10], for clothes and home style and gifts) and some market spill. This leads to Kensington Park Road, which is filled with cafes and bistros; then you can walk over to Holland Park (see below), where I promise there will not be a flock of German tourists just off a motorcoach.

Golborne Road

This street is the twilight zone of neighborhoods, one of the last truly funky and fabulous finds in Europe. You get here by walking on Portobello Road much farther than you thought possible. After you walk beneath the overpass of the highway, you're getting warm. The street is marked—simply turn right.

You'll enter a road filled with antiques dealers, architectural-building-parts shops, some street stalls, some fabric stores, a few cutie-pie boutiques, and several Portuguese cafes. You will be in the middle of nowhere, and you will have to walk back to Portobello Road in order to get out, but this is also heaven, filled with true charm and no tourists.

Holland Park

Holland Park is an extremely chichi residential area of London, on the other side of Portobello Road from the Ledbury Grove district. It has not had much retail over the years, but suddenly, in the middle of a bunch of row houses, a tiny enclave of sensational shops burst into the neighborhood. They are wildly creative and exciting (and expensive)—the fashion editors are mad for the area. You can walk from Portobello, although it's about 10 minutes.

If you don't want to walk, just take a taxi to the center of the big cluster of hotshot chic: **Summerhill & Bishop** (no. 100 Portland Rd.). Check out imports from France and Morocco, and just overall great stuff in a homey-chic environment. Then stop by **Virginia** (no. 98) for vintage clothing, and **The Cross** (no. 141) for cutting-edge pieces from up-and-coming designers—I was gaga for the cutout felt shawls, but they were very expensive. If you pride yourself on seeing the newest shops, this is your find for the day.

The Cross is on the corner of Portland Road and Clarendon Cross (hence the name). Clarendon Cross is a small street, mostly residential, but with a few little boutiques. Among the cutest is **Cath Kidston** (no. 8), and don't miss **Mary Moore** (no. 5) for upscale vintage.

Marylebone High Street

I can barely even pronounce this area—I find that I prefer to say *Marleybone*. But if I could afford it, I'd move here in a flash. If you're looking for a neighborhood to discover, this is it. A favorite of young locals, Marylebone High Street has a wonderful neighborhood feel, and a ton of stores, including **Brora** (no. 81) for contemporary cashmere; **Cologne & Cotton** (no. 88) for pure cotton linens and luxurious toiletries; **Little White Company** (no. 90) for natural fiber children's clothing; and **Shoon** (no. 94), where you'll find casual clothing, gifts, and comfortable shoes including Camper and Ecco. Marylebone goes from Oxford Street (more or less) right to a big, snazzy branch of **Conran** (no. 55), complete with good eats, some supermarkets, and a great street scene.

The highlight of shopping this neighborhood is the new flagship **VV Rouleaux** (102 Marylebone Lane), which used to be just one simple ribbon-and-trim shop at Sloane Square (it's still there); now the company has expanded to about five different locations that sell its knock-your-socks-off style. What's missing in this neighborhood? All the tourists.

TRAFALGAR, WESTMINSTER & COVENT GARDEN

Covent Garden

The area I call Covent Garden is actually a parcel of real estate that includes Covent Garden among a handful of other neighborhoods. This part of town begins at Trafalgar, but actually backs up at Mayfair on one end and Soho at the other.

The entire area around Covent Garden is filled with fabulous little shops and pubs that make the whole place a super shopping destination. It's also an officially designated tourist area, so stores are open on Sunday (not all, but many—unlike in other parts of London). Prowl everywhere, not just the festival marketplace. Include the two buildings of Covent Garden itself—a rehabilitation of the old marketplace—and make sure that you also see the two different markets that are more or less attached to Covent Garden (between the two buildings and Jubilee Market, which is out the back building).

Several multiples have branches in the red-brick mall stores; one of the most interesting is **Accessorize** (no. 22), an offshoot of Monsoon. I will admit that I flipped out when I discovered that a mere wisp of nothing but Thai silk and wire to wrap around the hair was selling for £18 ($36), but the clothes themselves are more moderately priced. **Lush,** my beloved bath-bomb supplier, has a storefront in Covent Garden piazza (no. 11). I like the King's Road and Carnaby Street stores better, but if you can't get there, be sure to stop in here. There's also a branch of **Culpeper the Herbalist** (no. 8), smaller than the one in Mayfair but stocked with the same great stuff.

Neal Street

Walk out the front end of Covent Garden and pass the Covent Garden Tube station. Here you'll see Neal Street, a pedestrian area that's home to several hip stores and lots of fun. There are pubs and people and shops galore, with a funky, friendly feeling that makes the whole Covent Garden adventure complete. A mall—**Thomas Neal's,** at 29–41 Earlham St.—adds to the excitement; this gentrified warehouse has been converted to a trendsetter's heaven for the young and hip. The stores here are mostly open on Sundays as well. Inside is **Space.NK,** the local cult makeup shop; it sells a lot of American brands (don't buy 'em; very expensive) but also some British and French brands. You'll also find **Hope & Glory** (men's streetwear; not related to the antiques shop on Kensington Church St.), **High Jinks** (street labels for hip urban commandos), and **Tabio** (an innovative sock specialty store).

Seven Dials

Seven Dials is easy to get to (use the Covent Garden Tube), it's where you want to be for shopping adventures, and it's a newly hot area known mostly for its old-fashioned cutie-pie. Vintage clothing stores are moving in, there's a well-known little French bistro here, and the various little shops seem to be at least 100 years old. Monmouth Street is home to a batch of high-profile shops, including **Koh Samui** (nos. 65–67), featuring labels like Balenciaga, Nina Ricci, and Dries Van Noten; **The West Village** (no. 44), where you'll find Susannah Hunter's appliquéd leather handbags; and **Poste Mistress** (nos. 61–63) for footwear by top designers, as well as their own line.

Leicester Square

Get here—the heart of the theater district and not much of a shopping district—via New Row so that you can take in a few more charming shops. New Row is only a block long, but there's something very quaint and very old-world about it that makes its combination of bookstores, antiques dealers, and crafts shops thrill you with a sense of discovery. Around the corner on Bedford Street, you'll find a **Tesco** (no. 21), where you can stock up on snacks, bottled water, and personal needs.

Charing Cross & the Strand

The Strand is a so-so tourist area where there are branches of the big-name shops, like **Chinacraft** (no. 98) and **Next** (no. 11), but where everything seems to have been in its prime back in 1960. It isn't a warm and fuzzy neighborhood, but it does lead to Covent Garden. Its midpoint is the Charing Cross train station, a few hundred yards past Trafalgar. The multiples around here cover everything you might need, including a **Superdrug** (nos. 49–50).

The Strand begins at Charing Cross and stretches along in the direction of St. Paul's Cathedral and the City. The Strand actually changes its name in a few blocks and becomes the infamous Fleet Street, but no matter. You can connect to Covent Garden or Charing Cross by walking, so the location can't be ignored, and it's certainly not as intimidating here as it can be for some in Mayfair.

The heart of the Strand as a shopping district is near Charing Cross and Covent Garden; here you've got the **Savoy Hotel,** along with a handful of multiples. Stamp collectors know the area well because several famous dealers are located here; there are also a lot of sporting-goods stores.

THE EAST END

Hoxton & Shoreditch

Pick up any magazine with an article about London in it and you are bound to read about the renaissance of the East End. A neighborhood that immigrants fought their way out of is now becoming gentrified and even chic. Right now it's the London version of Manhattan's Meat Packing District, so you can see the potential and smell the future. Market junkies will be in heaven here. You may want to have a taxi drive you around to look at **Hoxton Street Market** so that you can feel like you're part of it. You'll do your shopping in more fun zones, but this is the heart of the new world.

The most ready-for-prime-time area is surrounding the old **Spitalfields Market,** which is a funky version of Covent Garden. Unfortunately, it's shrunk to a third of its original size due to redevelopment, with many of the edgy-fashion stalls moving from Spitalfields to nearby Dray Walk's **Sunday (Up) Market,** which is open Sundays (duh) from 10am to 5pm in the Old Truman Brewery.

Still worth a visit, Spitalfields is an indoor market, Victorian or Edwardian in yummy wrought-iron-and-brick style. The outside is devoted to zillions of yuppie-like bistros and cafes. The scene is really on Sunday, when the young and trendy come out for brunch and browsing. Inside, there's a food court, and a so-so flea market with stores built around the sides. Among them are a dress agency (resale shop), up-and-coming designers, some artists, and even a small green market. Set up on tables in the market is **Savonnerie,** which uses Spitalfields as its flagship. Note that stores here open at noon on weekdays, open all day on Sundays.

By the way, **Petticoat Lane Market** is also held on Sundays; it's nearby—follow the signs to Middlesex Road—and a bit like Hong Kong, but if you like junk, it's a lot of fun. If you need a new suitcase to haul home all your purchases, there are tons of stores here that sell assorted pieces of luggage beginning at £10 ($20).

Off Petticoat Lane and past Commercial Street is **Brick Lane,** which is half yuck and half up-and-coming designers. Before you pooh-pooh it, keep in mind that Alexander McQueen came from this area.

Besides Spitalfields, the most fun here is the **Columbia Road Flower Market,** held only on Sundays from 8am to 2pm. You can take the Tube to Liverpool Street (the same stop you'd use for Spitalfields) or Old Street and then walk. If Columbia Road Flower Market were just a flower market, I'd have a lot of trouble sending you here, since few travelers are looking to buy flowers or trees. However, this is quite a scene, and the area boutiques sell home style, antiques, and whimsy. These boutiques, like the market, are open on Sundays only. The flower market is in full swing by 8:30am, but most of the stores open at 9am. There are plenty of places for a coffee or even breakfast.

Newly revived after a 30-year decline is the **Broadway Market,** a Saturday farmers-style venue that also has stalls selling vintage and new designer clothing, old *Vogue* patterns, and hand-knits. Along with market stalls, you'll want to check out **Black Truffle** (no. 74) for handmade funky shoes and **La Vie Boutique** (no. 18) for vintage fashion; **Fabrications** (no. 7) has recycled home accessories, and **Broadway Books** (no. 6) is a great literary browsing spot. The market opens at 8am on Saturday; take the central line to Bethnal Green Station, where

Brick Lane Market & More

—by Ethan Sunshine

As you're prowling the Brick Lane area, don't miss the following shops and stops.

If you're here on a Sunday, you'll likely head first to the **Old Truman Brewery,** 91–95 Brick Lane, E1 (Tube: Shoreditch or Liverpool St.), an 11-acre historic site that houses all kinds of vendors, including a few worthwhile vintage dealers in the alley. The highlights include **eatmyhandbagbitch,** for midcentury modern design; **Public Beware Co.,** for trendy clothes and shoes; and **Junky Styling,** which recycles old clothes into hip new fashions. Junky was by far my favorite; its classic Mr. T prints were priceless, but it was the custom-made neckties that won me over—these old thrift-store finds are sliced up and stuffed with packs of rolling papers, or glued with plastic cigarette butts, and come complete with the anti-smoking label ripped off a pack of smokes. (England's labels are much more direct, stating simply: SMOKING KILLS.)

After you finish browsing the Old Truman Brewery, you might as well make a whole Sunday of it and find Cheshire Road, off Brick Lane, and then go to the nearby **Spitalfields Market,** which is pretty good for vintage clothes and new designers. Whether or not you find the markets a bust, at least the other stores in the area more than make up for it.

The **Laden Showroom,** 103 Brick Lane, E1, is an amazing place. It features separate booths by different indie designers such as Red Mutha, Your Majesty, Charles of London, and many more. Some of the booths have cheesy stuff, but many clothes feature one-of-a-kind cut-ups, sew-ons, and paint-and-marker additions. A little pricey, but well worth it. Supposedly tabloid darlings Pete Doherty and Victoria Beckham have been spotted here.

Rokit, 101 and 107 Brick Lane, E1, is like a vintage-shopping conglomerate or almost-high-street multiple. Aside from this string of stores right on Brick Lane, it has a location on Camden High Street, as well as a newish one in Covent Garden. Rokit has quite a stranglehold on the local vintage scene—and thus is able to raise prices pretty high. I saw a dirty pair of used Nikes selling for £125 ($250) on Brick Lane.

Mendoza, 158 Brick Lane, E1, has a terrific selection of vintage clothes and modern styles. Among its best items are painted trucker hat one-offs and rare Nike Dunks. But the ultimate prize of my visit was to be found lying helplessly on the £10 ($20) rack: a red-and-white baseball tee sporting the slogan BORN TO $HOP.

you'll exit to the right and walk up Cambridge Heath Road to Regent's Canal. Take a left after the canal and follow Andrews Road to the market.

If you want to stay in this area, you can curl up in Frette linens for less than £125 ($250) at night at the new **Hoxton Hotel** (81 Eastern St.). In fact, you can actually stay here for £1 ($2)—that's right, two bucks. Every year on one day in early October, the hotel releases 595 rooms at £1 ($2) and another 595 at £29 ($58). This deal is available online on the hotel website, and the booking must be for the months of October through January. Needless to say, the rooms sell out in about 30 minutes, but if you're interested and have quick fingers, give it a try. © 207/550-1000. www.hoxtonhotels.com.

OTHER NEIGHBORHOODS

Camden Town

If you are older than 10 and younger than 30 (hmm, maybe you need to be younger than 25 . . .), you just may adore it here; I admit to having a recent change of heart and discovering some real finds here. This is an entire neighborhood dedicated to clothes and crafts and hippies and talented immigrants and those who just came back from holiday with an extra suitcase filled with lord-only-knows-what. The main street seems to be about buying black T-shirts and having your nose pierced, but when you get around the Lock and into some of the markets (don't miss the Stables), it's more crafty and funky and fun. It's particularly busy on Saturdays, as this is the day to shop and socialize among the many markets that line the high street.

You may have the urge to hold onto your handbag and to take a bath after you've been here, but your kids will consider this a very awesome part of town. Take the Tube to Camden Town and walk to your right.

Islington

The Tube stop for Islington is Angel, and you will be in heaven, especially on a Wednesday or a Saturday, when you wander for a while through fair Islington. You see, Wednesday and Saturday are market days, and there's an alley filled to overflowing with vendors—talk about charm galore. There's an indoor antiques market open every day, but the extra street (alley) action is what makes this fun. It's the population increase in nearby Clerkenwell (see below) that has made Islington really boom. The high street now has a branch of every multiple, there are plenty of pubs and cafes serving everything from Mexican food to pizza, and then there's lots of real-people stuff as well.

The antiques market is sort of the tag-sale type with people setting up tables, even in the rain; there are also some shops. Prices are not giveaway. There are several vintage-clothing shops that may interest collectors. Try **Cloud Cuckoo Land** (6 Charlton Place, Camden Passage, N1), and **Annie's** (12 Camden Passage, N1).

I also like the **city market,** which is for real people and is no different from any other market, except that this is where I buy my Arsenal team luggage. If you are looking for non-designer luggage, you, too, may want to stock up on the lines offered by the football vendors.

All these marvels are within walking distance of the Tube, so go and take cash. You're gonna love it. If you're looking for more than the flea market, walk from the Tube station along Upper Street—there are many shops on this street and in the area around where Upper Street gets to Cross Street. Once past Islington Green, the Upper Street shopping scene becomes more interesting. **Aria** (nos. 133 and 295), two shops facing each other across the street, carry everything from kitchenware to jewelry and leather goods; **Atelier Abigail Ahearn** (no. 137) features elegant home-style accessories; and at the **Gill Wing Gift Shops** (nos. 180–202), Ms. Wing offers jewelry, chocolate, cookware, plus a cafe. Crossing over to Cross Street, don't miss **Tribe** (no. 52) for handcrafted contemporary rugs; **Loop** (no. 41), featuring clothing and home accessories (along with knitting lessons); **Clusaz** (no. 56), for eclectic women's clothing, and **Fandango** (no. 50), for urban antiques and art.

Clerkenwell

Pick up any magazine that has a feature on the hot new areas of London, and you're certain to bump into hype about this neighborhood. Clerkenwell (do say *Clarkenwall*, dears) is the new-millennium area that is breaking through now and will be happening in the next few years. A neighborhood in transition, it's part blue-collar and ethnic unchic and part hot architecture and movin'-on-up money. It is still a commercial district where industrial buildings are being rehabbed for non-industrial usage. Lots of photographers have moved in, and there are also restaurants—it's all very downtown Manhattan. Try the **Bleeding Heart Tavern** (Bleeding Heart Yard, Greville St.) before browsing the jewelry ateliers around Clerkenwell Green. Check out the **Lesley Craze Gallery** (33–35a Clerkenwell Green) for selections by local jewelers.

Farrington is the closest Tube stop for Clerkenwell; if you have a car and want to drive around to see the lovely brick architecture and what's happening—great.

And if you want to stay in the middle of it, you can now actually book into a boutique hotel: The Rookery (Peter's Lane, Cowcross St.). © 207/336-0931. www.rookeryhotel.com.

Chiswick

This is a Born to Shop AP/Honors field trip—for devoted shoppers who want to mix with the locals, avoid the chains, and grab a taste of real London without breaking the bank. Chiswick is newly hip with young families moving in, just as London's music scene did—Sky TV and the BBC are part of the 'hood. Without a multiple to be found, small shops like **Zecca** (for home-style), the **Old Cinema** (an antiques collective), and **Winnie Buswell** ('50s textiles, glassware, and retro home design—very Cath Kidson) abound. Stop by **Theobroma Cacao** (43 Turnham Green Terrace) for homemade chocolates before taking a walk along the riverfront. For extra credit on the final, write me to tell me what famous Lady Brit is from this part of London.

Hampstead

To the north, and in a totally different frame of mind from the Docklands (described below), is the wealthy suburb of Hampstead, charmingly located right off its own heath. For those who want to see what upper-middle-class London suburbs (with good shopping) are like, and for those who may be browsing for just the perfect neighborhood to move to, Hampstead is a must. Note that Hampstead had Sunday shopping long before everyone else, so it used to be a big Sunday-brunch kind of village; but now it's more of an insider's place.

Hampstead still has the feel of an English country village. The Tube station is very deep and very ugly; I've found it frightening. You'll fall in love only when you get to street level. Trust me on this. After all, if it was good enough for Blake and Keats, it'll probably have something to please you, too. Beyond the immediate shopping area lies the famous Hampstead Heath.

In nearby Highgate Cemetery, a number of famous folk are buried.

The Docklands

The term *Docklands* has come to refer to all development along both sides of the Thames, below Tower Bridge and stretching to Greenwich. However, the development on the south side of the river, where the Design Museum is located, is not actually in the thick of what is generally known as the Docklands; this is confusing if you are an out-of-towner.

Canary Wharf is the heart of the true Docklands, and it has changed enormously in the past few years—back from the dead, filled with a series of malls and all kinds of good shopping, especially of the local nature. The branch of **Tesco** here has the makeup sponges I adore, which to me makes it worth the trip. The shopping has been developed in phases, so don't think you'll be limited to one building; oh no, this is shopping with attitude and altitude. For more on Canary Wharf, see the report by Jemma Griffiths, below.

To get here, take the Jubilee line of the Underground; this is the most fun line because it's clean and everything works. *Note:* Do not get off at Canada Water because you are not paying attention—you want Canary Wharf.

The **Four Seasons** has its second London hotel here, so the area is now hip and back in style. Many people come for the weekend in order to have a river view, be near the markets at Greenwich, shop the multiples without the London crowds, and enjoy the health club and spa.

Across the river from the Docklands and the Four Seasons, at **Butler's Wharf,** there's a lot to see and do and think about. Meanwhile, **Oxo Tower** has happened, with its fancy-dancy restaurant and shops. Open Tuesday through Sunday, the mall is home to local designers and artisans. **Gabriel's Wharf** is a community of craftsmen—with studios open Tuesday through Sunday from 11am to 6pm—but I found it dismally depressing. Someday, my love.

Canary Wharf: Insider's Retail Heaven

—by Jemma Griffiths

Canary Wharf, the center of London's financial district, isn't the first place you'd think of for shopping. However, steady improvement over recent years means Canary Wharf now boasts three malls: Jubilee Place, Canada Place, and Cabot Place, conveniently linked via the Tube station. These shopping complexes cater to the city's hassled, cash-rich, but time-poor workforce.

And now for a real insider's tip: Canary Wharf malls are virtually empty. Tourists are almost unknown in this part of London, and business folk don't shop during work hours. Apart from rush hour during lunch and around 6pm, you'll be free to browse at your own pace, practically undisturbed. It's a godsend if you want to investigate the British stores but cannot stand the crush of Oxford Street.

Jubilee Place, the newest mall, hosts a pleasing selection of British favorites: **Karen Millen,** one of my preferred local designers; **Fiorelli,** for stylish accessories normally found only in department stores; **Whistles** and **L. K. Bennett,** for luxury fashion and footwear; a fully stocked **Molton Brown,** featuring gorgeous bath and body products (ideal for gifts); and the quirky **Paperchase,** with unique photo albums, stationery, and cards.

Canada Place is home to an impressive number of high-street fashion labels. **Oasis** and **Warehouse** provide the more expensive fare, while the unbeatable **Topshop** and a reasonable **Dorothy Perkins** enable you to get the looks for less. There are also several high-end stores catering to the luxury market. For the gents, **T. M. Lewin** offers precisely tailored shirts of exceptional quality.

Cabot Place features branches of **Austin Reed,** for traditional British clothing; **Church's Shoes,** for traditional British wingtips; and **Thomas Pink,** for high-quality shirts. Don't go home without checking out **Sweaty Betty,** an Australian line of stylish workout gear.

As for munchies, there's a **PizzaExpress**, which towers over Cabot Place; **Crush,** the British answer to Jamba Juice, located in Jubilee Place; **Wagamama,** a Jubilee Place branch of the restaurant chain du jour, specializing in Asian noodle dishes; and, for a truly memorable experience, the modern French Conran restaurant called **Plateau,** in Canada Place. Top it off with a brownie from **Bene Bene** and coffee from **Starbucks.**

If you're in the vicinity, and in the mood for some pampering after a hectic shopping schedule, the luxurious spa at the fabulous **Four Seasons** provides an array of treatments. Better still, because its customers are usually businesspeople, the hotel has incredibly low and amenity-filled weekend rates.

The best way to see it all is to go to the **Design Museum,** eat lunch at one of the museum's several restaurants or cafes (take your choice—they're all Conran establishments and something to behold), pop into a few of the hot new galleries, browse the museums and their shops, and then take a boat and see the rest from the water.

Chapter Five

....

LONDON RESOURCES A TO Z

ACCESSORIES

....

You don't need to be born to shop to know that the ground floor of any department store sells all the lines of accessories, or that just about every boutique brand in the world carries some accessories. That understood, this is a list of those stores or brands you might not know or may find particularly well stocked or well priced. Jude Law, the ultimate British fashion accessory, is available but not listed.

ACCESSORIZE
22 The Market, Covent Garden, WC2 (Tube: Covent Garden); additional locations around town.

This chain, a division of Monsoon (p. 153), sells only accessories (duh) that are quite fashionable, quite well priced, and quite certainly going out of style in a year or two. Who cares? The colors and textures alone are enough to drive you wild with greed. Please note, a branch of Accessorize is often next door to a branch of Monsoon. Sometimes Monsoon or Twilight (another division, all about evening wear) will have its own accessories. The tiny beaded handbags are to drool for. ℂ 207/240-2107. www.accessorize.co.uk.

MICHAELA FREY
153 Regent St., W1 (Tube: Piccadilly Circus or Oxford St.).

This Viennese artist is known for her enamel bracelets and accessories and is rumored to make the enamelware for Hermès. Her specialty is historical art styles translated into cloisonné; the works are also sold at several museum shops. ✆ 207/287-7382. www.michaelafrey.com.

SWAINE ADENEY BRIGG
54 St. James's, SW1 (Tube: Piccadilly Circus or Green Park).

This 200-year-old firm makes the iconic Brit Brollies (umbrellas) that you picture when you close your eyes and think about a rainy day. They are handmade by master craftsmen and, contrary to popular myth, do come in other shades besides black. Along with Brollies, this firm makes a full range of proper accessories for gentlemen such as briefcases and small leather goods, and even luggage. Oh yes, and don't forget the canes and/or walking sticks, croquet mallets, and grooming kits. Prices are stiff upper lip. ✆ 207/409-7277.

BALLET & BALLET FLATS

BLUE VELVET
174 King's Rd., SW3 (Tube: Sloane Sq.).

Known primarily for their ballet slippers and moccasins, Blue Velvet also stocks a limited selection of dressy heels and boots. Their prices beat the competition by about 30%. ✆ 207/376-7442. www.bluevelvetshoes.com.

FREED OF LONDON LTD.
94 St. Martin's Lane, WC2 (Tube: Leicester Sq.).

If you're a ballet freak, you have long known of Freed of London, one of the most famous names in slippers and stuff. It also carries a dance and exercise line. The store is old and musty and not that charming, nor is the selection of leotards too great—but they do come with the hallmark of the Royal Ballet imprinted on them. © 207/240-0432. www.freedoflondon.com.

FRENCH SOLE
6 Ellis St., SW1 (Tube: Sloane Sq.).

This is the maker of the famous ballerina flats worn by Julia Roberts, Princess Diana, and so on. There are more than 100 varieties, made in solids and prints and glitter and with contrast toes. © 207/730-3771. www.frenchsole.com.

PRETTY BALLERINAS
34 Brook St., W1 (Tube: Bond St.).

Pretty Ballerinas, formerly available online only, has opened four boutiques in London, the largest being their flagship store in Mayfair. They stock thousands of shoes, including those little leopard-print numbers. © 217/493-3957. www.pretty ballerinas.com.

BEAUTY

See chapter 6, "Health & Beauty," for an entire chapter devoted to London bath, beauty, spa, and well-being sources.

BIG NAMES (BRITISH)

What's a British big name? It's either a major designer or a manufacturer whose name connotes a look that others imitate, yet it's based in the United Kingdom and may not be known outside of London. Note that some of the major names do not have their own stores and are sold either at Browns (see below) or at department stores.

ALEXANDER MCQUEEN
4 Old Bond St., W1 (Tube: Green Park).

I'd like to tell you that Alexander McQueen is a creative genius and nut case who does not make wearable clothes and whose prices are so high that you may as well forget him. When I got to his new store, however, I almost fainted from the wave of creativity and the inspiration I felt just from gazing in the windows. McQueen has been on his own of late and is still doing creative work that becomes more and more wearable and ever so chic. ✆ 207/355-0088. www.alexandermcqueen.com.

ALICE TEMPERLEY
6–10 Colville Mews, Lonsdale Rd., W11 (Tube: Notting Hill Gate).

It girl and designer Alice Temperley has become a fixture on the London social and fashion scenes and is now gathering international steam with her girly party dresses. Reminiscent of '70s hippie chic, the breezy frocks have become must-haves for young fashionistas with disposable income. She does a line for Target stores in the U.S. that may be more affordable. ✆ 207/229-7957.

AMANDA WAKELY
80 Fulham Rd., SW3 (Tube: South Kensington).

Big for locals with moola, Amanda Wakely is known for wedding dresses and special-event do's. Modern and not froufrou. ✆ 207/590-9105. www.amandawakeley.com.

AQUASCUTUM
100 Regent St., W1 (Tube: Piccadilly Circus).

The "other" Burberry, Aquascutum has hired a young designer (Michael Herz, considered one of the bright young things of his generation) and is watching its own checks make waves.

Established in 1851, Aquascutum has grown from a tiny cottage industry to a major international name. The Aquascutum line includes skirts, sweaters, and any accessory you could imagine. Instead of a plaid like Burberry's, Aquascutum is known for its checkered pattern. © **207/675-8200.** www.aquascutum. co.uk.

ASPREY
167 New Bond St. (Tube: Bond St. or Green Park).

Look at the old girl dance! If you think Asprey is staid and old-fashioned, then you haven't been into the store since it took on its new image. Asprey was losing market share to Tiffany & Co. and more modern brands, so it did the only thing it could do: pinched execs from Tiffany, closed shop for a year, and completely recast it. Now it's one of the snazziest stores in the world, selling luggage, handbags, gifts, some clothes, and lifestyle items for the rich and pampered. Just wander in and breathe deeply. © **207/493-6767.** www.asprey.com.

BROWNS
23–27 S. Molton St., W1 (Tube: Bond St.); Browns Focus, 38 S. Molton St., W1 (Tube: Bond St.).

Anytime you get the urge to pooh-pooh British fashion as dowdy, walk yourself right into Browns—the store, not the hotel—for a look-see at what has been London's temple of high fashion for decades. This is where it started and this is where the beat goes on.

Browns is filled with a ready-to-wear selection from the top designers in Europe: **Sonia Rykiel, Jil Sander,** and **Missoni** are all represented. **Calvin Klein** and **Donna Karan** were launched here before they opened their own stores in London.

The **Browns Focus** shop spotlights younger and hipper designers; a few of these lines are American (Lilly Pulitzer, Marc by Marc Jacobs), but many are local.

Browns usually has a sale shop that continues to move, depending on where empty storefronts turn up in the area. Ask at the main store. I visited this sale store and was horrified that it considered £125 ($250) for a cotton sweater a bargain price. ℂ **207/514-0000.** www.brownsfashion.com.

BURBERRY
Flagship: 21–23 New Bond St., W1 (Tube: Bond St.); 165 Regent St., W1 (Tube: Piccadilly); 2 Brompton Rd. (Tube: Knightsbridge); outlet shop: 29–53 Chatham Place, E9 (Bus: 55); factory outlet at Bicester Village (p. 278).

In keeping with its new image, Burberry has begun to take over the world. A few years ago, it was the new flagship on New Bond; now it has Scotch House in Knightsbridge. Both stores are large and modern, made of layers of glass and levels of display that feature everything known to man (or woman) that could possibly be made in plaid, including accessories for your dog. There's an outlet shop that can be reached by bus (it's a long schlep); for the factory outlet at Bicester Village, see p. 278. www.burberry.co.uk.

CAROLINE CHARLES
56–57 Beauchamp Place, SW3 (Tube: South Kensington).

There is an unwritten rule with British women that you can't go wrong with Caroline Charles, so if you're trying to impress the natives, one-stop shopping here will do it. ℂ **207/589-5850.** www.carolinecharles.co.uk.

DAKS
10 Old Bond St., W1 (Tube: Bond St.); 32–34 Jermyn St., SW1 (Tube: Piccadilly Circus).

Daks is the third of the plaid trio (along with Aquascutum and Burberry, described above) that comes from a veddy, veddy old tradition but has modernized itself in order to survive. Its plaid is beige with a rust, taupe, and charcoal–grayish black tattersall. You will faint when you see how with-it this store is—eat your heart out, Miuccia Prada! www.daks.com.

JAEGER
200–206 Regent St., W1 (Tube: Oxford Circus).

A basic, classic British resource, sold in its own shops and in many department stores. Jaeger has a way with wool in particular and strides the fine line between boring English clothes and high fashion. One of the good things about the Jaeger line is that it is totally color-coordinated each season, so you can buy a complete wardrobe of interchangeable pieces, which is great for travel; the bad news is that if you don't like the color palette for a season, you're out of luck.

The shop on Regent Street is almost a department store, with all the house lines, of which there are many. The newest is a knits range. This shop not only is easy to find, but also carries everything.

One warning: Jaeger may cost less in the United States! Shop carefully. © 207/200-4000.

JOHN SMEDLEY
24 Brook St., W1 (Tube: Bond St.).

This is actually the first John Smedley store ever, despite the fact that this cult maker of fine knitwear is very well-known in the United Kingdom. The mills make great knits—woolens and cottons and cashmeres—but Smedley is most famous for its Sea Island cotton shirts. The store is very tiny and not too exciting visually, but there's more stock downstairs. Prices are high. © 207/495-2222. www.john-smedley.com.

JOSEPH
77 Fulham Rd., SW3 (Tube: South Kensington or Fulham Broadway); 130 Draycott Ave., SW3 (Tube: South Kensington); 26 Sloane St., SW1 (Tube: Sloane Sq.); 23 Old Bond St., W1 (Tube: Green Park).

Not all Joseph stores are created equally, so attempt to see them all or else head straight to the flagship to observe the glory of the creator, Joseph himself. The man is incredibly inventive and creative; his stores provide visual stimulation that defines the best in hot British fashion, even though a raft of international labels are also for sale. It's the look and the mix that make the show, and sometimes the copies from more expensive brands. The home style has been Zen-ish since before Armani Casa, and the cafes are a good place to hang. It's a lifestyle, man. © 207/823-9500. www.joseph.co.uk.

MARGARET HOWELL
34 Wigmore St., W1 (Tube: Bond St.).

Margaret Howell offers clothes that are expensive, but so chic and elegant that they are very upper-class British. You'll see London dress-up clothes, but this resource is best for more casual, everyday attire and for weekend chic—hand-knit sweaters, twinsets, jackets, coats. © 207/009-9009. www.margarethowell. co.uk.

MATTHEW WILLIAMSON
28 Bruton St., W1 (Tube: Bond St.).

If you've been reading *Born to Shop London* over the years, you would have noted when the store Monsoon suddenly got hot and all I could do was ask for the smelling salts. Now we know the reason why: Matthew Williamson, who left Monsoon to become a cult darling with big-bucks clients and his first free-standing store. He's also the new face at Pucci. © 207/ 629-6200. www.matthewwilliamson.com.

NICOLE FARHI
158 New Bond St., W1 (Tube: Green Park); 202 West-bourne Grove, W11 (Tube: Notting Hill Gate); 193 Sloane St., SW1 (Tube: Knightsbridge); 27 Hampstead High St., NW3 (Tube: Hampstead); 11 Floral St., WC2 (Tube: Covent Garden).

This designer does the elegant-working-woman look with New York panache and would fit well into the American scene. Her tailored clothes are rich and simple, always elegant, but with sporty comfort. Branch locations are popping up so frequently that she may soon be considered a multiple. For those who like Armani but can't afford it, this line is less expensive and can serve the same purpose.

Farhi's Bond Street showcase is in the modern style; her restaurant, **Nicole's,** is the place to eat while on a shopping spree. It even serves breakfast. www.nicolefarhi.com.

PAUL SMITH
Westbourne House, 122 Kensington Park Rd., W11 (Tube: Notting Hill Gate).

That's Sir Paul to you. Although he began as a menswear designer offering funky chic before it existed, Smith was recently knighted for all his contributions to fashion and style, including women's and kids' clothes, too. His main store is in a funky little house near Portobello Road, although his designs are sold all over the U.K. and in most London department stores.

A Paul Smith furniture shop has opened at 9 Albemarle St., W1 (Tube: Green Park). The stores in Covent Garden, 40–44 Floral St., WC2 (Tube: Covent Garden), sell menswear and children's clothing. Don't forget the new Paul Smith chain located in international airports; try T5 at LHR.

There is an outlet store, at 23 Avery Row, W1 (Tube: Bond St.), for men's clothing, but I've never found it worth the visit. © 207/727-3553. www.paulsmith.co.uk.

STELLA MCCARTNEY
30 Bruton St., W1 (Tube: Bond St.).

Aren't you tired of hearing whose daughter she is? Stella went from St. Martins to Chloe to Gucci to H&M to Adidas, and has just launched **CARE by Stella McCartney,** a luxury organic skin-care line. Her designs are expensive, trendy, very feminine, and for those with good bodies. © 207/518-3100. www.stella mccartney.com.

VIVIENNE WESTWOOD
44 Conduit St., W1 (Tube: Oxford Circus).

When American fashion lion John Fairchild made up his list of the most influential and important designers of our time, Vivienne Westwood headed it up. She invents shapes, moods, and concepts of dressing and produces slightly way-out clothes that age well, though they are primarily for the young and moneyed. The Conduit Street shop is right in the heart of Mayfair shopping, so pop in. It sells off the samples at the end of the season, and prices can be reasonable. This is Viv's version of a markdown shop or factory outlet. The new fragrance, Boudoir, is super. © 207/439-1109. www.viviennewestwood.com.

BIG NAMES (INTERNATIONAL)

No shopping mecca is more international than London; no international resource can consider itself in the big time if it doesn't list a London address on its shopping bags. But there are very few bargains in international merchandise here unless you hit a big sale. Prices are almost always better in the U.S.—so think selection, not price.

Although American retailers and chain stores are opening right and left in London, don't think for a minute that you might save on American goods abroad. With very few exceptions, these stores offer merchandise that is much more expensive in Britain than in the United States. I go to **Gap** stores all the time just to laugh. The prices in pounds are exactly the same as the prices in U.S. dollars at home. (If you want to bring a gift to someone in Britain, buy it at Gap in the United States.)

I must report, however, that at **Harvey Nicks,** I did see merchandise from a major U.S. designer that I'd never seen in an American store. Granted, I don't live in the shipping department of a major mall—but it seemed incredible to go to London to fall in love with an American outfit (at full British retail, no less). Academics may want to note that one of the ways Harvey Nichols likes to differentiate itself from other London department stores is by being heavily committed to American designers and American brands.

ADOLFO DOMINGUEZ
15 Endell St., WC2 (Tube: Covent Garden).
© 207/836-5013. www.adolfodominguez.com.

AGNES B.
40–41 Marylebone St. (Tube: Bond or Baker).
© 207/935-5556. www.agnesb.fr.

AKRIS
30 Old Bond St. (Tube: Bond St.).
© 207/758-8060.

ALBERTA FERRETTI
205–206 Sloane St., SW1 (Tube: Knightsbridge).
© 207/235-2349. www.aeffe.com.

BOTTEGA VENETA
33 Sloane St., SW1 (Tube: Knightsbridge).
© 207/838-9394. www.bottegaveneta.com.

CELINE
160 New Bond St., W1 (Tube: Bond St.).
© 207/297-4999. www.celine.com.

CHANEL
278–280 Brompton Rd., SW3 (Tube: South Kensington); 26 Old Bond St., W1 (Tube: Bond St.); 167–170 Sloane St., SW1 (Tube: Knightsbridge); Heathrow Departure Terminals 3 and 4.
© 207/581-8620. www.chanel.com.

CHLOE
152–153 Sloane St., SW1 (Tube: Sloane Sq.).
© 207/823-5348. www.chloe.com.

CHRISTIAN DIOR
31 Sloane St., SW1 (Tube: Knightsbridge).
© 207/245-1300. www.dior.com.

COMME DES GARÇONS
Dover St. Market, 17 Dover St., W1 (Tube: Green Park); 59 Brook St., W1 (Tube: Bond St.).
© 207/581-0680.

DOLCE & GABBANA
55–56 New Bond St., W1 (Tube: Green Park); 175 Sloane St., SW1 (Tube: Sloane St.).
© 207/659-9000. www.dolcegabbana.it.

EMANUEL UNGARO
150 New Bond St., W1 (Tube: Bond St.).
© 207/629-0550. www.emanuelungaro.com.

EMILIO PUCCI
170 Sloane St., W1 (Tube: Knightsbridge).
© 207/201-8171. www.emiliopucci.com.

EMPORIO ARMANI
51–52 New Bond St., W1 (Tube: Bond St.).
© 207/491-8080. www.emporioarmani.co.uk.

ERMENEGILDO ZEGNA
37–38 New Bond St., W1 (Tube: Bond St.).
© 207/493-4471. www.zegna.com.

ESCADA
194–195 Sloane St., SW1 (Tube: Knightsbridge).
© 208/897-0412. www.escada.com.

ETRO
14 Old Bond St., W1 (Tube: Bond St.).
© 207/495-5767. www.etro.it.

FENDI
20–22 Sloane St., SW1 (Tube: Knightsbridge).
© 207/838-6280. www.fendi.com.

FOGAL
3A Sloane St., SW1 (Tube: Knightsbridge).
© 207/235-3115. www.fogal.com.

GIANNI VERSACE
183–184 Sloane St., SW1 (Tube: Knightsbridge).
© 207/259-5700. www.versace.com.

GIORGIO ARMANI
37 Sloane St., SW1 (Tube: Knightsbridge).
© 207/235-6232. www.giorgioarmani.com.

GUCCI
18 Sloane St., SW1 (Tube: Knightsbridge).
© 207/235-6707. www.gucci.com.

HERMÈS
179 Sloane St., SW1 (Tube: Knightsbridge); 155 New Bond St., W1 (Tube: Bond St.).
© 207/823-1014. www.hermes.com.

ISSEY MIYAKE
52 Conduit St., W1 (Tube: Oxford Circus).
© 207/851-4620. www.isseymiyake.com.

LOEWE
130 New Bond St., W1 (Tube: Bond St.).
© 207/493-3914. www.loewe.com.

LOUIS VUITTON
190–192 Sloane St., SW1 (Tube: Knightsbridge); 17–18 New Bond St., W1 (Tube: Bond St.).
© 207/399-4050. www.vuitton.com.

MARINA RINALDI
39 Old Bond St., W1 (Tube: Green Park).
© 207/629-4454.

MARNI
26 Sloane St., SW1 (Tube: Knightsbridge).
© 207/245-9520. www.marni.com.

MAX MARA
19–21 Old Bond St., W1 (Tube: Green Park).
© 207/499-7902.

MIU MIU
123 New Bond St., W1 (Tube: Bond St.).
© 207/409-0900. www.miumiu.com.

MOSCHINO
28–29 Conduit St., W1 (Tube: Bond St.).
© 207/318-0555. www.moschino.it.

NANETTE LEPORE
206 Westbourne Grove, W11 (Tube: Notting Hill Gate).
© 207/221-8889. www.nanettelepore.com.

PAUL & JOE
134 Sloane St., SW1 (Tube: Knightsbridge).
© 207/824-8844. www.paulandjoe.com.

PRADA
16–18 Old Bond St., W1 (Tube: Green Park).
© 207/647-5000. www.prada.com.

SALVATORE FERRAGAMO
*24 Old Bond St., W1 (Tube: Bond St.); 207 Sloane St., SW1
(Tube: Knightsbridge).*
© 207/838-7730. www.ferragamo.com.

SONIA RYKIEL
27–29 Brook St., W1 (Tube: Bond St.).
© 207/493-5255. www.soniarykiel.com.

VALENTINO
174 Sloane St., SW1 (Tube: Knightsbridge).
© 207/235-5855. www.valentino.it.

YOHJI YAMAMOTO
14 Conduit St., W1 (Tube: Oxford Circus).
© 207/491-4129. www.yohjiyamamoto.co.jp.

YVES SAINT-LAURENT
33 Old Bond St., W1 (Tube: Green Park).
© 207/493-1800. www.ysl.com.

BIG NAMES (NORTH AMERICAN)

Paul Revere's ghost could well be riding the Tube and shouting, "The Americans are coming! The Americans are coming!" Indeed, many American brands have their own stores and are sold in the big department stores here.

Tiffany & Co. (25 Old Bond St.) and **Ralph Lauren** (1 New Bond St.) act like they have been in town forever; **Marc Jacobs** (24–25 Mount St.) and **Abercrombie & Fitch** (7 Burlington Gardens, off Bond St.) have opened in Mayfair, and **Gap** is everywhere. What is London coming to? There are now so many American retailers here that I am not going to waste space listing them. I've already made it pretty clear how I feel about this shopping option.

Donna Karan, 46 Conduit St., W1 (Tube: Oxford Circus), has moved her flagship into a stunning town house, and you may also want to poke into the flagship **Ralph Lauren/Polo**, 1 New Bond St., W1 (Tube: Bond St.), because it's decorated in true Brit Ralph style and is something to behold. But please, we didn't come here to buy American brands, now did we?

BOOKS

Below are listings of booksellers who carry recently published books, bestsellers, and other titles in print. If it's first editions, rare or antiquarian books, or out-of-print titles you seek, please see chapter 9, "Antiques, Used Books & Collectibles." For business books, try the major multiples or **Foyles** (see below). There are also bookstores at Heathrow Airport. Note that the only time you would be saving money, or even breaking even, on a British book is through an international edition (sold at airports and international train stations) or at discount shops, where you can sometimes get hardback bestsellers for £11 ($22); see below. The real reason to buy in Britain is the selection.

Small Wonders

While we all buy books online and patronize the chains, many Londoners still prefer the indies, as local shop owners can provide a better, more informed service and more select titles. Good examples include **Broadway Books** (6 Broadway Market, E8) and **Crockatt & Powell** (119–120 Lower Marsh, SE1), which are good browsing spots and offer quality literature selections plus choice nonfiction titles. **Pan Bookshop** (158 Fulham Rd., SW10) is good for signed copies, while **Metropolitan Books** (49 Exmouth Market, EC1) and **Blenheim Books** (11 Blenheim Crescent, W11) have created in-house areas for neighborhood mingling. **The Talking Book Shop** (11 Wigmore St., W1) has more than 6,000 titles on CD if you need a book to plug into your Bose for the return flight. **Travel Bookshop** (13–15 Blenheim Crescent), another Notting Hill favorite, has a literary vibe; they focus on travel novels as guides. Sorry, but Hugh Grant isn't in residence.

BORDERS
203 Oxford St., W1 (Tube: Oxford Circus).

Despite this being an American chain, it has a wide selection and fair prices—and this branch is located right next to Superdrug, so you can kill a few shopping birds with the same tote bag. © 207/292-1600. www.borders.co.uk.

BRITISH BOOKSHOPS & SUSSEX STATIONERS
530 Oxford St., W1 (Tube: Marble Arch).

This is a rather average-looking bookstore from the street, but it's a real find. It sells hardback bestsellers at excellent prices (about 40% less than regular retail)—and at the same time as the major booksellers, so there's no wait to read your favorites. There are also nonfiction and some stationery items. © 207/377-1391.

Building Centre Bookshop
Building Centre, 26 Store St., WC1 (Tube: Goodge St.).

For design freaks, this is the last word. Just camp out and order in. This is a bookstore for the design trade, with specialty titles for architects, designers, do-it-yourselfers, and the like. On Saturdays, it closes at 1pm. ℂ **207/692-4040**. www.building centre.co.uk.

Foyles
113–119 Charing Cross Rd., WC2 (Tube: Leicester Sq.).

Foyles is the largest bookstore in London, with more than four million volumes in stock. It's as crowded as ever, but the somewhat lackadaisical staff has been replaced by earnest and mostly helpful college students. There are large children's and fiction sections on the main floor; upper floors are devoted to technical books, a small antiquarian library, and huge sections on hobbies, art, and commerce. The business section is particularly noteworthy. ℂ **207/437-5660**. www.foyles.co.uk.

Hatchards
187 Piccadilly, W1 (Tube: Piccadilly Circus).

Looking for me in London? Stop by Hatchards at Piccadilly. I spend part of almost every visit to London here. Far and away the most complete of the modern booksellers, the main Hatchards is in a town house near Fortnum & Mason and is filled with just about everything. Hatchards is owned by Dillons as a sort of boutique bookstore. There are bigger stores in London, but I like the size of this one, and I love its travel section. ℂ **207/439-9921**. www.hatchards.co.uk.

RD Franks
5 Winsley St., W1 (Tube: Oxford Circus).

Located on a small lane north of Oxford Street, this small shop is one of the fashion industry's best-kept secrets; along with thousands of books from design and photography to sewing and crafts, the shop stocks London's most comprehensive range of U.K. and international media and fashion magazines, journals, and trend books. ✆ **207/636-1244.** www.rdfranks.co.uk.

WATERSTONE'S
88 Regent St., W1 (Tube: Piccadilly Circus); 99–101 Old Brompton Rd., SW7 (Tube: Knightsbridge); 193 Kensington High St., W8 (Tube: High St. Kensington); 121–125 Charing Cross Rd., WC2 (Tube: Tottenham Court Rd.).

Yes, it's a chain—but with a large selection of everything and many locations near the shopping areas to which you'll gravitate. This is simply a good basic source for extra guidebooks (no one can survive in London without an *A to Z*), stuff to read on the plane, and art books. www.waterstones.co.uk.

ZWEMMER
Oxford University Press Bookshop, 72 Charing Cross Rd., WC2 (Tube: Leicester Sq.).
ZWEMMER ART
24 Litchfield St., WC2 (Tube: Leicester Sq.).
ZWEMMER BOOKSHOP
80 Charing Cross Rd., WC2 (Tube: Leicester Sq.).

Ready to keep this straight? Zwemmer has three stores in Charing Cross: (1) Zwemmer, the Oxford University Press Bookshop, company store for one of the most respected publishers in the world; (2) Zwemmer Art, which is devoted to the fine arts; and (3) Zwemmer Bookshop, which focuses on the graphic arts—illustration, photography, and so on (there were three different books on Issey Miyake the last time we looked). ✆ **207/240-4157.**

BOUTIQUES

....

DAY BIRGER ET MIKKELSEN
133A Sloane St., SW1 (Tube: Sloane Sq.).

Where the boho crowd comes to worship and buy the rich hippie look. You'll find clothes, accessories, and even lingerie. Prices are very high. But so is the glam factor. © 207/267-8822. www.day.dk.

DOVER STREET MARKET
17 Dover St., W1 (Tube: Green Park).

This is a designer marketplace located on Dover Street. It's a gorgeous London double-size town house that works on the open format and showcases both big-name designers and the kind of people you are waiting to discover. There's lots of Japanese designer clothing, which makes sense since this is the brainchild of Rei Kawakubo from Comme des Garcons. You may not buy anything, but this could be a museum of cool; go here for people-watching, if nothing else. © 207/493-2342. www.doverstreetmarket.com.

EGG
36 Kinnerton St., W1 (Tube: Hyde Park Corner or Knightsbridge).

This tiny Kensington shop is so tucked away in a residential mews that you may think you're lost as you wander down Kinnerton Street. Don't give up—Egg is a real find. One of London's best-kept secrets, Egg features clean-lined clothing with an Asian feel by a select group of up-and-coming designers. Egg's ethos is very Zen and ignores the whims of trendy high-end fashion; this doesn't stop Issey Miyake and Donna Karan from shopping here. Surprisingly, most items are under £175 ($350). © 207/235-9315.

SHOON
94 Marylebone High St., W1 (Tube: Baker St.).

This is a small concern with one location in London and one in Bath. Shoon is very hippie/politically correct, with a green attitude, world music, and a mélange of men's, women's, and kids' clothes in what is possibly the store of the future for the environmentally concerned. It carries lots of linen for spring and summer—I really like the brand Oska for its big droopy feel. Don't miss the basement if you're looking for comfortable walking shoes. ✆ 207/487-3001. www.shoon.com.

THE SHOP AT BLUEBIRD
30 King's Rd., SW3 (Tube: Sloane Sq.).

Conceived by the couple who successfully launched Jigsaw, this former Sainsbury's grocery store has been transformed into a one-room megashop that's part lifestyle boutique and part design studio. There's a huge book section illuminated by 1,000 light bulbs, and the ever-shifting inventory includes jewelry, clothing, and accessories from a roster of independent designers. Fashion-wise, the styles are more traditional than edgy. Short-term collaborations, such as a promotional Blue-Bird shirt by Turnbull & Asser, keep the inventory fresh and unique. There are also a cobbler, tailor, chocolatier, and minispa. ✆ 207/351-3873. www.theshopatbluebird.com.

YACCO MARICARD
10 Kensington Church St., SW1 (Tube: High St. Kensington).

I discovered this Japanese designer in Bangkok, and was thrilled to find another shop in London. His designs are casual and relaxed yet very sophisticated; think CP Shades with an edge. You'll find lots of shirt styles, most with drape and flow, and some that can double as jackets. I bought a skirt/skort/capri number made of two contrasting textured cottons in a soft shade of sand. ✆ 207/376-9151. —S.R.L.

BUTTONS

....

BUTTON QUEEN
19 Marylebone Lane, W1 (Tube: Bond St.).

Don't let the address throw you; this store is only 2 blocks from Oxford Street. Get here through Cecil Court, and you won't mind the walk—especially if you sew, knit, or collect. The small shop has everything in buttons, from old to new, hand-painted to Wedgwood. The latter set is rather *cher,* but other prices begin at about a quarter per button. If you're considering making a sweater or having one made from a designer kit, come by here to get the buttons. ☎ **207/935-1505.** www.thebutton queen.co.uk.

CHILDREN'S CLOTHING

....

Please note the recent trend of the midrange multiples to add on clothing lines for kids, or at least for little girls. Some of these have free-standing stores (**Jigsaw Junior**); others, such as **John Lewis,** have dedicated a separate area or entire floor to children's goods. **Brora** cashmeres for kiddies are incredible, as are the prices (see store listing on p. 166), and **Paul Smith** for children is worth a look (p. 122).

CARAMEL
291 Brompton Rd., SW3 (Tube: South Kensington).

Most of the things in this store were designed by the Greek owner, who was disheartened by kids who wore only frills or Gap togs. Her house collection is called Caramel Baby & Child. Madonna bought young Rocco a pair of cashmere trousers for just over £50 ($100). Oy. ☎ **207/589-7001.**

MAMAS & PAPAS
256–258 Regent St., W1 (Tube: Bond St.).

Eco Kids

For children's clothing, toiletries, and other essentials that are preservative- and pesticide-free, organically grown, and manufactured from recycled materials, check out these London sources:

Green Baby (354 Upper St., N1; Tube: Angel) sells baby clothing that is made in South India as part of a community project that supports the education and employment of young girls. Along with the 100% organic bib and tucker, there are organic sheets, and baby balms and lotions based on pure lanolin and cocoa butter. © 207/359-7037.

The Natural Mat Company (99 Talbot Rd., W11; Tube: Ladbroke Grove) sells mostly mattresses (they won't fit in the overhead bin), but you'll also find baby clothes in organic cotton and cashmere. © 207/985-0474.

Mamas & Papas is a huge chain selling maternity and brand-new-baby needs as well as kids' clothes and things such as strollers and toiletries. Their new flagship store on Regent street features "Cibo at Mamas & Papas," a cute cafe on the first floor catering to the nutritional needs of expectant and nursing mums. © 870/830-7700. www.mamasandpapas.co.uk.

MARIE CHANTAL
61A Ledbury Rd., W11 (Tube: Notting Hill Gate).

I'm not listing this shop because you'll find great prices, or even good value, but because it carries some of the most beautiful baby's and children's clothing I've ever seen. This is a place for wealthy grams and hedge fund mums. It was created by Marie Chantal, otherwise known as the next Queen of Greece who is one of the infamous Miller Sisters. With all the creds, she still has amazingly simple and chic fashion for toddlers. © 207/243-0220.

TROTTERS
34 King's Rd., SW3 (Tube: Sloane Sq.).

Trotters is an adorable shop that sells kids' toys and clothing.
© 207/259-9620. www.trotters.co.uk.

CIGARS

A woman is a woman, but a cigar is a smoke—everyone knows
that—and everyone who knows it has known it for a very long
time. Now that London has banned indoor smoking, "smok-
ers," which were actually PR events created by hotels and cigar
stores to boost interest and sales, are a thing of the past. Not
to worry: London is still a leading cigar capital of the world,
partly because Cuban cigars are not illegal in Britain. But
because it is currently still illegal to bring in or sell Cuban cigars
in the United States, my reporting on this subject is going to
be limited.

There are a few major cigar retailers in London, and you
can discuss your needs specifically with them. I happen to like
to hang out at Davidoff because the men who shop there are
so handsome. But don't mind me. **Harrods** and **Selfridges** also
sell cigars.

DAVIDOFF
35 St. James's St., SW1 (Tube: Green Park).

Davidoff, from Geneva, has shops in all the major capitals. Its
London location is on the corner of St. James's Street right near
Jermyn Street, firmly entrenched in Man Territory. The atmosphere is not as forbiddingly formal as that of Dunhill. © 207/
930-3079.

DUNHILL
*48 Jermyn St., W1 (Tube: Green Park); 159 Sloane St., SW1
(Tube: Knightsbridge).*

Alfred Dunhill is more than a cigar shop, but it does have cigars, humidors, and smoking paraphernalia galore on the mezzanine, where the atmosphere is masculine and clubby. If you're looking for the perfect gift for the man who has everything, surely one of Lord Linley's bespoke humidors will do the trick. (Non–royal watchers will note that David Linley is the son of Princess Margaret and a major force in new British design.) ℗ 207/458-0779. www.dunhill.com.

J. J. Fox
19 St. James's St., SW1 (Tube: Green Park).

Old cigar hands may know this shop as Robert Lewis. J. J. Fox is the newer name. Indeed, we're talking about a merger here, the joining of two of London's top cigar dealers, James J. Fox and Robert Lewis. Now then, if you think Dunhill is intimidating, you have not visited this clubby little nook, where men speak Cohiba in quiet tones. The setup is simple: The ground floor is devoted to sales, and yes, there's a cigar museum. This is the shop noted for its Churchill memorabilia—Winston Churchill opened his account here in 1900 and used it right up until a month before he died, 64 years later. ℗ 207/930-3787. www.jjfox.co.uk.

COMPACT DISCS & DVDs

The heavyweights—HMV and Virgin—have all the amenities and services you'd expect to find in a warehouse, but they do have mammoth selections, literally something for every taste. HMV and Virgin stores open at 9:30am and stay open until at least 7pm.

Tip: If you're buying DVDs, know your zones! DVDs sold in London may be playable in the U.K. only. My international DVD player normally plays discs from anywhere, but was just stumped by a legally bought (from HMV) DVD set. Ouch!

FOPP

220–224 Tottenham Court Rd., W1 (Tube: Goodge St. or Tottenham Court Rd.).
© 207/299-1640.

HMV

150 Oxford St., W1 (Tube: Oxford Circus).
© 207/631-3423. www.hmv.co.uk.

VIRGIN MEGASTORE

14–30 Oxford St., W1 (Tube: Oxford Circus).
© 207/631-1234. www.virgin.com.

DEPARTMENT STORES

American department stores are mostly patterned on British ones, so you'll feel right at home in just about any department store in London. All are in big, old-fashioned buildings and offer the kind of social security that enables you to know you could live in them. Most have several restaurants or tearooms. And all have clean bathrooms, although Harrods makes you either pay to use the loo or show a sales slip to prove you have bought something.

During the Christmas shopping days, department stores are open later than usual, which may mean until 7pm. They are rarely open until 9pm. Other than at Christmastime, department stores have 1 night a week—either Wednesday or Thursday—during which they stay open until 7 or possibly 8pm.

All department stores have export desks that will help you with VAT forms; all allow you to collect your receipts over a period of time to qualify for the VAT. Some may charge £4 to £6 ($8–$12) for the administrative work they must do on their end. The minimum amount of money that you must spend to qualify for a VAT refund varies dramatically from department store to department store.

When you go to the VAT desk in any given store, allow some time not only for getting your paperwork processed, but also for standing in line while others ahead of you deal with theirs. If you can move right through, the process will take about 10 minutes. Do have your passport on hand or know your number by heart.

DEBENHAMS
334–338 Oxford St., W1 (Tube: Oxford Circus).

Debenhams was remodeled a few years ago and is continuing to pursue new brands by way of famous names doing clothing exclusives—what it calls "autograph lines." It is the fastest-growing department store, in terms of revenue, in the United Kingdom. For Debenhams's youngest shoppers, **The Restaurant** offers **VIP Baby** services including baby food on the menu, baby food and bottle warming service, and changing facilities next to the restaurant. © 844/561-6161. www.debenhams.com.

FENWICK
63 New Bond St., W1 (Tube: Bond St. or Oxford Circus).

I adore Fenwick (say *Fennick*). In fact, I almost count it as my favorite stop on Bond Street. I've shopped Fenwick top to bottom and am happy to say this is a great source for affordable designer bridge lines, such as Tara Jarmon and Nanette Lepore; upscale lines include Collette Dinnigan, Anna Sui, and Sonia by Sonia Rykiel. There's also plenty of cheap-junk fashion looks, and terrific hair accessories. It now has a branch of Carluccio's in the basement for quick eats. This place isn't as large as a full-size department store, so you can give it a quick once-over and not be exhausted. © 207/629-9161. www.fenwick.co.uk.

HARRODS
87–135 Brompton Rd., Knightsbridge, SW1 (Tube: Knightsbridge).

If you are serious about spending time in Harrods, pick up its free *Store Guide* at any of the doors—it has detailed maps of all floors and even a two-page list of the customer services offered within the store, which is really a city unto itself.

There is no question that this store is a landmark and that it offers one hell of a lot of merchandise. The china department and the food halls are what become legends most; the children's toy department is almost as good as Hamleys (p. 172).

Before I even give you the scoop on what's inside, let's hope that you can indeed enter the store to see it for yourself. Harrods has recently enlarged its list of no-nos for visitors and enforces a very strict dress code. I got a postcard from an angry reader who said she was denied entrance because of her backpack. Jeans that are torn—even fashionably so—are also on the banned list.

The food halls, located on the ground floor, are internationally known, with 17 departments in all. The department store itself covers 1.8 hectares (4½ acres) of land and has 6 hectares (15 acres) of selling space. This is good to remember when your feet are telling you to stop, but you don't even feel that you've made a dent yet. The food halls are open from 9am to 9pm Monday to Saturday, and noon to 6pm on Sunday.

Don't forget that Harrods prides itself on being a full-service department store. Therefore, on the lower level, you will find a complete travel agency, export department, London Tourist Board office, bank, and theater-ticket agency. There is a hair salon upstairs on five; it opens at 9am, even though the rest of the store doesn't open until 10am. ✆ 207/730-1234. www.harrods.com.

HARVEY NICHOLS
109–125 Knightsbridge (at Sloane St.), SW1 (Tube: Knightsbridge).

Harvey Nicks, as it's called here, is a *real* store—not a tourist trap trading on an old reputation. Its styles are always the latest, and most of the major design houses are represented; there are lots of American lines, but the idea of the store is to offer thrills via new brands and new stuff. It's also taken the show on the road and opened many new branches around the world (and across the U.K.), but this is the flagship.

I have checked out the hat department of every department store in London, and this is the single best one. It's not huge, and it's not overly dramatic—it's simply solid. I also like the home-decor floor, which has recently added Italian luxury lifestyle brand's **Culti** boutique. The fifth floor—named "The Fifth Floor"—has the new food hall and a hotshot restaurant called, get this, Fifth Floor. There is also a place for coffee, a snack, sushi, or a quick lunch between the fancy eats and the food halls. Note that as a political statement, the store no longer sells furs. © 207/235-5000. www.harveynichols.com.

HOUSE OF FRASER
318 Oxford St., W1 (Tube: Bond St.).

House of Fraser has a good selection of its own private-label items and many designer names. The ceilings are low, and the store is rather dense; so it's not as glamorous as other options. But you'll see things here that you just won't find in other shops; you'll also find that it billboards midrange designers who can get buried in glitzier stores. It's not the fanciest place in London, but if you like bread-and-butter clothes, you may want to give it a try. © 870/160-7258. www.houseoffraser.com.

JOHN LEWIS
278 Oxford St., W1 (Tube: Bond St.).

John Lewis is one of the many department stores standing on Oxford Street, but despite its recent $120-million face-lift, you won't see much of a change in the merchandise. Now spiffed up with new transparent-sided elevator banks and skylights, it's a very special creature unto itself—a real-people store with a stiff upper lip. While it does have fashion, it's much more of a meat-and-potatoes store for fabrics, crafts, household items, and the like. There's an excellent accessories department and a good drugstore, both on the ground floor. *Warning:* This store does not accept credit cards or bank cards—only cash or its own store card. © 207/629-7711. www.johnlewis.com.

LIBERTY
Great Marlborough St., W1 (Tube: Oxford Circus).

Formerly occupying two buildings, Liberty recently lost the lease of its Regent Street wing, so now all departments are cozily tucked into the Tudor-style building on Great Marlborough Street. This building has always been my favorite as it has a fabulous old-fashioned market-spree feel to it. If you enter through the main entrance (at the corner of Regent and Great Marlborough sts.), you find yourself in the gift room, smack in the middle of the soaring atrium.

After browsing the signature Liberty scarves and hand-bags, turn left to visit rooms devoted to cosmetics, fragrance, and skin care. The upper floors feature home goods, where you'll want to buy and ship everything you see. On my last trip, I found some stunning silk throw pillows for under £100 ($200). Don't miss it for the world. © 207/734-1234. www.liberty.co.uk.

MARKS & SPENCER
458 Oxford St., W1 (Tube: Bond St.).

M&S is back from the dead and even has some style to sell, along with the bread-and-butter clothing items. There are some lines created by famous designers, some lines that are exclusives (available only for a few weeks), and the old faithfuls, too. M&S's designer Autograph collection for men and women and George Davis's Per Una fashion line are winning rave reviews. The food divisions have always been fabulous, but now the clothes and many other products are making news. The Marble Arch flagship is by far the best—best selection and best renovation. © 207/935-7954. www.marksandspencer.co.uk.

PETER JONES
Sloane Sq., SW1 (Tube: Sloane Sq.).

Another makeover, another contemporary scene. I wish I liked it. Not that there's anything to dislike, but the store looks like Barneys now. I liked it a tad more frumpy. Still, this is the source for trimmings, home fabrics, and bed linens. Sale prices on designer textiles such as Designers Guild and Sanderson range from £10 to £50 ($20–$100) per meter, and you'll find even better deals on fabric end bolts and closeouts. *Tip:* Peter Jones is now open on Sundays 11am to 5pm; its hours Monday through Saturday are from 9:30am to 7pm. © 207/730-3434. www.peterjones.co.uk.

SELFRIDGES
400 Oxford St., W1 (Tube: Bond St.).

Selfridges is surely the Avis Rent A Car of Britain: There's no question that it tries harder. In the past few years, the store has all but reinvented itself and has worked hard to upgrade both its image and its merchandise. Many now say it's the best department store in Britain.

It's all here. For big spenders, the new Wonder Room arcade is home to big-ticket miniboutiques ranging from Chanel to Tiffany. There's a new section between the beauty hall and Spirit (young women's fashion with a Topshop outpost) devoted to mid-priced handbags; Selfridges's beauty hall, the largest in Europe, houses all the global names.

Dining options include three restaurants, four coffee shops, a juice bar, a cafe in Stella McCartney, and a Krispy Kreme franchise in the basement. There's a good magazine selection on the ground floor, plus a small food hall, making this a convenient place to do some "real" shopping. In short, the store has everything. © 0870/837-7377. www.selfridges.com.

ECO-CHIC

••

BAMFORD & SONS
31 Sloane Sq., SW1 (Tube: Sloane Sq.).

Bamford is a veddy proper provider of clothes for gentlemen and boys, but they also have a particularly lush and luxurious accessories line and a green policy toward home gear and clothing. Its eco range of organic fabrics and non–chemical-treated leathers is in sync with environmental issues; there's even a Daylesford Organic Café in the basement. © 207/881-8010. www.bamfordandsons.com.

EQUA
28 Camden Passage, N1 (Tube: Angel).

Equa is London's first stand-alone shop dedicated entirely to fair trade and organic fashion. The collection is limited, but features designers like Ciel, whose clothes have a vintage feel; Edun, the couture creation of Ali Hews (Bono's wife), and NYC transplant Rogan Gregory; and cutting-edge denim from organic jeans brand Loomstate. © 207/359-0955. www.equa clothing.com.

POTASSIUM
2 Seymour Place, W1 (Tube: Marble Arch).

On a tiny street behind Marble Arch lies the electric blue storefront of Potassium, a contemporary eco-lifestyle boutique stocked full of clothes, furniture, and home style. Prices are reasonable (for London); check out the organic T's for £12 ($24) and cashmere-mix V-necks for under £30 ($60). Embroidered reclaimed-fabric pillows (£50/$100) stack up next to tea towels made from recycled flour sacks (£12/$24). Here's proof that you don't have to sacrifice style to save the planet. © 207/723-7800. www.potassiumstore.co.uk.

FOODSTUFFS

A trip to any supermarket is always fun. Most of the department stores have food halls: **Harrods** has the most famous one, but **Harvey Nicks** has interesting choices, and **Selfridges** has expanded its market. Grand old dame **Fortnum & Mason** has reopened after a major face-lift with a new food hall worthy of her $50-million nip and tuck. The biggest news on the food front is the opening of U.S. giant **Whole Foods** on Kensington High Street. This three-story, 75,000-square-foot flagship offers organic and additive-free groceries, an organic pub, and eco clothing lines to those who can afford to shop here.

Most **Marks & Spencer** locations have a grocery store on their lower level that carries only the store's own brand of foodstuffs. I swoon for the tandoori chicken in the cooked-foods department. M&S is also opening 50 **Simply Food** stores in the next few years; there's even one across the street from the Ritz, right in the heart of Mayfair.

The main supermarket chains often have branches—albeit small ones—in areas where travelers may be shopping. You'll find **Waitrose** branches on King's Road, Marylebone High, and Motcomb streets. **Canary Wharf** is out of town but has a big mall, and has large-format grocery stores. If you're a true supermarket devotee, you may want to go to the **Sainsbury's** on Cromwell Road—you will need a car or taxi and an arranged pickup.

Don't miss **Borough Market,** 8 Southwark St., SE1 (Tube: London Bridge), where you'll find fresh produce, cheeses, breads, and gourmet foodstuffs. It's open Thursdays, 11am to 5pm, Friday from noon to 6pm, and Saturday from 9am to 4pm. This market is a very "in" place so try to get there early. © 207/407-1002. www.boroughmarket.org.uk.

If you're a purist and find Borough Market has become too hip or touristy, head farther south to **Northcote Road,** in Battersea. This is the place for those in search of old-fashioned neighborhoods, a place where everyone knows your name, the days gone by without supermarkets. This well-off residential

Green Grocers

For PC picnics and organic fare, these markets will give you some local choices while providing everything you need to eat healthy. **Daylesford Organic**'s three-story outpost in Pimlico offers groceries plus a market-style deli selling home-baked bread, fruit, veggies, meats, and pastries. They also have a good selection of organic wines. **Whole Foods** on Kensington High Street offers much of the same in an equally gorgeous store. **Planet Organic** has grown from a single organic supermarket into a minichain, with locations throughout London. Other options include **Total Organics** on Moxon Street, **Bushwacker Wholefoods** on King Street, and **Alara Wholefoods** on Marchmont. Located inside the Chelsea Farmer's Market, **Here** sells food and drink that's certified organic and biodynamic (free of chemicals).

area is chockablock with small family-run food resources. Don't miss the **Hive Honey Shop** with its indoor 5-foot-high beehive, home to around 20,000 bees. EpiPens are allowed. There's also a food market, open Thursday through Saturday from 9am to 5pm, as well as the **Northcote Road Antiques Market,** 155 Northcote Rd., SW11 (Tube: Clapham Junction; © 207/228-6850).

Top take-away resources include **The Grocer on Elgin** (6 Elgin Crescent, W11; Tube: Ladbroke Grove or Notting Hill Gate), where you'll find prettily packaged gourmet meals like chicken with alsace bacon, and mushrooms with truffled mashed potatoes; **Ottolenghi** (63 Ledbury Rd., W11; Tube: Notting Hill Gate or Westbourne Park), featuring Mediterranean and Middle Eastern dishes; and **Tavola** (155 Westbourne Grove, W11; Tube: Notting Hill Gate), offering a daily changing Mediterranean lunch box meal.

Tip: If you're returning to the U.S. from the U.K., remember to keep in mind what you can and can't bring back legally. (See p. 44 for details.)

CHARBONNEL ET WALKER
1 The Royal Arcade, 28 Old Bond St., W1 (Tube: Green Park).

During "the season" (as in Social Season, m'dear), this chocolatier to the queen makes strawberries dipped in cream and chocolate. Their specialty holiday chocolates are worth schlepping. © 207/491-0939. www.charbonnel.co.uk.

FORTNUM & MASON
181 Piccadilly, W1 (Tube: Piccadilly Circus).

Your visit to Fortnum & Mason actually begins before you enter the store. The clock outside is very, very famous, so stand back and take a look. Then go through the revolving doors into a food emporium of fun.

After a $50-million refurbishment, the store has reopened with a return emphasis on gourmet foodstuffs. While the upper floors have been transformed into a classy gift shop (you can find beautiful antique china), the food hall has been expanded into the basement, so there are now two floors of gourmet sweets, teas, jams, meats, and fish, along with dishes-to-go prepared by on-site chefs. There's a new wine bar and the famous Fountain Restaurant has been revamped as well. Fortnum & Mason's hampers are a must for a status Christmas gift or for the picnics that you must eat (in the car park, no less) when you attend Royal Ascot or any of the events of "the season." Order ahead, prices be damned! © 207/734-8040. www. fortnumandmason.co.uk.

LOUIS PATISSERIE
32 Heath St., NW3 (Tube: Hampstead Heath).

You might not want to make a special trip all the way out here just for the pastries (or maybe you would), but if you find yourself in Hampstead anyway, stopping at Louis is considered an important part of the ritual and one of the pleasures of the Heath. The cakes are Eastern European, although it's the

French pastries that bring in the crowds. Cash only. © 207/
435-9908.

NEAL'S YARD DAIRY
17 Shorts Gardens, WC2 (Tube: Leicester Sq. or
Covent Garden).

Part of the Covent Garden experience and an important icon
for foodies, this English cheese shop is considered the grand-
daddy of British cheeses. © 207/240-5700. www.nealsyard
dairy.co.uk.

O & CO.
114 Ebury St., SW1 (Tube: Knightsbridge).

O & Co., also known as Oliviers & Co., is a purveyor of all
things olive—from oils to soaps—and was created by the same
French genius who brought us L'Occitane. The olive oils are
fabulous and much less pricey in Europe than in the United
States: Some cost £15 ($30) here and $36 in the U.S. © 207/
823-6770. www.oliviers-co.com.

THORNTONS
353 Oxford St., W1 (Tube: Oxford Circus); additional
locations around town.

This chain is popular with many locals for its chocolates and
its novelty items for seasonal holidays. I happen to be such a
toffee nut that even my dog is named Toffee, partly because
of his color and partly because I got him right after a trip to
London—where I consumed boxes and boxes of the "original" flavor. © 207/493-7498. www.thorntons.co.uk.

TWININGS
216 The Strand, WC2 (Tube: Temple or Charing Cross).

One of the most famous names in British tea, this old-world
firm makes loose tea, tea bags, and even iced tea. They have a
new line of green teas. While there is most likely distribution

in your local supermarket back home, the London shop carries gift packs, tastes, and combinations not available in the States. © **870/241-3667**. www.twinings.com.

HANDBAGS

In these days of $2,000 handbags—and, yes, £2,000 handbags—the competition is fierce, leaving the shopper one of the few treats to be found in London: the mere possibility of striking it rich with a rich handbag that no one else at home has latched onto yet. Prices here are bound to be astronomical, but if you care about novelty and not cost, you've come to the right destination.

Some of these sources have stores in the U.S.—and of course merchandise can always be bought online—but London branches may offer choices that you can't find elsewhere, especially at your local mall.

ANYA HINDMARCH
15–17 Pont St., SW1 (Tube: Sloane Sq.).

Anya Hindmarch is revered for her classic, chic collection of handbags, luggage, shoes, and accessories. Her latest must-have is a THIS IS NOT A PLASTIC BAG plastic bag. Who says the British don't have a sense of humor? © **207/838-9177**. www.anyahindmarch.com.

ASPREY
167 New Bond St., W1 (Tube: Bond St. or Green Park).

Goodbye, Margaret Thatcher and Queen Mum handbags. Hello, rich-bitch and chicer-than-thou blue-stocking types, who are into classic but stunning bags with a twist of style and modernity to match the price tags. Those who know will know immediately what an Asprey bag means. If you have to ask, you aren't in the right crowd. © **207/493-6767**. www.asprey.com.

DOLLARGRAND
124A King's Rd., SW3 (Tube: Sloane Sq.).

The famous British cheapie brand has just opened its first free-standing store on King's Road, but the line is still available in all department stores. You'll find great fashion bags in the £25 to £50 ($50–$100) range. Honest. The shop is not much to look at (I was surprised at the lack of finesse); but Dollargrand is famous for fab finds, so home in on the value per pound. © 845/108-4454.

LULU GUINNESS
3 Ellis St., SW1 (Tube: Sloane Sq.).

Lulu Guinness is one of a handful of handbag mavens in the cult heroine role in British social ranks; she made her name with evening bags topped with flowers and has continued to produce clever and whimsical designs ever since. Prices are high. © 207/823-4828. www.luluguiness.com.

MULBERRY
41–42 New Bond St., W1 (Tube: Bond St.).

How I long for the simple days way back when, when you knew what a Mulberry bag looked like. Now Mulberry handbags and Marc Jacobs handbags look surprisingly alike, and Mulberry is chasing the cutting edge. It's managed to combine its bag status with classic bag style. *Insider's tip:* The brand has recently opened in NYC, so you might want to compare prices before you fly across the pond. © 207/491-3900.

MULTIPLES (BRITISH)

A few successful chain stores dominate British retail, but don't look now: With finances as screwy as they've been in the past few years, some of the most popular high-street merchants are fighting to stay alive. Many are closing branch locations, although basically there's still one of these shops in every shopping neighborhood in London. There are so many of them that they call them, uh, multiples.

AUSTIN REED

103–113 Regent St., W1 (Tube: Piccadilly Circus); additional locations around town.

This chain sells men's and women's traditional (read: boring) British clothing from the big makers. It's the place to shop if the Brit look—in its most conservative incarnation—is your need. All the sturdy and steadfast British names are sold here, but you can sometimes bump into something fashionable as well.

Branch stores tend to be in need of renovation. Some locations open early in the morning for the business crowd running an errand or two on the way to the office. © 207/734-6789. www.austinreed.co.uk.

DOROTHY PERKINS

508 Oxford St., W1 (Tube: Marble Arch); additional locations around town.

Petite clothes are sold in specialty sections of some of the major department stores, but this high-street multiple gives particular attention to the smaller sizes and sells clothes for the professional woman at low-to-moderate prices (for Britain, anyway). It has changed the range slightly to include some street fashions as well. © 207/494-3769. www.dorothyperkins.co.uk.

EAST

105 King's Rd., SW3 (Tube: Sloane Sq.); additional locations around town.

Come here for everyday looks that have a slightly exotic feel to them. The clothes are made in India and have more than a few details in common with style from Kenzo. This is a lifestyle fashion store, with dress-up, casual, and weekend wear at moderate prices. © 207/376-3161. www.east.co.uk.

FRENCH CONNECTION
396 Oxford St., W1 (Tube: Bond St.); additional locations around town.

I spent years thinking this was a French firm, so sophisticates, beware—this line is not only British, but is also made by the same firm that owns designer Nicole Farhi's brand.

The line specializes in wearable men's and women's fashions that have a touch of trendy around the edges, but are not over-the-top. Prices are meant to be midrange, but in the U.K. that means they start out high. Sale prices may be more impressive. © 207/629-7766. www.frenchconnection.com.

JANE NORMAN
262 Oxford St., W1 (Tube: Bond St.); additional locations around town.

Low-end hot stuff, with stores all over town. © 207/499-7454. www.janenorman.co.uk.

JIGSAW
126–127 New Bond St., W1 (Tube: Bond St.); additional locations around town.

Jigsaw is a chain selling hip-but-wearable fashion for women; many of the designs are inspired by the latest big-money Euro trends. A lot of the merchandise is on the cutting edge (which means good, frequent sales), and much of it is geared toward those under 40. Prices are moderate, and there's always something to see and be impressed with—even if you're just sizing up the hot looks. It also does a men's line as well as Jigsaw Junior for preteen girls.

This chain is just beginning to move into the international market; they have recently opened in the U.S. But still, don't leave Britain without at least checking out one of the stores. Other convenient locations include 91–97 Fulham Rd., SW3 (Tube: Notting Hill Gate), and 65 Kensington High St., W8 (Tube: High St. Kensington). © 207/491-4484. www.jigsaw-online.com.

Miss Selfridge

216 Oxford St., W1 (Tube: Oxford Circus or Bond St.); additional locations around town.

Miss Selfridge is right next door to Topshop and can be accessed through the store itself. It holds a similar array of cheap high-fashion looks, but aims for a younger audience—young teenage girls will coo in delight over the trendy goods, while moms relax comfortably once they've surveyed the prices. It's good for novelty pieces that you fancy at the time, but might not necessarily wear next season. A recent face-lift has brought in London design duo Odie and Amanda, creating their own line for the store, as well as the Miss Vintage line, tapping into the recent obsession with all things dated. © 207/927-0214. www.missselfridge.co.uk. —J.G.

Monsoon

5–6 James St., WC2 (Tube: Covent Garden); additional locations around town.

This women's chain features fashions made in India in the current styles, but in fabrics inspired by the mother country (India)—thus resulting in a gauzy, colorful, sometimes ethnic (but not always), and very distinctive look. Prices are low to moderate. Very popular with the 'tweens-through-20s set.

Monsoon does such enormous business, and is so popular during hard times, that there are now spinoffs. **Accessorize** (p. 114) is a chain of small stores selling only accessories, while dress-up clothes can be found at the appropriately named **Twilight.** There's also a line for girls. © 207/379-3623. www. monsoon.co.uk.

New Look

Flagship: 500–502 Oxford St., W1 (Tube: Marble Arch); additional locations around town.

New Look is the fashion student's secret weapon. In my teen days, I avoided this store like the plague. In recent years, however, it's had a serious makeover and is now doing a roaring trade. The Oxford Street flagship is brilliant fun, with whee-lable shopping trolleys and funky music and lighting. The shiny entrance steps make you feel like you're walking into a runway show. New Look's "boutique" line is becoming a firm favorite, and several hot new designers have been enlisted to continue its success. The buys are definitely the shoes, some going for as little as £20 ($40). There are numerous locations around town, including another branch down the road at 175–179 Oxford St. (Tube: Oxford Circus). © 207/290-7860. www.newlook.co.uk. —J.G.

PRIMARK
499–517 Oxford St. (Tube: Marble Arch).

This is the leading value-for-money store in the U.K. It's a store (and scene) not to be missed. © 207/495-0420. www.primark. co.uk.

PRINCIPLES
260 Regent St., W1 (Tube: Oxford Circus); additional locations around town.

Hot, with-it fashions at low (for Britain) prices, with plenty of designer knockoffs and in-step accessories. Many of the stores look—from the outside—like the Next chain; don't be confused because the styles inside are definitely different. © 207/287-3365. www.principles.co.uk.

TOPSHOP
36–38 Great Castle St. (at Oxford and Regent sts.), W1 (Tube: Oxford Circus); additional locations around town.

Now then, there are small branch locations of Topshop around London, but I don't want you to go to them until you have "done" the mother ship, because otherwise you won't under-stand what I am raving about.

Topshop is simply heaven for those who love the latest looks at the lowest prices. For some dumb reason, the men's clothes

(Topman) are on the street level on Oxford Street, so you may not even be tempted to go inside. Mistake.

Go in, go down, and gawk. Every possible trend has been translated into two floors of women's cheapie fashions, and you will go nuts touching and feeling and shopping. Many big-name designers do specialty lines exclusively for Topshop. This is my new favorite store in London. © 207/636-7700. www.topshop.co.uk.

WHISTLES
20 The Market, Covent Garden, WC2 (Tube: Covent Garden); additional locations around town.

An on-the-edge chain with high-fashion looks and prices too high for the young people who can actually wear these clothes. The prices are even too high for me, though I may be a little old for some of this stuff. When droopy is in, it does droopy. When wrinkled is in, it does wrinkled. Very L.A. styles that actually work in London fashion circles. © 207/379-7401. www. whistles.co.uk.

MULTIPLES (INTERNATIONAL)

MANGO
235 Oxford St., W1 (Tube: Bond St.); additional locations around town.

These are young, trendy, Spanish-made clothes, somewhat competitive to Topshop's. Mango has more than 500 locations the world over, so it must be doing something right. © 207/534-3505. www.mango.com.

NITYA
118 New Bond St., W1 (Tube: Bond St.).

I love this brand because it's good for tall women with a little extra weight. Hmmm. Well, anyway, the clothes are luxe but usually have elastic waistbands (or no waist). They have an ethnic feel, somewhat droopy and Indian (the subcontinent, not Native American), and often with embroidery. Prices are moderate to high but not outrageous; many of the items can be hand-washed and travel well. ℂ 207/495-6837.

VENTILO
193 Westbourne Grove, W11 (Tube: Notting Hill Gate).

The cut of many items in this line is similar to Nitya, but Ventilo is more BoHo, glamour puss. The clothes are clever, ethereal, and possessed of a specific look that is timeless and somewhat in the Rich Hippie category. Who else but Armand Ventilo would mix black-and-white polka dots, stripes and lace, and beading and embroidery in one outfit and get away with it? Don't fret, there are some simple items, too. ℂ 207/243-8907.

ZARA
118 Regent St., W1 (Tube: Piccadilly Circus); additional locations around town.

Zara is a Spanish brand with stores all over the world, including a handful of stores in the U.S. Zara makes well-priced, chic, fashionable clothes for work and weekend. Without being silly or cheap, it copycats the latest jacket shape or skirt silhouette or whatever fashion gimmick is cutting edge so that you can look on-the-minute, fashion-wise, but not go broke along the way. ℂ 207/534-9500. www.zara.com.

PAPER GOODS & FILOFAX

FILOFAX
21 Conduit St., W1 (Tube: Bond St.).

This is a free-standing Filofax boutique, not a stationery store that sells the stuff. It's rather fancy, considering the Mayfair neighborhood and the clientele, and is replete with pages, inserts, and various notebooks in many sizes. Prices are still half of what they are in the United States, and the store has sales and closeouts. I always have a ball here. © 207/499-0457. www.filofax.co.uk.

PAPERCHASE
213–215 Tottenham Court Rd., W1 (Tube: Goodge St.).

The "in" place for paper goods, Paperchase offers a wide range of products—everything from greeting cards, stationery, Filofax pages, and party items to a variety of materials for the serious artist. I often buy my Christmas cards here; part of the proceeds goes to charity. © 207/467-6200. www.paperchase. co.uk.

SMYTHSON
44 New Bond St., W1 (Tube: Bond St.).

If you're looking for stationery fit for a queen, stop by this very elegant shop, which has been producing top-quality paper since the beginning of the last century. Aside from the selection of papers, there's a wide variety of leather goods, including address books, notebooks, diaries, and lovely desktop accessories. This is an old-fashioned, blue-blooded, very regal kind of place; personally, I find it way too expensive. © 207/ 629-8558. www.smythson.com.

PLUS SIZES

Marks & Spencer is known for its wide range of sizes, including larger sizes, and **New Look** has a line called Inspire, which comes in sizes 16 to 28. **Long Tall Sally** (21–25 Chiltern St., W1; Tube: Baker St.) carries contemporary designs for tall gals over 5'9", and **Base** (55 Monmouth St., WC2; Tube: Covent Garden) has upmarket, continental designer wear in sizes 16 to 28. Remember to use a sizing chart, as U.K. sizes are different from U.S. sizes. (See the "Size Conversion Chart," on p. 288.)

ANN HARVEY
266 Oxford St., W1 (Tube: Oxford Circus); additional locations around town.

This multiple has a wide range of looks for weekend, office, and dress-up at moderate prices. © 207/408-1131.

EVANS
538–540 Oxford St., W1 (Tube: Marble Arch); additional locations around town.

Another multiple, but with various lines for different "looks" and even a made-to-measure department. There's a new lingerie range for the well-endowed, with bras up to a 50H (H as in Huge) cup. © 207/499-0434. www.evans.ltd.uk.

MARINA RINALDI
39 Old Bond St., W1 (Tube: Green Park).

Marina Rinaldi is a branch of the famous Italian design house Max Mara; it offers the same style and quality in plus-size clothes. The sizes begin at what is an American 14, which is a 16 in the U.K. © 207/629-4454.

RESALE SHOPS

THE DRESS BOX
8 Cheval Place, SW7 (Tube: Knightsbridge).

This dress agency sells new and next-to-new designer clothing. © 207/589-2240.

THE LOFT
35 Monmouth St., WC2 (Tube: Covent Garden).

Designer resale shops are the latest retail rage—they're popping up everywhere. This one, which carries men's clothing on the ground floor and women's in the basement, tries to specialize in the big international designers. You have to be the right size to make out like a bandit (as they say), but I was knocked out by the choices for my 28-year-old son. © 207/240-3807. www.the-loft.co.uk.

PANDORA
14–22 Cheval Place, SW7 (Tube: Knightsbridge).

Locals call this a dress agency; I call it heaven. I'm talking £63 ($126) for a YSL blouse, £50 ($100) for an Hermès scarf. Armani jackets go for about £200 ($400). The store is fairly large, with a dressing room in the back. It has a strange system of automatic markdowns, which is explained on handwritten signs with a color code. Pandora is around the corner from Harrods, grandmother of all dress agencies. © 207/589-5289.

SEX TOYS

If you're shy, don't get your knickers in a twist over this entry. I don't consider myself particularly prudish but I was gobsmacked silly to find that sex toys—especially for women—are considered run-of-the-mill merchandise in London these days, and are available at places like **Boots** and **Superdrug.**

Both drugstore chains have new departments selling sex toys, feminine lubricants, and designer sex products for men and women. I tested a few, but frankly, my dear, I couldn't tell why anyone would spend 12 bucks for a product that seemed no different from good old K-Y jelly. Still, it is amusing and possibly educational.

Not to be outdone, bookseller **WHSmith** has *Je Joue* (French for "I Play"), which is being sold as an "intelligent" sex aid for women.

ANN SUMMERS
37 Long Acre, Covent Garden, WC2 (Tube: Covent Garden); additional locations around town.

Ann Summers has lingerie and sex toys, but they're more the Frederick's of Hollywood style. And, yes, if you want to play nanny or nurse, you can get the get-up here. ✆ 870/053-4109. www.annsummers.co.uk.

COCO DE MER
23 Monmouth St., WC2 (Tube: Covent Garden).

Coco de Mer is probably the most glamorous sex shop in London. Lingerie by D & G and Christian Lacroix may be tried on in a changing room with an adjacent "confessional" where your partner can take an approved peep. Or you can use the built-in camera with upload capability to e-mail a .jpeg to your loved one. For the ultimate in designer sex toys, check out the Shiri Zinn line—many are made of solid quartz or molten glass and trimmed with silver, Swarovski crystals, and fox fur. *Warning:* It may be the price tag that'll make you moan. ✆ 207/836-8882. www.coco-de-mer.co.uk.

MYLA
166 Walton St., SW3 (Tube: South Kensington); additional locations around town.

The real talk of the town is Myla, which sells lingerie as well as sex toys in its own boutiques and also has distribution through other stores, making the brand the Rolls-Royce of private moments. Note that Myla also has U.S. distribution and a boutique in Manhattan. What ever happened to that old saying, "No sex please, we're British"? ✆ 207/581-6880. www.myla.co.uk.

SHOES

I've listed only the special, traditional, or unusual shoes. See "Big Names (International)," earlier in this chapter, for addresses of stores such as Ferragamo and Prada.

BERTIE
25 Long Acre, Covent Garden, WC2 (Tube: Covent Garden); additional locations around town.

A famous London shoe resource at the moderate price level, Bertie has shops all over the city, as well as branches and department store distribution in the United States. © 207/836-7223. www.bertieshoes.co.uk.

CHRISTIAN LOUBOUTIN
23 Montcomb St., SW1 (Tube: Knightsbridge).

Prepare to part with anywhere from £350 to £750 ($700–$1,500) for a pair of Louboutin's coveted shoes with their signature red soles. © 207/245-6510. www.christianlouboutin.fr.

CHURCH'S SHOES
133 New Bond St., W1 (Tube: Bond St.); additional locations around town.

What did you come to London for, if not to buy Church's shoes for him? These are traditional wingtips and slip-ons at high prices. There are actually branches in the United States as well; the prices in London are usually equal to the American ones (though, get this—there are outlet stores in the U.S.). © 207/493-1474.

EMMA HOPE
53 Sloane Sq., SW3 (Tube: Sloane Sq.); additional locations around town.

Emma Hope does creative shoes in heels, flats, and boots—and up to a size 9, considered large for Brit feet and a near-fit for an American size 11. Excellent sales. © 207/259-9566. www.emmahope.co.uk.

F. PINET
47 New Bond St., W1 (Tube: Bond St.).

This is where I spend time musing at the stock in the windows and wondering if I can ever wear "that kind of shoe." Locals count on this resource for special-occasion footwear—dress-up shoes, colored leather shoes, creative inventive designs, sexy stilettos, and so on. It does carry flats as well as heels, but I'm always attracted to the high heels in green snakeskin. © 207/629-2174.

GINA
189 Sloane St., SW1 (Tube: Knightsbridge).

The shoes are high-fashion, expensive, and sometimes innovative. Locals seem to consider this the cat's meow. I find it a good store, but not the last word. © 207/235-2932. www.gina shoes.com.

JIMMY CHOO
32 Sloane St., SW1 (Tube: Sloane Sq.); 27 New Bond St., W1 (Tube: Bond St.).

Mr. Choo has shops in New York, Los Angeles, and Las Vegas, and he now has a couture line of shoes. Prices begin at £250 ($500) and go up from there. © 207/823-1051. www.jimmy choo.com.

L. K. BENNETT
31 Brook St., W1 (Tube: Bond St.); additional locations around town.

A source that has really taken off in the past year or two, Bennett actually sells clothes as well as shoes, but is famous for its footwear in wild colors. Prices are moderate, considering how much style you get. © 207/629-3923. www.lkbennett.com.

MANOLO BLAHNIK
49–51 Old Church St., SW3 (Tube: Sloane Sq.).

Okay, so maybe the average reader can't pronounce his name or afford his shoes. But those who are truly in the know, know Blahnik. Manolo is one of the leading designers of expensive, creative shoes with vamp for the vamps of the world. They do not come cheap (in either case). He has a few boutiques dotted here and there in the shopping capitals of the world. *Note:* Prices in the U.S. may be lower. ✆ 207/352-3863.

NIKETOWN
236 Oxford St., W1 (Tube: Oxford Circus).

Just do it? Why not, since the store is next door to Topshop and you'll be here anyway. Go here for the scene. ✆ 207/612-0800. www.nike.com.

OFFICE
57 Neal St., WC2 (Tube: Covent Garden); additional locations around town.

One of the small trendy stores located across from Covent Garden, with a gigantic selection of fashionable shoes at excellent low prices. ✆ 207/379-1896. www.officeholdings.co.uk.

PATRICK COX
129 Sloane St., SW1 (Tube: Knightsbridge).

Cox originally made waves in the international world of fashion with his pink (and orange) patent leather loafers on lug soles. ✆ 207/730-8886. www.patrickcox.co.uk.

POSTE MISTRESS
61–63 Monmouth St., WC2 (Tube: Covent Garden).

Stop by for hard-to-find brands, little-heard-of designers, and funky, funny, much fun. ✆ 207/379-4040.

SHELLY'S
266–270 Regent St., W1 (Tube: Oxford Circus); additional locations around town.

Not only does Shelly's carry every shoe known to the U.K., but it also goes up to a British size 9, which is about a size 11 in the U.S. and is not that easy to find in London. There's a great selection of Doc Martens, along with cheapie skimmers and leopard-print ballet flats for around £23 ($46). Most of the customers are under 30, but that shouldn't stop you. ✆ 207/287-0939. www.shellys.co.uk.

SHOOTING & FISHING

....

JAMES PURDEY & SONS LTD.
57 S. Audley St., W1 (Tube: Green Park).

Gun and rifle makers, with three royal warrants. Keep the Purdey catalog on your coffee table merely for the fun of it. Take your kids, as if you were going to a museum. Pretend you're going on safari with Clark Gable or going shooting with David, the Duke of Windsor. Don't miss it. This store is right behind the Dorchester Hotel. ✆ 207/499-1801. www.purdey. com.

SWEATERS & SHAWLS, CASHMERE & PASHMINA

....

The perfect sweater requires three ingredients: chilly weather, homegrown wool, and long winter nights. Today's sweater's value is based on who made it and how. A hand-knit sweater is more valuable and will always cost more than a machine-knit one. Sweaters made with synthetics have the least value, while those made with wool or cashmere (or any other natural fiber, such as cotton, silk, or linen) have far more value.

Cashmere sweaters are valued by the number of plies or strands in the yarn—one to four is common. The higher the number of plies, the heavier the sweater, and the more expensive it is. Cashmere sweaters are sold year-round in the many cashmere shops for which London is famous.

Keep in mind that cashmere is quite tricky to buy, as the price is very much related to the quality of the yarn and the way in which it is combed and knitted. The cashmere all comes from Mongolia, but the best cashmere sweaters come from Scotland, the United Kingdom, and Italy—this is what you pay for.

The $99 cashmere sweater you can find at any U.S. discount store is not the same quality as the $300 cashmere sweater you'll see on sale at N.Peal or one of England's other icon sweater dealers. Any cashmere that has been produced in Scotland will cost more than a cashmere from the Far East, and the difference between a $200 sweater and a $500 sweater is invariably the quality of the cashmere itself and the way it has been processed.

In recent years, a pashmina craze has broken out on both sides of the pond. Pashmina is a cashmere-like fiber that also comes from goat hair. It's incredibly fine and soft, and it dyes very well. (It is legal, whereas *shahtoosh,* a softer-than-cashmere goat's hair, is not.) Pashmina is most often made into the softest mufflers and shawls; it can be dyed in the yummiest colors. Although some fashionistas will tell you pashmina is over, as I see it, a classic is a classic.

BALLANTYNE
153 New Bond St., SW1 (Tube: Bond St.).

Ballantyne means traditional styles plus a few with a bit of flair (usually in the texture of the knit itself rather than the style of the sweater), twinsets galore, and fabulous colors. You can also order a bespoke classic diamond argyle with your choice of colors. No bargains. © 207/495-6184. www.ballantyne.it.

BELINDA ROBERTSON
4 W. Halkin St., SW1 (Tube: Hyde Park Corner or Knightsbridge).

You'll practically want to spring for a taxi so you can arrive in style at this shop, in an enclave of Belgravia that is only for the rich and famous. It's a good option for color and chic, such as the excellent cashmere shells to wear under suits. The RobertsonB line is less expensive. Custom colors and items can be ordered. ✆ 207/237-0519. www.belindarobertson.com.

BRORA
344 King's Rd., SW3 (Tube: Sloane Sq.); additional locations around town.

This Scottish source was doing plaids and tartans way before the new Burberry hit the scene. Now it has a Baby Brora line as well as plenty of cashmeres worn by models, socialites, and rock stars because the designs are so fresh and young. ✆ 207/352-3697. www.brora.co.uk.

LORO PIANA
47 Sloane St., SW1 (Tube: Knightsbridge).

Stop by the newly opened London branch of this famed Italian cashmere source, which also features home style and loungewear. The little bedroom slippers are the country-house gift of choice. ✆ 207/235-3203. www.loropiana.com.

N.PEAL
37–40 Burlington Arcade, W1 (Tube: Piccadilly Circus).

For the quality- and convenience-conscious, N.Peal offers a variety of wool and cashmere in a multitude of colors and styles. N.Peal is one of the few stores that sell fashion merchandise made of cashmere. Notice that its sweaters are entirely different from the look-alikes you see everywhere else. The color palette will leave you drooling, and the quality puts cheap cashmere to shame. It is top-of-the-line in the business, but frankly, I could faint from the prices. I have, however, found one of the best gifts in the world here—N.Peal makes its own cashmere wash, sort of a fancy version of Woolite. Very clever! ✆ 207/499-6485. www.npeal.com.

PICKETT
32–33 Burlington Arcade, W1 (Tube: Piccadilly Circus);
additional locations around town.

I must give Pickett a lot of credit for being flexible: It was once one of the best pashmina sources in London, but although it still carries pashmina, it has changed the focus of the store so it doesn't appear to be out of it from a fashion standpoint. It also sells chunky ethnic-styled jewelry in semiprecious stones, as well as leather goods. I bought a pair of teal leather gloves here that bring tears to my eyes—they're *that* beautiful. ℂ 207/ 493-8939. www.pickett.co.uk.

PORTOBELLO CHINA & WOOLLENS
89 Portobello Rd., W11 (Tube: Notting Hill Gate).

If you love crazy fun, this one's for you. This is Bargain Sweater City. Sweaters that would cost $100 elsewhere are $75 here. Sweaters that would cost $150 elsewhere are $100 here. There are seconds; some of the merchandise is big-name without labels, but the help will tell you what it is. Note that it is worse than mobbed on Saturdays, so you have to be the kind who likes this sort of stuff to endure it. ℂ 207/727-3857. www. portobello-ltd.com.

PRINGLE
112 New Bond St., W1 (Tube: Bond St.).

Pringle has always been great for classics, but now it's added fashion and even what it calls "washable" cashmere. I don't mean hand washable (that's how I've always done mine), but machine washable. Sweaters cost about £125 ($250) and actually seem a relative bargain. ℂ 207/297-4580. www.pringle- of-scotland.co.uk.

THE WHITE COMPANY
8 Symons St. (Tube: Sloane Sq.); additional locations
around town.

Tartans & Tweeds

Americans have so mangled British English over the centuries that there is now some confusion as to the difference between a tartan and a plaid—a difference that will get you in deep water when you come to buy one or the other.

A *tartan* is a pattern of fabric, with alternate colors in the warp and the weft in which the colors repeat themselves in a set order. A *plaid* is a piece of clothing worn as part of a Scottish dress uniform. In the U.S., the term *plaid* has come to mean a pattern of alternating colors set in a sequence, but in Scotland a plaid is *not* a tartan. Or vice versa.

Tartans signify the great clans of the Highlands, each clan having its own special way of weaving its colors and stripes into a particular sequence, which no one else can copy. There is usually a battle tartan and a dress tartan for each family or clan. The men who fought for a certain clan all wore the same pattern, and certain areas of the Highlands became known for these patterns.

Now then, if you want to get all gussied up in proper Highland attire, you probably want to wear the right tartan. In London and Edinburgh, retailers will gladly help you use a chart that lists surnames or look on a map to find the village your family came from. You can also choose one of the two tartans authorized by Queen Victoria to be worn by those who don't have Scottish ancestry. Of course, a lot of people just pick what they like best.

By the way, a *tweed* has nothing to do with a tartan, and the two are rarely worn together. Tweed fabric, named for the River Tweed, is a blend of various colors of wool so that a pattern emerges. Many tweeds are named for the places that created them, such as the Harris tweed. Tweeds are 100% wool and often nubby with a rough hand. They can be bought by the meter or as ready-made garments. Men's tweed jackets can be less expensive in the U.K. than in the U.S. Tweed fabric bought off the bolt will be considerably cheaper—expect a 50% savings. If you're really into saving money, buy the fabric in Scotland and then take it to Hong Kong to have the tailoring done. Even if you're not Hong Kong–bound this year, think about it. The best thing about tweeds is they never go out of style. You can hang on to the fabric, get a classic suit made, and it will last 20 years—or longer.

Don't worry—The White Company sells more than just white stuff. And, yes, this is where you can buy a cashmere hot-water-bottle cover for £75 ($150). It may not be the bargain of the century, but it's a great gift for the person who has everything. © 207/823-5322. www.thewhitecompany.com.

TAILOR-MADE FOR WOMEN

COUTURIERE
33 Brook St., 2nd Floor, W1 (Tube: Bond St.).

Although the workspace is cramped, Couturiere will do everything from a simple adjustment to transforming your wedding gown into a classic frock. They'll even make clothes from scratch. You'll pay top dollar for excellent workmanship. © 207/493-1564.

NICOLA DONATI
51 Kinnerton St., SW8 (Tube: Sloane Sq.).

This tiny tailor recently moved to tiny Kinnerton Street from Mayfair, and is now located across the street from one of my favorite boutiques, Egg. They'll be happy to take up a simple hem, do complicated alterations, or work with you to design and create a unique garment. © 207/254-6414.

TEENS & 'TWEENS

··

There are several acceptable teen looks these days, and London has them all, from vintage clothes to designer catwalk copies. There are entire streets, even neighborhoods, where the retail scene is geared to this age group. Don't forget **Mango** and **Zara,** both Spanish chains (p. 155 and 156). Also see the "Vintage" and "Trendy" sections, later in this chapter.

H&M (Hennes & Mauritz)
261–271 Regent St. (Tube: Oxford Circus); additional locations around town.

You're probably very embarrassed for me, but the truth is, I love this store and make it a regular place to check out. H&M specializes in teen clothes and hot trends and cheap junk and copies of the latest runway looks, and yes, I buy for myself, too, so there. That is, I buy when I can find something that fits.

Note: I'm faithful to the Oxford Circus main store, but there are tons of branches around town, with several on Oxford Street closer to the Marble Arch end. © 207/493-4004. www.hm.com.

Kew
123C Kensington High St., W8 (Tube: South Kensington); additional locations around town.

This is the low-cost division of Jigsaw—more basic than the high-fashion multiple, but good for rounding out the wardrobe. © 207/937-8850. www.kew-online.com.

Primark
499–517 Oxford St., W1 (Tube: Marble Arch); 1King's Mall, Hammersmith, W6 (Tube: Hammersmith).

The opening of this budget megaretailer on Oxford Street was the biggest news to hit the London retail scene in years. In fact, opening day was a riot. Yeah, really—young fashionistas lined up for blocks and there was madness when the doors opened.

This is the best source in town for low-priced fashion. Everything in the store is ridiculously affordable; there's not much for sale for over £10 ($20) and most items are 10 bucks or less. At these throwaway prices, you can choose from the latest imitation of catwalk trends—tops, trousers, dresses, jackets—along with lacey lingerie and cheap accessories. This is the home of the £5 ($10) T-shirt. © **207/495-0420.** www.primark.co.uk.

TOPSHOP
214 Oxford St., W11 (Tube: Oxford Circus); additional locations around town.

I've already listed this chain under "Multiples (British)" (p. 154), but since it's basically across the street from H&M and is teen heaven, I must remind you that it's here. Don't miss it! © **207/ 121-4519.** www.topshop.co.uk.

UNIQLO
84–86 Regent St., W1 (Tube: Piccadilly Circus); additional locations around town.

This Japanese chain, inspired by the Gap, has intentions of taking the world by storm. World domination has not quite followed, as some branches have closed—but not this one. Uniqlo is a lifestyle store with clothing for men, women, and children; unisex dressing rooms; and low, low, low prices. Not long on style, but good for basics. Uniqlo opened its first American store, in New Jersey, in fall 2005. © **207/434-9688.** www.uniqlo.co.uk.

TOYS & KID STUFF

DISNEY STORE
140 Regent St., W1 (Tube: Oxford Circus or Piccadilly Circus).

Give me a break. © **207/491-9136.** www.disneystore.com.

HAMLEYS
188–196 Regent St., W1 (Tube: Oxford Circus).

Whether or not you have children, know any children, or even like children, Hamleys deserves attention. If you're interested in retail, go out of your way to visit this London masterpiece theater. And if you're looking for that unusual toy not readily available in the U.S., then Hamleys is a must. The gift shop on the street level is the best (and easiest) place I know of to buy gifts for all your friends and neighbors.

If you begin to feel dizzy by the selection, you'll be relieved to find a snack bar in the basement. The prices, however, will not make you dizzy (although American toys are more expensive), and Corgi toys are a bargain.

Forget schlepping your packages home—Hamleys will ship them to your door. The paperwork takes about 20 minutes, but is well worth the time. Make sure, of course, that you are sending home an unsolicited gift valued at less than $50; otherwise, you will pay duty.

There are several branches at LHR, but you deserve the mother ship. © 870/333-2455. www.hamleys.com.

HARRODS
87–135 Brompton Rd., SW1 (Tube: Knightsbridge).

Harrods has a fabulous toy department on the fourth floor—possibly as good as Hamleys. There's a sample of every toy imaginable, and the kids can play, ride, climb, bite, or torture the toys and each other. © 207/730-1234. www.harrods.com.

TRENDY

You will find plenty of trendy-ish stores listed in the "Teens & 'Tweens" section of this chapter (p. 170), but those sources tend to have only copies of the latest styles. For truly trend-setting sources, read on. The look very often is a version of rock-star chic or rich hippie; forget the pearls. Note that the original is usually expensive, but if you have to be the first on your block to own it, or even see it, then step this way.

CATH KIDSTON
8 Clarendon Cross, W11 (Tube: Holland Park); additional locations around town.

Kidston is a fabric designer, but her small store sells clothes, accessories, and home-design items made from those fabrics. Some of her inspiration comes from American textiles from the '30s to the '60s, but the prints are refreshing and especially fun when made into travel bags or totes. This store is part of the ritual walk from Portobello Road Market to The Cross (see below). © 207/221-1400. www.cathkidston.co.uk.

THE CROSS
141 Portland Rd., W11 (Tube: Holland Park).

The Cross has a religious following, though the name actually comes from the fact that the store is located at the crossing of Portland Road and a street named Clarendon Cross. It's a small store, filled with one-off looks made by the city's up-and-coming designers and snatched up by regulars, who include magazine editors and movie stars. Prices are high, but that's part of the cachet. © 207/727-6760.

MATCHES
60–64 Ledbury Rd., W11 (Tube: Notting Hill Gate); additional locations around town.

Matches has eight stores in its small chain, but this one, on one of London's most famous streets for trendsetters, is the one you want to see. The clothes are worthy of a stare because they're so light and fresh and inspirational in terms of creativity and color. It helps to be thin here. © 207/221-0255. www.matches fashion.com.

OG2
367 Portobello Rd., W10 (Tube: Ladbroke Grove).

A newish Notting Hill address for those who simply have to have the latest in trendy—and expensive—dresses that everyone else knows are trendy and expensive; dresses cost close to £1,000 ($2,000). © **208/960-7570.**

WILLMA
339 Portobello Rd., W10 (Tube: Ladbroke Grove).

This is not really part of the Portobello Road Market—it's located close to the Golbourne Road end of the stores and is possibly best on a nonmarket day (any day but Sat) so you can enjoy the creativity of the mix without being mobbed. © **208/960-7296.**

UNDERWEAR

AGENT PROVOCATEUR
6 Broadwick St., W1 (Tube: Piccadilly Circus).

I just don't get it about this brand. It's expensive and not worth the hype, as far as I can tell. Nonetheless, everyone else adores it and finds it cutting edge, sexy, and oh-so-naughty. Beats me. But wait! I've just gone to the website. Ohmygoshgollygee, oh me oh my. © **207/439-0229.** www.agentprovocateur.com.

BODAS
38B Ledbury Rd., W11 (Tube: Notting Hill Gate).

Known for knitted little-boy shorts for gals. © **207/229-4464.** www.bodas.co.uk.

MARKS & SPENCER
458 Oxford St., W1 (Tube: Bond St.); additional locations around town.

M&S has long been famous for its undergarments, although the iconic St Michael brand has been discontinued. There's still everything from plain Jane to ooh-la-la. Prices are not low, but quality is high; and there's a good selection in all sizes. © 207/935-7954. www.marksandspencer.co.uk.

MYLA
166 Walton St. (Tube: South Kensington).

Myla is just as famous for its saucy underwear as for its discreet sex toys. (See p. 160 under "Sex Toys.")

RIGBY & PELLER
22A Conduit St., W1 (Tube: Oxford Circus).

This shop is the corsetiere to the queen so you can be assured they know how to fit a bra; their specialty is measuring and fitting. Rigby & Peller's own brands are surprisingly modern and reasonable in price; you can buy a top-quality undergarment for around £25 ($50). Made-to-measure specialty bras can run as high as £250 ($500). Ouch. © 845/076-5545.

VINTAGE

London has always had a large market for used, gently worn, and vintage clothing—partly because of the variety of street looks and partly because prices are so dear that many women prefer resale shops (see "Resale Shops," p. 158). You'll find the London outpost of LA vintage couture emporium **Decades in Dover Street Market,** and there are vintage dealers at almost all of the markets, including **Portobello, Shepherd's Bush, Camden Passage,** and **Camden Lock.** You may also do well at London's many charity shops, although these days they seem to be selling old Voyage sweaters for £200 ($400) and calling them vintage.

Vintage Finds

- For big-name labels: **Rellik** (8 Golbourne Rd., W10; Tube: Westbourne Park) and **Appleby** (95 Westbourne Park Villas, W2; Tube: Royal Oak).
- For trendy styles: **Bang Bang** (21 Goodge St., W1; Tube: Goodge St.) and **Absolute Vintage** (15 Hanbury St., E1; Tube: Liverpool St.).
- For the thrifty bride: **Annies** (12 Camden Passage, N1; Tube: Angel) and **Dolly Diamond** (51 Pembridge Rd., W11; Tube: Notting Hill Gate).
- For all-out glamour: **Circa Vintage Clothes** (8 Fullham High St., SW6; Tube: Putney Bridge) and **One of a Kind** (253 Portobello Rd., Unit 8, W11; Tube: Ladbroke Grove).
- For kitsch: **The Girl Can't Help It** (Alfies Antique Market, 13–25 Church St., NW8; Tube: Edgware Rd.) and **Radio Days** (87 Lower Marsh, SE1; Tube: Waterloo).
- For the unusual: **One** (30 Ledbury Rd., W11; Tube: Notting Hill Gate) and **Gallery of Antique Costume & Textiles** (9 Connaught St., W2; Tube: Marble Arch).
- For accessories: **Shikasuki** (67 Gloucester Ave., NW1; Tube: Camden Town) and **Hoxton Boutique** (2 Hoxton Sq., N1; Tube: Liverpool Station).
- For handbags: **French Touch** (11 Shelton St., Covent Garden, WC2; Tube: Covent Garden).

Vintage Fairs

The **London Vintage Fashion, Textiles & Accessories Fair** is held every 4 to 6 weeks at the Hammersmith Town Hall on King Street. Call © **208/543-5085** for the current sked. www. pa-antiques.co.uk. Another good bet is the **Battersea Vintage Fashion, Accessories, and Textiles Fair.** Vintage dealers from all over the U.K. exhibit at this bimonthly fair held at the Battersea Arts Centre, Lavender Hill. © **208/325-5789.** www. vintagefashionfairs.com.

Absolute Vintage
15 Hanbury St., E1 (Tube: Aldgate East or Liverpool).

These feet were meant for vintage. There are thousands of shoes organized by color here, along with clothing and accessories. © 207/247-3883. www.absolutevintage.co.uk.

Annie's
10 Camden Passage, N1 (Tube: Angel).

This cramped shop is good fun, with lots to look at—but you'll find no giveaway deals, and it's pricier than any teenager would want. Still, Annie's is a well-known source for alternative bridal and big-name designers who have found inspiration here. © 207/359-0796.

Arthur Morrice
11 Beauchamp Place, SW3 (Tube: Knightsbridge).

Vintage glasses frames!

Bentley's
204 Walton St., SW3 (Tube: South Kensington).

Vintage Vuitton trunks.

Hoxton Boutique
2 Hoxton Sq., N1 (Tube: Liverpool St.).

Vintage sunglasses.

Mary Moore
5 Clarendon Cross, W11 (Tube: Holland Park).

Like Stella, this is another British-design case study in "who cares who her father is?" Mary Moore began her shop by selling her own personal collection of vintage; she traveled in jet-set circles and simply kept everything she wore. The location is sublime, right near The Cross. © 207/229-5678.

An Excellent Vintage Year

—Ethan Sunshine

You needn't wait for the market day. Any day of the week, you can check out Pembridge Road's Retro shops duo, aptly named **Retro Man** and **Retro Woman,** at 30–34 Pembridge Rd., W11 (Tube: Notting Hill Gate). The men's store has an enormous diversity of discount designer denim. It features a large selection of denim pants and jackets with huge names to match: Paul Smith, Helmut Lang, Armani Jeans, and Levi's Engineered, to name a few.

All are expensive, but there are serious bargains to be had if you're willing to be a relentless tag-checker. Items that haven't sold are marked down until they do, and the prices do drop. Most jeans are under £79 ($140), and I saw some Evisus for £40 ($80), almost four times cheaper than regular retail! Just be sure to scrub 'em good when you get home.

Beyond Retro, 112 Cheshire St., E2 (Tube: Liverpool St.), is a huge warehouse with more than 10,000 items in stock at any time; there's treasure to be found among the (often appealing) trash.

The best bargains are still waiting for you at Saturday's **Portobello Road Market.** As you make your way there, you'll see some great vintage shops—but the real deals are with the outdoor vendors. In this case, you lose the option of a fitting room (unless you're willing to climb into the back of a truck), so know your sizes well. (Check the "Size Conversion Chart," p. 288, for help.)

The more popular items, as in the States, tend to be old track jackets, ironic T-shirts, jeans, and worn hats. Most track jackets are above £25 ($50), and many T-shirts, strangely enough, are imported from America . . . so stick to Goodwill and the Salvation Army back home for those items. The biggest bargains here, once again, are the jeans. I found one vendor with Levi's, Diesel, and G-Star for 20 bucks—in the case of Diesel and G-Star, that's 10 times cheaper than retail!

POP BOUTIQUE
6 Monmouth St., WC2 (Tube: Covent Garden).

This shop is a retro haven with garb galore from the '60s to the '80s. A favorite with fashion students, it features a mix of original vintage and reworked items.

SHEILA COOK
105–107 Portobello Rd., W11 (Tube: Notting Hill Gate).

Cook has moved several times, so don't be confused; this is the latest address. The new shop is actually right smack in the middle of the Portobello Road Market, and is open by appointment only. She specializes in textiles and her vintage clothing has always been exceptional, which every movie company in the area knows. Prices tend to be a little high, but I've bought some items I thought were reasonable. ✆ **207/792-8001.** www.sheilacook.co.uk.

STEINBERG & TOLKIEN
193 King's Rd., SW3 (Tube: Sloane Sq.).

Perhaps the best vintage clothing store in London and maybe one of the best in the world. Each microcentimeter of this two-level shop is crammed with stuff. The prices are not low, but the quality and selection more than make up for that. Note that there is no terribly convenient Tube stop; you can either walk from Sloane Square or take a bus along King's Road. ✆ **207/376-3660.**

VIRGINIA
98 Portland Rd., W11 (Tube: Holland Park).

Virginia was a movie star, and her small shop looks like a movie star's dressing room or boudoir around 1932. The store is in the trend-niche real estate right around the corner from The Cross and not too far from Portobello Road, so it's handy and often visited by models and celebs. ✆ **207/727-9980.**

Chapter Six

·················

HEALTH & BEAUTY

A BEVY OF BEAUTY BUYS

London is working its way to becoming the beauty capital of Europe, the international queen of drugstores/chemist shops. Maybe this is historically related to Vidal Sassoon and Mary Quant, who got here first, or maybe it's simply a sign of the times. Maybe no one can afford to shop anywhere more expensive than Boots or Superdrug, so that's why all the fun stuff is being launched at those stores.

The day Boots's **No. 7 Protect and Perfect Beauty Serum** was introduced, hundreds of women queued outside the Oxford Street flagship store to buy the £17 ($34) wrinkle buster. A month later, it was still hard to come by.

Sarah was first in line when the Boots Piccadilly branch opened; she attempted to buy two bottles of the goop, but was politely told "one per customer." Luckily, a young lady with flawless skin in the pay station queue offered to purchase a second bottle. Is the stuff worth it? Too soon to say, but since all this is now available at many Target stores, it takes the pressure off your next trip to London.

Maybe you should concentrate instead on any of the dozen different designer hair-care brands on the shelves at Boots (most of which cannot be bought in the U.S.). There are simply scads of brands and products for every purpose, in an ever-changing parade of beauty needs.

Sunday Beauty

As you know, most major **department stores** are open on Sunday from noon to 5pm, and some throw open their doors at 11am, if you need a beauty fix. Some **Boots** stores are also open. **Bliss Chemist,** 5–6 Marble Arch, W1 (Tube: Marble Arch), is not only open on Sunday, but also open until midnight every night of the week.

Boots has gone for beauty in such a big way that its **Boots Well-Being Centre,** on Kensington High Street, is one of the most exciting retail adventures in the U.K., and it's looking to open more such concept stores. **Sephora,** the French beauty supermarket, has opened in two locations, and there's a branch of **Sally Hair and Beauty** on Shaftesbury Avenue in Soho, if you need emergency hair color. We've all been there. Sally is an American brand. **Space.NK** is expanding like mad; Selfridges is competing with French department stores for the bragging rights to square footage on beauty products.

Spas are also here to stay. A few years ago, the **Dorchester** was considered almost over-the-top when it opened a spa; that spa has since been redesigned and now every luxury hotel in London has its own spa. There is much competition among them for the latest in treatments and philosophies. There are also day spas, which have nothing to do with hotels, and which often sell their branded treatment lines through drugstores.

UNSUNG HEROES

Finding brands you've never heard of that turn out to be great discoveries is one of the reasons we travel and shop. Here's a list of lines I have tested that are either exclusive to the U.K. or hard to find in the U.S. As I've said over and over, **Selfridges** has the largest beauty department in Europe. For a list of British hair-care brands, see p. 198.

Note: Some American and Canadian lines have free-standing shops in London, but these brands can be bought at lower prices in department stores back home—or else online, if you don't have hometown access to MAC, Kiehl's, and so on.

ANGELA FLANDERS   Therapeutic pillow spray for 20 bucks—what can I say? The brand is sold in many department stores as well as at Angela's own store, at 96 Columbia Rd., E2 (© 207/739-7555; Tube: Liverpool St.), in the snazzy "new" East End. Her shop is open only on Sundays from 9:30am to 2pm, in keeping with the Sunday-only nature of the Columbia Road Flower Market (p. 7). www.angelaflanders-perfumer.com.

AUTOGRAPH   A makeup line with some treatment products created for Marks & Spencer and sold only in its stores. There is also a clothing line named Autograph. www.marksandspencer.com.

BOOTS NO. 7   Sarah swears by this mascara, which is available in both waterproof and regular formulas. Also available online from Amazon and Target.

DR. HAUSCHKA   This German brand is found in the U.S., but not easily. It consists of a very large range of mostly treatment products, all made from natural ingredients. The rose products are the most famous; many supermodels swear by this line. I use the rose oil on my cuticles. www.drhauschka.com.

ORIGINAL SOURCE   Original Source is a low-end Australian line, available in drugstores and grocery stores, that really needs a distributor in the U.S. The most expensive item costs £6 ($12). The line itself is bath-oriented—my favorite is still Tea Tree & Mint, although various scents come in and out of fashion. The Lemon & Honey liquid soap is also a winner.

What I hate is that stores rarely stock Original Source by the total range of the brand, so various pieces of the collection are in all different aisles. The best selection I've found is at the Tesco on Cromwell Road. Some Boots carry it as well; some don't. www.originalsource.co.uk.

RUBY & MILLIE A color-cosmetics line that is now getting mainstreamed, in the U.K. at least. Moderate price range. www.rubyandmillie.com.

ST. TROPEZ Despite the French name, this is a brand from Nottingham that's essentially a fake-tan system, sold in three parts. The whole set costs well over £50 ($100), but you can often buy just Step 3, the tanning gel—for about £20 ($40). That may strike you as outrageous, but wait! I've tested this product and it is simply worth the money. Speaking as someone who has been testing fake tans since they were invented—I've been through orange, streaks, and even salon rip-offs—this is the first product I've found that actually gives you a natural tan and is easy to use. (*Note:* Steps 1 and 2 are exfoliating and moisturizing processes that you can do on your own; Step 3 is the tanning gel itself.) You can buy this in the U.S. now through various online sites. www.st-tropez.co.uk.

HEALING & WELL-BEING

While the French have been using the slogan *bien-etre* (well-being) as the catchall phrase of the decade, and day spas are multiplying in London, there is also a resurgence in Chinese medicine and in various health and holistic treatments. My best new find was Sen, a very fancy studio right on South Molton Street in the high-rent district.

SEN
59 S. Molton St., W1 (Tube: Bond St.).

When China awakes, the world will tremble—so spake Napoleon. We all know how true this is—and now, how chic. Sen offers Chinese herbal medicine, full-body acupuncture, head and neck acupressure, reflexology, beauty products, and more—all based on ancient Chinese medicinal philosophy. Its various treatments are designed to address anything from insomnia to impotence to stress and pain management. The studio has coupons for discounts on services. © 207/629-2243. www.sen health.com.

PHILOSOPHIES & GIMMICKS

Speaking of philosophy, note that several lines offer therapeutic pillow spray these days. **Boots** has a complete range of Sleep products, including pillow spray. Meanwhile, **Tesco** is the exclusive supplier for the **Feng Shui** line of bath products. This brand has just begun distribution in the U.S., but is less expensive when bought at the grocery store. Aromatherapy is old news, but Zen is a hard concept to package . . . it's even hard to grasp.

AROMATHERAPY

Aromatherapy began its international push from London years ago, has been popularized in the United States, and breathes on. A recent scientific study, reported on the front page of most British newspapers, revealed that aromatherapy works for those who *think* it works.

Shoppers, please note: There is a difference between American and British aromatherapy. Although the effectiveness of both may be in the mind of the beholder, the British product usually has more juice in it.

The philosophy behind aromatherapy is that different smells affect your mood and your body in different ways. It posits that you can manipulate your feelings and your health by surrounding yourself with certain types of fragrances. This has become such a big business that just about every manufacturer in the world has jumped on the bandwagon. You'll have no trouble walking into **Boots, Superdrug,** and **Tesco** and finding a score of different types of aromatherapy products and treatments.

Even airlines offer samples of aromatherapy products that are designed to fight jet lag; most hotel spas offer jet-lag treatments with aromatherapy massages; and most of the new spa centers have some form of aromatherapy.

For an overview of available products, regardless of the brand, check out any large department store and any large **Boots** store. Remember that American brands, such as Origins and Crabtree & Evelyn, cost less in the United States.

CULPEPER THE HERBALIST
8, The Market, Covent Garden, WC2 (Tube: Covent Garden).

This small source for oils, soaps, potpourri, and even cooking items is a British multiple with several locations around the country. The store has an old-fashioned and charming feel to it. The oils are of excellent quality; the best product is the aromatherapy fan. ℂ 207/379-6698. www.culpeper.co.uk.

FRESH LINE
55 King's Rd., SW3 (Tube: Sloane Sq.).

Greek beauty firms have gone crazy opening up new shops on the King's Road (see the listing below for Korres). Fresh Line is so much like Lush that I had to ask if I was indeed in Lush. As it turns out, Lush is farther up the street. There are very similar beauty and bath products here, and, of course, bath bombs. ℂ 207/881-0900. www.freshline.gr.

JO MALONE
Flagship: 150 Sloane St., SW1 (Tube: Knightsbridge).

The Sloane Street flagship is probably the best bet; this could be your second stop after robbing the Bank of England because this stuff is pricey. However, wait: It's 30% less in the U.K. than in the U.S. Those on a budget may feel shy. On the other hand, if you're looking for the perfect gift for the person who has everything, this could be it.

I gave a bottle of this juice to a woman who offered a weak "thank you" to me; she obviously had no idea that I had spent the moon on her or that this item is the cult must-have of the U.K. Don't go all out for someone not in the know.

The Mandarin Oriental Hyde Park uses Jo Malone bathroom amenities—and it may just be cheaper to book a room, take the products each day, and give them as gifts.

For those who don't have time to get to the flagship, try to stop by the new store right off Bond Street, at 23 Brook St., W1, or look for Jo Malone kiosks in major department stores. © 207/730-2100. www.jomalone.co.uk.

KORRES STORE
124 King's Rd., SW3 (Tube: Sloane Sq.).

It's all Greek to me—and will be to you, too, when you shop this stylish new free-standing store representing a Greek line of bath, beauty, hair-care, and men's grooming products. The packaging is in Greek and English; the products are all natural. Price-wise, the line costs less than many other high-end brands, so it's attractive for those who want to test a few products. The Korres print support and educational materials are excellent. © 207/581-6455. www.korresstore.co.uk.

LUSH
123 King's Rd., SW3 (Tube: Sloane Sq.); 11 The Piazza, Covent Garden, WC2 (Tube: Covent Garden); 40 Carnaby St., W1 (Tube: Oxford Circus); 80–82 Regent St. (Tube: Piccadilly Circus); 96 Kensington High St., W8 (Tube: High St. Kensington).

I'm not sure if it's proper to classify Lush as aromatherapy—maybe it's just bed, bath, and beyond. Quite beyond, my dears, quite, quite. Even all these years later, I am still amazed and amused. If you tend toward asthma, you may find that you cannot even enter a Lush store, as the scent is heady.

Like all aromatherapy, it's in the mind. Still, breathe deeply, think of your gift-giving list, cope, and smile. Buy the Red Rooster soap, if nothing else.

I can't say that every product here is the best in the world; I have tested many and am smitten with many, but some are just average. The bath bombs are a fabulous novelty and a great gift for someone who has seen it all; but they fizzle, so to speak, once dropped in the tub, and the aroma doesn't last that long. Never mind; it's still very clever. However, you can buy them in the U.S. The black-bread face mask is the best mask I've ever used. There are prepackaged gift packs in the under-£10 ($20) price range. Expect to wait in line during the Christmas season. *Web tip:* You can shop online in the U.S.

There are also a zillion Lush knockoff stores and products in London these days (see Fresh Line, listed above), if you like the gimmick but don't want to spring for the real thing or if you want to try something new. www.lush.com.

NEAL'S YARD REMEDIES
15 Neal's Yard, Covent Garden, WC2 (Tube: Covent Garden); Chelsea Farmers' Market, Sydney St., SW3 (Tube: Sloane Sq.); 9 Elgin Crescent, W11 (Tube: Notting Hill Gate).

This well-known brand has become an icon for its cobalt-blue jars, although it also has products in tubes and other means of conveyance. It offers excellent literature and do-it-yourself materials for using aromatherapy and essential oils and treatments and cures, as well as many natural products. There's even a library. You'll find cosmetics and toiletries, homeopathic cures, body-care products, shampoos, bath goods, soaps, and more. International mail order is available should you run out of products, and the line is sold at a number of stores in the U.S. as well. www.nealsyardremedies.com.

BATH & BEAUTY

Also see "Aromatherapy" (above) and "Cosmetics & Makeup" (below); and for heaven's sake, don't miss **Lush** or **Jo Malone**.

THE BODY SHOP

Covent Garden, WC2 (Tube: Covent Garden); 374 Oxford St. (Tube: Bond St.); additional locations around town.

For me, no trip to London is complete without a raid on at least one branch of The Body Shop, but nowadays I wait for the one at Heathrow, where prices are slightly better. Some of the stores also have a "well-being centre" (Brit-speak for spa treatments).

The brand has not been doing so well financially and is not as famous as it was when it first made retail history for creating fair-trade items and green products. Nonetheless, it's still fun. Inside the easily recognizable, dark-green shops is a world of environmentally and politically correct soaps, scents, and other beauty products; some aromatherapy; and full men's and baby lines. Everything comes in sample sizes to meet the new airline regs; I think the best fun in the world is to buy tons of these little jars and bottles for my own travel kit, for Christmas stocking stuffers, and for making up gift baskets.

The Body Shop has a branch in every trading area of London; I frequent the one on Oxford Street. Savings are currently about 20% over U.S. prices. www.thebodyshop.com.

BOOTS THE CHEMIST

Piccadilly Circus, W1 (Tube: Piccadilly Circus); additional locations around town.

In the Queen's English, Boots is a chemist. To Americans, Boots is a drugstore. To me, it's a way of life. No day in London is complete without a dose of Boots. But please remember my motto: *Not all Boots are created equal.* This means never pass a Boots without going in for a half-hour.

The best thing about Boots is that it has a huge selection of health and beauty aids, usually at reasonable prices. Its house lines offer choices in many pharmaceuticals and beauty products. And speaking of beauty products, see the separate listing below for the Boots Well-Being Centre.

There is always a pharmacy, sometimes an optical shop, and always a selection of small appliances, such as hair dryers, should you discover that your French model will not work in England. (It won't—different plugs.) You can find pantyhose, film, some costume jewelry, and just about any brand of makeup or perfume.

Boots carries the **Bourjois** line of makeup from France and has its own line of ecologically sound bath and beauty products that imitate what's sold at the Body Shop. (I buy the cucumber face scrub.) It also has its own brand of Chanel-inspired products, such as **No. 7** (it's a joke—like Chanel No. 5, get it?), which is the single-best-selling cosmetics line in the U.K. The **No. 7 Protect and Perfect Beauty Serum** caused quite a stir when it launched and still sells out quickly. The eyeliner pencils are better than Chanel's, and Sarah swears by the mascara. A makeup line for teenagers, **No. 17,** is less expensive than No. 7.

There is a Boots in almost every city in England and Scotland, most often located on the high street. In London, there's a branch in every major trading area. Some are open on Sunday, and some are not. The newer stores are better than the older ones. There's a great store in Canary Wharf, and the Green Park one is awfully good. www.boots.co.uk.

BOOTS WELL-BEING CENTRE
128 Kensington High St., W8 (Tube: High St. Kensington).

Be still, my heart: I am in love. If you are looking at this Boots from the street, it seems small and average, and you will think I am nuts—so trust me on this. If you enter from the Tube, you will get a better idea of size and selection but not the total scope. Sooooo, in this new incarnation, Boots sells more upscale brands of makeup and fragrance as well as zillions of hair-care lines and all bath products big and small, great and tall. Upstairs, you'll find a spa, a Chinese herbal treatment center, a manicure station, and much more. Just drop me off here and pick me up on the way to the airport. Call ℂ **0845/121-9001** for spa appointments. www.boots.co.uk.

SAVONNERIE
Spitalfields Market, E1 (Tube: Liverpool St.).

This is a newish firm, sort of Lush-like, whose products are sometimes sold at markets such as Covent Garden and always at Spitalfields. It does natural glycerin soaps with flowers and herbs and spices. Not cheap, but great fun. www.savonnerie soap.com.

SUPERDRUG
197–213 Oxford St., W1 (Tube: Oxford Circus); additional locations around town.

Superdrug is a multiple with branches all over town. Not each branch is as fabulous as its sister, so I pop into as many as I can find; the Oxford Street store is my regular. It is often my first stop in London, and then I walk to Regent Street.

With a hair salon in the rear and both a pharmacy and a drugstore, this is a younger, hipper version of Boots, and may be a few pence less expensive. I've often found brands to test here that later came to Boots, but that was before Boots started its "well-being centres." Still, it's worth a look and a few minutes of browse time—plus, it opens at 8am, if you have jet lag and happen to be up early and want a treat. www.super drug.com.

COSMETICS & MAKEUP

I also discuss this subject in the "Bath & Beauty" section above; there's a lot of overlap, as **The Body Shop** also has a makeup line and so on. Also, **Boots the Chemist** sells two very important lines: **Bourjois,** the French dime-store brand made in the same factories as Chanel, and **No. 7,** the house brand; makeup for teens is called **No. 17.**

Note that British women have traditionally bought most of their cosmetics in the major department stores. **Harrods** is an old staple, but the in crowd goes to **Selfridges,** 400 Oxford St., W1 (Tube: Bond St.), now the single largest piece of beauty real estate in all of Europe.

While we're on the subject of the big department stores, **Liberty,** 210–220 Regent St., W1 (Tube: Oxford Circus), has a just-okay makeup department, but I adore its house brand of soaps (grapefruit and jojoba) and bath items.

Several of the lifestyle stores have branched into makeup, aromatherapy, and bath goop. These include **Topshop, Miss Selfridge, Next, French Connection** (which is a British firm, not a French one), and **Principles.** Famous-name stores that also sell makeup include **Mary Quant.** Beauty salons have gone into spa treatments, aromatherapy, and makeup colors—**Molton Brown** is a good example here.

Space.NK, with several locations around town, sells hard-to-find brands. It has been so influential that it now has branches all over the U.K. and is being copied in some Euro cities. Many of the brands are American, however, so you don't want to load up on those while in London.

The problem with makeup in Britain is usually price—so look for less-expensive brands or items you can't find back home. The hottest local line is **Ruby & Millie,** which is sold in most Boots stores. Note that **MAC** is more expensive in the United Kingdom, as are most American and Canadian brands.

English Mavens

BECCA
91A Pelham St., SW7 (Tube: South Kensington).

Becca means boudoir and makeup bins. This place gives whole new subtlety to the expression "beauty parlor"—it's more like a living room where you *parlez beaute.* Stop by to get makeup tips or select by color palette. ✆ 207/225-2501. www.becca cosmetics.com.

MOLTON BROWN
58 S. Molton St., W1 (Tube: Bond St.); additional locations around town.

Famous hairdresser and maker of Molton Browners (hair twists), the salon has a product range that is so successful, it's sold at Harrods and all over the world. It has bath and spa items, aromatherapy, a men's line, and makeup. Check out the new **Davana Blossom** body collection sourced from a village in India called Mysore. For my sore body? I had a ball at the outlet store in Bicester Village (p. 278). ✆ 207/499-6474. www.moltonbrown.co.uk.

PIXI
22A Fouberts Place, W1 (Tube: Oxford St.).

Located right off Carnaby Street, this itty-bitty shop sells a makeup brand created by a team of Scandinavian girls. It also does facials and massages and lets you play with the makeup all day. Prices begin at £10 ($20). ✆ 207/287-7211. www.pixi beauty.com.

POUT
32 Shelton St., Covent Garden, WC2 (Tube: Covent Garden).

A newish brand that is expanding like crazy and is even represented in major department stores. Pout was more or less inspired by Space.NK (see below) and strives to carry lines not easily found elsewhere, such as Ole Henriksen from Beverly Hills—a skin-care line—and Essie, the leading beauty-salon brand of nail polish in the U.S. but little known in the U.K. It also has its own brands. ✆ 207/379-0379. www.pout.co.uk.

SCREENFACE
24 Powis Terrace, W11 (Tube: Notting Hill Gate); 48 Monmouth St., Covent Garden, WC2 (Tube: Covent Garden).

A stage-makeup resource often used by celebs and their makeup artists. ✆ 207/221-8289. www.screenface.com.

SPACE.NK

Thomas Neal's, 37 Earlham St., WC2 (Tube: Covent Garden); 45 Brook St., W1 (Tube: Bond St.); additional locations around town.

Space.NK specializes in cult brands, which is great, but many of them (Nars, for example) are American. Doesn't sound American, but it is—and it's priced accordingly. We don't buy American in London, now do we? Shu Uemura is a Japanese line carried to some small extent in the U.S., but it's also sold here, which is a great place to play with all the colors. You'll discover many brands you haven't heard of; spend a few hours and have a ball. There's enough selection that you can buy British and come out with many unique products. ✆ 207/379-7030. www.spacenk.co.uk.

International Names

Department stores fight to carry the big international brands, some of which have exclusive relationships with specific retailers. These brands also have free-standing stores; all are available in the United States as well.

AVEDA
28–29 Marylebone High St., W1 (Tube: Marylebone).
✆ 207/224-3157. www.aveda.com.

FRESH
92 Marylebone High St., W1 (Tube: Baker St.).
✆ 207/486-4100. www.fresh.com.

KIEHL'S
29 Monmouth St., WC2 (Tube: Leicester Sq.).
✆ 207/240-2411. www.kiehls.com.

L'OCCITANE
149 Regent St., W1 (Tube: Oxford Circus).
✆ 207/494-0467. www.loccitane.com.

MAC
109 King's Rd., SW3 (Tube: Sloane Sq.).
℡ 207/349-0022. www.maccosmetics.com.

SHU UEMURA
55 Neal St., Covent Garden, WC2 (Tube: Covent Garden).
℡ 207/240-7635. www.shuuemura.com.

BEAUTY STROLLS

If you just want to see several famous beauty and cosmetics brands in a short period of time, take a little walk along South Molton Street (Tube: Bond St.) or go to the King's Road, where there are several new shops. Note that Brook Street runs perpendicular to South Molton Street when it dead-ends.

South Molton Street

JO MALONE
23 Brook St., W1 (Tube: Bond St.).
℡ 207/491-9104. www.jomalone.co.uk.

MOLTON BROWN
58 S. Molton St., W1 (Tube: Bond St.).
℡ 207/499-6474. www.moltonbrown.co.uk.

SEN
59 S. Molton St., W1 (Tube: Bond St.).
℡ 207/629-2243. www.senhealth.com.

King's Road

FRESH LINE
55 King's Rd., SW3 (Tube: Sloane Sq.).
℡ 207/983-8810. www.freshline.gr.

KORRES STORE
124 King's Rd., SW3 (Tube: Sloane Sq.).
℡ 207/581-6455. www.korresstore.co.uk.

LUSH
123 King's Rd., SW3 (Tube: Sloane Sq.).
© 207/376-8348. www.lush.com.

MAC COSMETICS
109 King's Rd., SW3 (Tube: Sloane Sq.).
© 207/349-0022. www.maccosmetics.com.

ORGANIC PHARMACY
369 King's Rd., SW10 (Tube: Sloane Sq.).
© 207/351-2232. www.theorganicpharmacy.com.

HAIR

Who knew that in a country where it rains so often, so many hairstylists would become stars? There's so much going on in this section that I have broken it down into two parts: stylists and products. Better-known salons are invariably located in the Covent Garden area or the West End. There are hair salons in all major department stores and hotels; neighborhoods also have their share of local hairdressers.

As for products, the choices are absolutely astounding. Some lines have unique products you may have never heard of, while others simply offer packaging gimmicks.

Stylists

CHARLES WORTHINGTON
34 Great Queen St., WC2 (Tube: Covent Garden); additional locations around town.

Worthington is sort of an older-generation name; he was basically puttering along at an average pace until he went to America and became famous. Prices are affordable, and the Covent Garden salon is very hip and worth going to, if only to be part of the scene and to hang out at the juice bar and eavesdrop on Bridget Jones. Worthington has other salons around town. Wash,

cut, and dry: about £63 ($126). © 207/831-5303. www.cw
london.com.

DANIEL GALVIN
58–60 George St., W1 (Tube: Baker St. or Bond St.).

Galvin is one of several hairdressers who rode the Princess Diana
tresses to fame and fortune. He is known in the fashion magazines for his Midas touch with color. © 207/486-9661.
www.daniel-galvin.co.uk.

JO HANSFORD
19 Mount St., W1 (Tube: Marble Arch or Bond St.).

Known as the best hair-color artist in London, Hansford has
a salon near the Dorchester, but also sells hair-color products
in Boots stores. © 207/495-7774. www.johansford.com.

JOHN FRIEDA
75 New Cavendish St., W1 (Tube: Great Portland St.).

Although John Frieda is indeed a British hairstylist, he made
his name and his fortune in the United States. He's known for
his products, not for his salon, and most who come to the salon
do so because they like the products, including one collection
designed for straightening curly hair. Cut and dry will run you
about £63 ($126). © 207/636-1401. www.johnfrieda.com.

MICHAELJOHN
25 Albemarle St., W1 (Tube: Green Park).

I have been friends with the John (and also the Michael) of
Michaeljohn for more than 30 years; I did their *People* magazine story when they first opened in Beverly Hills. Now,
John's daughter Kate, whom I've known since she was 6, does
my hair in London when she's available.

To be honest, for several years I didn't take the time to have
my hair done in London, partly because the bad exchange rate
made it awfully expensive. But after many color disasters, I

went back to Michaeljohn, and even though my old team had moved on, there were complete files on my hair and I was back to naturally glorious in no time at all. Although the salon is one of the royal hairdressers, there is nothing stuck-up about the place. Wash, cut, and dry: £100 to £200 ($200–$400).

After Born to Shop Editorial Director Sarah Lahey told me she had the best manicure of her life at Michaeljohn, I booked several spa treatments to test it out. The downstairs space has been renovated and is now very luxe. I had a salt scrub, shea-butter renewal treatment, and massage that left my skin glowing for a week. Next time, I'm booking pulsed-light therapy to combat signs of aging. ✆ 207/491-4401. www.michaeljohn. co.uk.

Nicky Clarke
130 Mount St., W1 (Tube: Bond St.).

I believe Nicky Clarke became famous as the hairdresser to Sarah Ferguson when she was the Duchess of York. He's been doing models and editorial pages for years, and has become the newest John Frieda of hair-care products. He specializes in products for colored hair, with a complete line called Colour Therapy (buy it at Boots or Superdrug). They say the wait for a cut from Mr. Clarke himself is 6 months; he charges about £300 ($600). ✆ 207/491-4700. www.nickyclarke.com.

Toni & Guy
8 Marylebone High St., W1 (Tube: Marylebone); additional locations around town.

Toni & Guy began as sort of a hip, funky, slightly punk, and a little bit outrageous fashion source, truly on the cutting edge. They've worked hard to keep a touch of the outlaw in their style, while simultaneously becoming so mainstream as to have many salons and the beginnings of an international empire. There are numerous branches around town, including locations in Canary Wharf, Covent Garden, Kensington, and Knightsbridge. Prices are much more moderate than at the other big names. Wash, cut, and dry: about £40 ($80). © 207/ 935-7900. www.toniandguy.co.uk.

TREVOR SORBIE
27 Floral St., WC2 (Tube: Covent Garden).

Another name made famous in the Diana years; he is best known for being on the floor himself, a real working stiff who is available to real people. A cut with him costs a mere £100 ($200), which is a steal compared to the star-snipper prices in New York and London. © 207/379-6901. www.trevorsorbie. com.

VIDAL SASSOON
45A Monmouth St., WC2 (Tube: Covent Garden).

Vidal Sassoon was the first celebrity hairstylist and is possibly still the most famous name in hair in the world. Although he rarely does hair personally, and lives mostly in California, the beat goes on. He has not only an important salon, but also a training school where you can get a bargain haircut: the Vidal Sassoon School, 56 Davies Mews, W1 (Tube: Bond St.; © 207/318-5205), open Monday through Friday from 10am to 3pm. Prices at the school begin at about £10 ($20); in the regular salon, you will pay £45 ($90). © 207/240-6635. www.vidalsassoon.co.uk.

Products

These products are usually sold at the salons themselves, but can also be found at most chemist shops. Not all Boots stores carry all brands; the big **Boots Well-Being Centre,** 128 Kensington High St., W8 (Tube: High St. Kensington), has the best selection.

CHARLES WORTHINGTON TAKEAWAYS   This is a genius concept in marketing and packaging: a complete line of travel-size products that fit in your handbag or travel kit. Each product comes in a different shade of pastel package, with

2.5 ounces (75ml) of product in it. Each unit costs about £1.50 ($3). I bought a selection as a gift—great for the person who has everything, likes to try new products, or travels a lot. www.charlesworthington.co.uk.

JOHN FRIEDA   Although British-born, Frieda actually made his name and his product line in the United States before taking on the United Kingdom. Now he has a large brand with many products for curly hair and blond hair, as well as concept items including a new line for the beach. The products are almost fashion accessories. www.johnfrieda.com.

NICKY CLARKE   What attracted me to Nicky Clarke products was the Colour Therapy line; I've had a lot of fun using a copper goop that's called a polisher and texturizer. There is a huge range of products, some for specific shades of colored hair and some for normal hair, whatever that is. www.nicky clarke.com.

NAILS & MANICURES

Manicures are very expensive in London (like everything else), but if you're used to American manicures, at least you have a shot at getting what you're accustomed to or the kind of repairs you may need. Many spas and most hair salons have manicurists; there is also a manicurist at the **Boots Well-Being Centre,** 128 Kensington High St., W8 (Tube: High St. Kensington).

AMAZING NAILS
53 S. Molton St., W1 (Tube: Bond St.).

This is what it's come to on South Molton: The once-fanciest retail street in London now has nail salons. These people really are amazing, though not as keen for your business as at Nails Inc. (see below), with hours at a civilized Monday through Saturday from 10am to 5:30pm. © **207/355-3634.**

Manicure at Michaeljohn

—*Sarah Lahey*

Shopping is tough work, and schlepping heavy bags back to the hotel is even tougher. Not to mention what it does to your nails. After an intense week of Born to Shop research, I was in trouble—and it wasn't glove season yet. I realized I would have to pay more in London for a manicure than I do at home in Marin County, so I decided to go for the best. I called **Michaeljohn,** 25 Albemarle St., W1 (Tube: Green Park; ℂ 207/629-6969; www.michaeljohn.co.uk), and booked a fill with Kerry.

I didn't know what to expect from this upscale salon; but Suzy's hair always looks great after her visits, so I figured my nails would, too. I was right. Not only did I get a fabulous manicure and fill, but it also lasted over 3 weeks with no chips; the whole experience was worth every pound.

From the minute I walked in the door, I felt comfortable and pampered. I opted for my usual French manicure and fill; the whole process took a little over an hour. The thing I hate about acrylic overlays is that they often look heavy and puffy. Not here: Kerry meticulously applied several very thin layers and the final result was perfect, natural-looking nails. Price? £60 ($120)—ouch!—but everything was top-notch.

NAILS INC.
41 S. Molton St., W1 (Tube: Bond St.). Additional locations around town.

Like I said, there goes the neighborhood—although this is quite a chic nail salon. Note that the hours are most helpful: Monday through Friday from 8am to 8pm, Saturday from 10am to 7pm. ℂ 207/499-8333.

NYNC
17 S. Molton St., W1 (Tube: Bond St.).

This one is a chain, a very successful one, with salons all over town and products for sale in department stores and drugstores. At least the prices are reasonable: Manicures cost less than £15 ($30). The brand may just conquer Europe. ℂ 207/409-3332.

PERFUMES & TOILETRIES

. . . .

CZECH & SPEAKE
39C Jermyn St., SW1 (Tube: Piccadilly Circus or Green Park).

Trendy Italian and old-fashioned English in the same breath, this bath shop specializes in brushes and bath-time accessories, as well as its own brand of fragrances, which have somewhat seeped into the cult of better-known, little-known brands. The shop is all gray, black, and brass; the packaging is very special in a simultaneously high-tech/traditional manner. It's one of the most interesting shops in London, with a product line that not too many Americans know about. ℂ 207/439-0216. www.czechspeake.com.

DIPTYQUE
195 Westbourne Grove, W11 (Tube: Notting Hill Gate).

This age-old French cult maker of scented candles, soaps, and cologne has branched out in the past few years, with stores in cities like Boston and San Francisco and now this London branch. Prices may be lower in the U.S. and surely in France, but the candles are on every fashionista's must-have list. ℂ 207/727-8673. www.diptyqueparis.com.

D. R. HARRIS & CO.
29 St. James's St., SW1 (Tube: Piccadilly Circus or Green Park).

This is one of my best secret London finds, although I sort of owe it to a Jilly Cooper novel. This old-fashioned apothecary sells its own line of goods; Skinfood is the cream that I learned about in the novel. There are also men's colognes and shave products, quill toothpicks, and almond-oil moisturizers. © 207/930-3915. www.drharris.co.uk.

FLORIS
89 Jermyn St., SW1 (Tube: Piccadilly Circus or Green Park).

London has two leading local perfumers; Floris is one of them. This place is so classically English—the firm was begun in 1730 and kind of looks it, with true Brit style, old-fashioned vibes, and royal warrants. Even the packaging is fabulous. There is a lemon-curd shower cream that I can't get enough of. Special floral perfumes include Roses, Lilies, Lavender, and on and on. © 845/702-3239. www.florislondon.com.

MILLER HARRIS
21 Bruton St., W1 (Tube: Green Park or Bond St.); 14 Needham Rd., W11 (Tube: Notting Hill Gate).

Book 6 months ahead for a private consultation to create your own scent. Oh yeah, that might cost you about $10,000. But wait, there's other stuff, too: the ready-made scents, which are all perfumes and last longer than colognes. © 207/629-7750. www.millerharris.com.

ORMONDE JAYNE
12 The Royal Arcade, 28 Bond St., W1 (Tube: Green Park).

This little cutie-pie shop is located in one of London's prettiest old arcades. Although the boutique has been redesigned, the fragrances—from light floral to romantic musks—are as tempting as ever. There's a complete line of lotions and potions, but I buy the scented candles. © 207/499-1100. www.ormondejayne.com.

PARFUMS DE NICOLAI
101A Fulham Rd., SW3 (Tube: South Kensington).

Tiny French brand created by a member of the Guerlain family. © 207/581-0922.

PENHALIGON'S
*41 Wellington St., WC2 (Tube: Covent Garden); 16
Burlington Arcade, W1 (Tube: Piccadilly Circus).*

The other leading perfumer, alongside Floris . . . except Penhaligon's is much more than Floris and has really widened its range and image over the past several years. Now it even makes great little leather goods.

Although well known for toilet water and soap that men adore, Penhaligon's also holds a royal warrant. The products are produced according to the original formulas of William Penhaligon, who began his business as a barbershop in 1841. It's very "olde England" in here and fun to sniff around. For a whole lot of fun, check out the outlet store at Bicester Village (p. 278). © 207/434-2608. www.penhaligons.co.uk.

SPAS

Spas have become the jewel in the crown of many a luxury hotel, beauty center, and airport. Virgin Atlantic has incredible spas at both Heathrow and Gatwick airports, and British Airways installed a Molton Brown Travel Spa in Terminals 1 and 5 lounges for business- and first-class passengers (who actually get the treatments for free).

For the poor man's spa, see **Boots Well-Being Centre** (p. 14). Department stores also have spas, as do most hotels. Treatments for men and male-only spas are the new rage; check out **WholeMan** (67 New Bond St., W1; Tube: Bond St.; © 207/629-6659) and **Gentlemen's Tonic** (31A Bruton Place, W1; Tube: Bond St.; © 207/297-4343).

ELEMIS DAY SPA
2–3 Lancashire Court, W1 (Tube: Bond St.).

I became addicted to Elemis bath products long before this spa opened. Now you can wallow in the products and be smoothed out of stress or jet lag or cellulite or whatever; treatment packages begin at £113 ($226). About the address: This is just off New Bond Street. ℭ 207/499-4995. www.elemis.com.

SPA AT MANDARIN ORIENTAL
66 Knightsbridge, SW1 (Tube: Knightsbridge).

The addition of the spa is part of the remake of this hotel and the enrichment program to keep it in tune with the luxuries of the Mandarin Oriental brand. The spa is large, has many therapies, and is best known for its stone therapy. ℭ 207/838-9888. www.mandarinoriental.com.

Chapter Seven

....

HOME FURNISHINGS & DESIGN RESOURCES

THE LOOK

Maybe you can blame it on all those TV makeover shows, but the Brits have become more design conscious than ever. Just as high-street chains have knocked off the latest catwalk styles, the looks from glossy home style magazine pages have been brought within the means of the average bloke. Just take a stroll through **Zara Home's** (129 Regent St., Tube: Piccadilly Circus) recently opened flagship store. You'll be amazed at the inexpensive designer look-alikes.

If you think British home style is all cabbage roses and dark wood, you can think twice and get a look at the Tate Modern. Contemporary styles have become popular, and the Continental/Zen style has arrived, epitomized by Giorgio Armani's cool **Armani Casa** home-furnishings store on Bond Street.

Even the traditional British makers divide themselves into several schools of thought, from the classic cozy chic of **Nina Campbell,** who epitomizes the new version of old-fashioned English style, to **Tricia Guild,** who blazes forward with crafts and hot colors and lots of wow, to **Terence Conran,** who stands for a very clean, graphic, simple sort of cross-culture. The craft-luxe of **David Linley** takes a classic place in local design—his store is now huge and business is booming. He's possibly the only royal who has found a calling early in life and thrived in it.

"Smalls" are seen in every shop window, and a new boutique featuring unique home accessories seems to pop up every week. Check out **Mint** (70 Wigmore St., W1; Tube: Bond St.), a favorite with photo-session stylists; **Willer** (12 Holland St., W8; Tube: High St. Kensington or Notting Hill Gate); and **Suzy Hoodless** (10 Clarendon Cross, W11; Tube: Holland Park). **Hygge** (35 Camden Passage, N1; Tube: Angel) in Islington and **Maiden** (9 Princess Rd., NW1; Tube: Camden Town) in Primrose Hill are two more good bets for handpicked accessories and decorative items.

PROFESSIONAL SOURCES

For those of you who prefer to go to the trade sources, here are a few rules you ought to be aware of when buying in London:

- Have plenty of business cards on hand—if you are working as a member of the trade, introduce yourself when you enter a shop; ask upfront what trade discount or courtesies are offered.
- It is proper etiquette for dealers to identify themselves; they usually give themselves away by their knowledge anyway, but go ahead, tell 'em who you are.
- British decorating and design houses are not in the business of reducing prices unless you are an established client with an open account. Be prepared to show that you are indeed a professional, that you have a credit rating, and so on. It's best to have at least three references from big U.S. firms where you hold open accounts.
- Very often, English design firms will not take personal orders from out-of-towners. This is especially true if the firm has an agency in the country where you wish the goods to be shipped. They will not compete with their own overseas agents.
- Unlike U.S. design firms, British design firms will sell goods directly from their London showrooms to anyone. You

don't even need to pretend you're a member of the trade. (If you are a member of the trade, however, there's a 10% discount; be prepared to show resale number and business card.)

- Be prepared to handle your own shipping.

In flea markets and at fairs:

- When shopping in a market or on Portobello Road, expect to bargain. If you pay the price as marked, you will be overpaying. "Can you do better?" is all you need to say.
- Deal with cash when possible. Often, a store will offer a discount for cash transactions because then it does not have to deal with credit card fees. In the markets, only cash is accepted; many stalls will not even take traveler's checks. If the store does not offer a discount for cash, ask to see the owner and make your point.

While you're there:

- When you're in the fabric house, ask if there are any close-out bins. Quite often, fabrics are discontinued or half rolls are sold, and the showroom cannot sell the leftover pieces. There just might be some wonderful leftovers that are perfect for your home or for a piece of furniture you hadn't thought of re-covering.
- If you are buying fabrics that need trimmings to match, buy them at the same time and with the fabrics in hand. The English trimmings (fringes, ropes, tassels, and so on) are designed and colored to match the fabrics. Do note that, in Britspeak, the word *fringe* refers to the bangs of a hairstyle. Use the word *trim*. These trimmings are not cheap, but they can be much, much less in England than in the U.S. Also, the London selection is superior to what you'll find back home.
- When buying wallpaper, ask about the life expectancy of the paper. Once again, printing processes differ, and the wallpaper you are dying for could, in fact, be printed on a paper that is not as sturdy as your needs.

BASIC SOURCES

. . . .

Several of the department stores have recently reinvented themselves to beef up their home-decor offerings. Aside from department stores, the big names of European design all have shops in London; the question is whether you have such a shop near where you live in America or whether the VAT refund will make the price better.

Other tips:

- If you're planning to buy a lot of furniture, make arrangements with a shipper before you start your spree (see "Shipping," p. 215). Very often, the fabric houses will ship for you, but the furniture dealers prefer that you make your own arrangements. If you're buying antiques valued at over £2,000 ($4,000), you will need to have an export license from the British Customs office. A good shipper will also help arrange this for you. Keep in mind that it's easier to have all your goods arrive in one container than in dispersed shipments. Ask your shipper whether it will pick up from a variety of sources and whether there is any charge for this extra service. Be sure to get the best insurance possible on your goods. Don't try to save money on shipping. Shop the options, but buy the best.

- When buying at auction, be aware that you will be bidding against dealers who know their goods and what they are worth. Do a very careful inspection of the auction items the day before and check carefully for repairs and/or replacement of parts. The technology of furniture repair has made it possible to repair and/or replace damaged parts without the untrained eye being able to see the work. If you are not buying to collect but only to enjoy, this won't matter. However, if you're collecting Georgian antiques, every repair changes the value of the piece. If the dealers are not bidding, take their cue that something is wrong.

- If you want a piece badly enough, you can very often outbid the dealers. They need to resell the piece to make a profit

ℳeasure for ℳeasure

English fabrics are sold by the meter or the yard—ask. Always verify the width of the fabrics (most American fabrics are 54 in. wide) and the size of the repeat, as both will affect the amount you need to purchase. If you're buying for a particular piece of furniture, take the measurements of the piece and a photo with you. Most fabric houses have trained staff who will help you determine how much fabric is necessary for your job. If there is any question, buy extra. Yes, you may be able to find the same fabric at home, but the dye lot will be completely different, and your two pieces will never match. You can use the extra for pillows, if you don't end up needing it for your job.

Allow for the repeat. If you have no idea what I am talking about, you should reconsider your abilities as an interior designer.

Wallpaper rolls are very often double rolls, not single rolls. That is to say, one single British roll measures almost as long as two American-size rolls. Ask.

and, therefore, need to stop well under the street value for that piece. This is where you will have the advantage. You can save money and get a valuable collectible, piece of furniture, work of art, or carpet while having the fun of beating the dealer.

- When buying period pieces, whether at auction, through a dealer, or at a stall, remember to get papers of authenticity. Any item 100 years or older is free of U.S. Customs duties. However, you will be asked for proof of age by officials. They are on to tricks in this area, so don't try to pass off a new tea service as antique. But this is also a gray area in British law. For instance, if you buy a chair that is Georgian but has had some parts replaced, this would be considered a reasonable restoration and would be fine. But if more than half of the chair has been restored so that most of the parts are new, the law is not clear, and your chair may not be considered duty-free.

- If your favorite important antiques dealer has closed his doors, fret not. Many have done so because of the strength of the auction houses.
- Don't expect to be able to buy a national treasure. Important pieces must be approved for export by the country of origin before they are granted an export license.
- Be sure that the price you are paying is not more expensive (taking shipping, insurance, and so on into account) than it would be to buy a similar piece through a dealer in the United States.

BOOKING ENGLISH STYLE

If you're as interested in English style and decor as I am, you'll have a ball with all the magazines your news agent can sell you.

British publishing has far more choices in the subjects of design, architecture, style, crafts, and reference for buying antiques. Alas, British book prices are also outrageously high. Make sure there is no American edition of a book you are planning to buy before you go hog-wild at your nearest **Hatchards** or **Dillons.** Note that if you buy price guides, prices will be in pounds sterling pegged to local values; many items are more (or less) valuable across the pond.

Also pick up brochures in design showrooms; they frequently announce sale events. There are also ads in the newspapers about such special sales and clearances.

DESIGN SHOWS

DECOREX Almost 20 years old and still ticking, this is a popular show for the trade and for pros, although you can possibly wangle a way in. ✆ 207/833-3374. www.decorex.com.

LONDON DESIGN WEEK   This is an event for the trade: It includes complimentary chauffeur-driven cars to whisk you to various participating showrooms, where they lay it on thick. Only the big names play. One day is open to the public. The event is usually in March. www.designcentrechelseaharbour. co.uk.

ORIGIN, THE LONDON CRAFT FAIR   Annual event, usually in October, open to the public and featuring more than 300 artisans. www.craftscouncil.org.uk.

100% DESIGN   Another trade show, but wait—the public is invited on the last day! It's usually in September. www.100 percentdesign.co.uk.

AUCTIONS

The designer's best secret is the London auction, where more and more people are hoping to get a deal. Because prices are set at auctions and then determined for similar items throughout the art and furniture world, you may not find a bargain at all. Naturally, the London auction scene is the big time, whereas country auctions are easier to deal with and may offer better prices. I must admit, with a warning, that we went to a country auction and found that the furniture was desirable and well priced, but the cost of shipping it back to the United States did not justify buying anything.

Nevertheless, auctions are a tremendous amount of fun and should be given consideration for pure entertainment's sake. In London, however, there are certain auctions that are quite serious and important and, while fun, are taken without much of a sense of humor. If you attend a big auction at a prestigious house, ask around about proper wardrobe. Women should plan on simple suits or silks for day. Evening auctions can be black-tie events (they're seldom white-tie). Viewings are almost always during the day, as are the majority of auctions. Proper business clothes are essential, even if one isn't bidding.

Like all major cities, London has an auction season: October through May. Country auctions are often held in the summer, but fancy auctions are held only at auction houses in the city during the season. Occasionally auctions are closed to the public (such as the fur auctions in St. Petersburg, Russia, where pelts are sold to furriers in lots), but usually, you can be admitted to an auction by catalog or for free. Weekly auction programs are published in the *Times* on Tuesday and in the *Daily Telegraph* on Monday. Some houses sell certain types of works on specific days of the week, such as china on Monday and European oil paintings on Friday. In season, there will be about 100 auctions a month in London alone.

Various auctions have various functions in their respective fields; often, it is to set the prices for the rest of the world. On the other hand, you shouldn't be intimidated. You may indeed get a real "steal," or you may be shopping in a country where the market price for an item you're interested in is considerably less than in the United States.

Please note that there is no VAT on antiques. Do be wary of fakes at auctions, particularly from the less famous houses. If you buy an item because you love it, and if it doesn't matter to you whether it's real or not, that's one thing. But if you are buying for investment, name-dropping, or status-seeking purposes, use a house expert or, better yet, a private expert as a consultant. The better houses will not intentionally sell you a forgery or a fake, but small-time auctioneers may not care what's in the lots, as long as they move them out. A house may even admit that it doesn't know if a piece is authentic. Sotheby's, for example, uses the full name of an artist in the catalog listing when it knows the work is authentic, but only the initials of the artist if it has some doubt as to the provenance of the work.

The experts at the big auction houses are trained not only to know their stuff, but also to be informative and polite. If you want to bone up on a point of curiosity or just pick someone's brain, wander into a good auction house and speak to someone at the front desk. They may well give you information you never knew or turn you on to a free and expert opinion.

The most famous auction houses in London are **Sotheby's** and **Christie's,** but don't underestimate **Phillips** or **Bonhams,** which have been around since 1793. See below for contact info for all these houses.

There are also stamp and coin auctions. **Harmers,** 111 Power Rd., Chiswick, W4 (Tube: Gunnersbury; © 208/747-6100; www.harmers.com), is the leading stamp auction house. **Stanley Gibbons,** 399 The Strand, WC2 (Tube: Charing Cross; © 207/836-8444; www.stanleygibbons.com), another famous house, has an auction about six times a year. Don't forget country auctions that you may find on a weekend outing; these are usually charming (but remember that if there were something truly important to sell, it would have gone to a big house in a major city to command a big price). At a country auction, expect to pay cash for your purchase. Be prepared to make your own shipping arrangements (see "Shipping," below).

When you shop at an auction of any kind, remember:

- The house is not responsible for the authenticity of the article.
- There is a house commission charged to the seller, but the buyer will have to pay taxes. Some houses also commission the buyer—ask, as this can raise the price by another 10%. This is called "the buyer's premium." There's a recent trend, in order to reel in the big auctions, for the house to cut the commission but raise the premium. Know your terms and ask questions.
- You are entitled to know the price a similar item went for in previous years and the price the house expects the item to go for at the current auction. Often these prices are posted at the viewing or may be published in the catalog. The house's expectation of what something will go for at auction proves meaningless several times a year, but it is a beginning.
- Find out before you bid what currency you must pay in. International houses often accept many currencies, and you may

do better with your dollar converting to one rather than another. This can pay off with a large purchase.

- If bidding is not in U.S. dollars, keep a calculator in your hand during the bidding to know what the prices are; remember to calculate at the current American Express rate of exchange rather than the bank rate. The bank rate will be more favorable than the one you will actually be paying, so don't cheat yourself by an inaccurate conversion.
- Expect to pay tax on the item when you call for it. Find out the tax ahead of time. VAT is not paid on antiques.
- The auction house may pack and ship your purchase for you, but it may be cheaper to do it yourself, or ask your hotel concierge to handle it for you.
- Make sure that the item you are about to buy may leave the country! Some countries won't let you out with what they consider to be items that are part of their heritage. Conversely, make sure that you can get it into the United States. You will not be reimbursed if the government confiscates any of your property. If the item is an antique, get the papers that verify its age. According to Customs, an antique is any item 100 years old or more.
- Don't bid against Bill Gates.

Major Auction Houses

BONHAMS
Montpelier St., SW7 (Tube: Knightsbridge); 101 New Bond St., W1 (Tube: Bond St.).
© 207/393-3900; www.bonhams.com.

CHRISTIE'S
8 King St., SW1 (Tube: Green Park).
© 207/839-9060; www.christies.com.

PHILLIPS
25–26 Albemarle St., W1 (Tube: Green Park).
© 207/318-4010; www.phillipsdepury.com.

SOTHEBY'S
34–35 New Bond St., W1 (Tube: Bond St.).
© 207/293-5000; www.sothebys.com.

SHIPPING

The good news: You've just found the most wonderful, gorgeous, fabulous, chic, and inexpensive sideboard. You've longed for one for years. The bad news: It certainly won't fit into your suitcase.

Whether the item is as cumbersome as a sideboard, as small as a few bottles of perfume, or as fragile as dinner plates, you can arrange to ship it home. All it takes is a little time and a little more money.

To make shipping pay, the item—with the additional cost of shipping, duty, and insurance (and Customs agent, if need be)—should still cost less than it would at home, or be so totally unavailable at home that any price makes it a worthwhile purchase. If it's truly unavailable at home (and isn't an antique or a one-of-a-kind art item), ask yourself why. There may be a good reason—such as it's illegal to bring such an item into the country! If you are indeed looking for a certain type of thing, be very familiar with American prices. If it's an item of furniture, even an antique, can a decorator get it for you with a 20% rather than a 40% markup? Have you checked out all the savings angles first?

Your Options

There are basically two types of shipping: surface and air. Air can be broken down two ways: unaccompanied baggage and regular airfreight.

Surface mail is the cheaper of the two. Surface mail may mean through the regular mail channels—a small package of perfume would be sent parcel post—or it may require your filling an entire shipping container, or at least paying the price for use of an entire container.

Many people make the mistake of assuming that only the weight of an item will matter in the shipping. Although weight matters, there may be a 500-pound difference per price bracket! For instance, a piano may weigh more than two Queen Anne chairs, but they may cost the same to ship.

Surface mail may take 3 months, but we've had delivery in 3 weeks. Allow 3 months to be safe, longer if so advised by the dealer. If you are shipping books (antique or otherwise), note that there are special surface rates and no U.S. duties. Otherwise, generally speaking, rates are per cubic foot and include:

- Picking up the purchase.
- Packing the goods (crating may be extra).
- Handling export documents.
- Sea-freight charges.
- Customs clearance on the U.S. end.

If you want to save money, ask about "groupage" services. Your goods will be held until a shipping container is filled. The container will then go to the United States, to one of only four ports of entry (Los Angeles, New York, San Francisco, or New Orleans), where you can meet the container at the dock, be there when your items are unpacked, and pay the duties. A full container is 1,100 cubic feet of space (or 8.5 ft.×8.5 ft.×20 ft. long—or big enough for about 100 pieces of furniture) and will not be delivered to your door (no matter how much you smile). There are also 40-foot containers, if you're furnishing your cottage in Newport.

Shipping a 20-footer to New York will cost you at least £3,000 ($6,000), probably more. This price includes wrapping, shipping, and London paperwork. U.S. collections and bills of lading usually add £250 ($500) to the bill. Insurance costs 1.5% of the total value of the goods.

Airfreight is several times more expensive than surface, but it has the assurance of quick delivery. You can airfreight small items up to 50 pounds (in weight, not price) through traditional business services such as DHL and FedEx. Or you can use freight services that send larger packages and even furniture.

If your purchase is so delicate and so important as to need to be flown, it may require an international courier, which is a person who hand-carries the item for you. (This is often done with pieces of art or valuable papers.)

You can find a list of shippers and packers in the back of the annual *Guide to the Antique Shops of Britain,* published by the Antiques Collectors Club. When you choose a shipper, ask for a "buying kit," which includes all necessary paperwork.

Among the most famous names in the trade:

- **Davies Turner,** ℂ 207/622-4393; fax 207/720-3897; www. daviesturner.com.
- **Gander & White,** ℂ 208/971-7171; fax 208/946-8062; www.ganderandwhite.com.
- **Lockson Services Ltd.,** ℂ 208/957-2889; fax 208/597-5265; www.lockson.co.uk.

But Wait!

Here's one more source, which I actually discovered in France. It may be your best bet yet because it has offices in New York and London and three different ones in France—in Paris, at the St. Ouen Flea Market, and in the South of France at the big flea market city of Isle Sur la Sorgue:

- **Hedley's Humpers,** 3 St. Leonard's Rd., London NW10 (ℂ 208/965-8733; fax 208/965-0249; www.hedleys humpers.com); New York office: 21–41 45th Rd., Long Island City, NY (ℂ 718/433-4005; fax 718/433-4009).

I've found another service that might be helpful if you don't have enough for a container but need some help with your parcels. Stop by any British post office and investigate **Parcel Force,** the parcel delivery branch of the U.K. postal service. ℂ 870/850-1150.

Insurance

Insurance is usually sold by the package by your shipper. Don't assume that it's included in the price of delivery, because it isn't. There are several different types of insurance, with deductibles or all-risk (with no deductible), so you'll have to make a personal choice based on the value of what you are shipping. *Remember:* When figuring the value of the item for insurance purposes, include the price of the shipping.

If you bought a desk for $1,000 and it costs $500 to ship it home, the value for insurance purposes is $1,500. If you have the replacement-cost type of insurance, you should probably double the price, since that is approximately what it would cost to replace the item in the United States.

THE DISH ON DISHES

The British are blessed with a crazy location in the sea of geography: They've got coal and they've got clay. As a result, they have a centuries-old tradition of producing bone china. Yeah, I know that they don't mine the coal anymore, and no one wants to breathe near coal-belching factories—but historically speaking, coal has a lot to do with dishes. You can visit the china factories in the countryside or you can visit all the china stores in London. Keep in mind:

- Most china stores in London sell only first quality. The prices are usually 30% lower than in the U.S., but if the dollar is bad, that savings may shrink. During sales, especially in January, you may discover a 50% savings. Some of the biggies (like **Harrods**) truck in seconds, which are so marked, for the sale season.
- The problem with really saving big on china comes with the shipping. China must be packed, crated, insured, and—in some cases—you must pay duty on it (but not if it comes home in parcels worth under $50 and marked "Unsolicited

Gift"). Even with VAT refunds, you will still raise the cost of your purchase appreciably. But that doesn't mean you shouldn't consider a big haul. It just means you need to mentally register the landed price, not the asking price.

- Prices on the same items are supposed to be the same in each retail outlet but may vary by as much as £2 ($4) per place setting. If a retailer is overstocked with a certain pattern, he may deal on the price of a large order.

- If you want to buy seconds, consider a trip to Stoke-on-Trent; if not, come to London for the January and June/July sales, or even order by phone during a sale period. **Harrods** has a toll-free phone number during the January sale to make it even easier.

- Silver, even silver plate, is getting more and more expensive each year, but is still a good bet when bought secondhand. Avoid the fancy stores and stick to street markets or the famous **London Silver Vaults** (p. 220). By law, silver must be hallmarked—look for marks or ask. To bring silver (or plate) into the U.S. tax-free, it must be over 100 years old. Get a receipt that says so from the dealer at the time of purchase.

- England is also famous for its lead crystal, although the most famous brands come from Ireland or Scotland. You can shop for crystal during the big sale periods when you buy china, or head for the factory-outlet stores, which usually feature the best prices on discontinued patterns. If you're filling in an existing pattern, you may want to buy at the airport in either London or Shannon.

RESOURCES: CHINA, CRYSTAL & SILVER

....

CHLOE ALBERRY
84 Portobello Rd., W11 (Tube: Notting Hill Gate).

This is a good resource for mirrors, chandelier drops, and unique pulls for lights and shades. They also carry a complete range of door fittings including whimsical door handles, mail slots, cut crystal knobs, and those fab brass door knockers with lions' heads and curlicues. ✆ 207/727-0707. www.chloealberry.com.

LONDON SILVER VAULTS
53–64 Chancery Lane, WC2 (Tube: Chancery Lane).

This takes a little getting to, but if you love silver, I beg you to include the Silver Vaults on your shopping list. It's just great, good fun. Originally founded in 1882 as a large safety-deposit box and now in the Holborn section of London, the Silver Vaults comprise 35 shops selling a variety of large and small items at all prices. Only one shop is at street level; the rest are underground. Expect to find everything from silver buckets to Fabergé jewelry. ✆ 207/242-3844. www.thesilvervaults.com.

REJECT CHINA SHOP
183 Brompton Rd., SW3 (Tube: Knightsbridge.).

News flash! This longtime china source has downsized to one London location. The stores on Regent Street and Covent Garden have closed, but fortunately, the best one on Brompton Road in Knightsbridge is still going strong, where you'll find a good selection of Portmeirion, Spode, and other British brands.

Okay, let's get this straight: There are no bargains here. Sometimes, there are seconds, which are priced lower than firsts, but this store is marketed to imply that you are getting a bargain—when, in fact, prices are the same as elsewhere. In fact, prices are the same as at Thomas Goode! Shocking, huh? Still, the store is convenient to the tourist trade and is stocked to make you think you've found rock-bottom prices. ✆ 207/581-0739.

THOMAS GOODE
19 S. Audley St., W1 (Tube: Green Park or Hyde Park Corner).

If you're looking for the ultimate shopping experience for your selection of china, glassware, silver, or exquisite accessory pieces, this elegant shop is a must. In fact, if you're looking to pick one simple, very London, very elegant shopping experience that epitomizes why you travel, why you have to shop in foreign cities, and what can be gained by educating your eye in the world's best cities, well, Thomas Goode just might be your choice. This is theater as well as shopping.

The store is almost the size of a city block and rambles through a variety of salons; don't miss any of them—including the far back where the antique knickknacks are sold, or the far side where there is now a tearoom (with very high prices). Also check out the bomb. Yes, the bomb. Don't bring your children. Do bring your credit cards. And possibly your camera.

Thomas Goode carries top European brands of china and crystal and has monogram services available on the premises. They will even work with you to create a personal pattern. The sales help is incredibly well-bred and nice. © **207/499-2823.** www.thomasgoode.co.uk.

VESSEL
114 Kensington Park Rd., W11 (Tube: Notting Hill Gate).

With an emphasis on Italian and Scandinavian glass as well as top British design, this gallery store displays and sells unusual contemporary tableware. Each product is chosen for quality, innovative form, and, of course, function. Alongside classics like Orrefors crystal, you'll see sculptural glassware, animal figurines, and tableware designed by local artisans. © **207/727-8001.** www.vesselgallery.com.

RESOURCES: ENGLISH MODERN

Contemporary looks are frequently combined with old-fashioned architectural styles in London; the look has moved through the 1960s and come out the other end with clean lines and moderate prices.

THE CONRAN SHOP
Michelin House, 81 Fulham Rd., SW3 (Tube: South Kensington); 55 Marylebone High St., W1 (Tube: Baker St.).

The Conran Shop should not be confused with the now-defunct Conran's in the United States. The flagship store on Fulham Road, with its Art Deco tiles and hoopla, welcomes you first into a cafe, then into a store of mini-showrooms with modern yuppie furniture. Go downstairs for a less stark and more moderately priced version of the first floor. Here's where you'll find the fun: baskets, gifts, dried flowers, china, toys, books, foodstuffs, coffees, luggage, umbrellas—everything. © 207/589-7401. www.conran.co.uk.

HABITAT
121–123 Regent St., W1 (Tube: Oxford Circus or Piccadilly Circus); 208 King's Rd., SW3 (Tube: Sloane Sq.); 26–40 Kensington High St., W8 (Tube: High St. Kensington).

Habitat made British home-furnishings history, although not in the same way as Mr. Chippendale. After the spare Scandinavian look came the modern British look—an update of the old Nordic chic with a touch of high-tech. It all began with Terence Conran, who was later knighted for his contributions to the world. Habitat, although no longer owned by Sir Terence, is still a glorious place to shop; the new grade-II listed Regent Street flagship store is located in a former cinema where Queen Victoria apparently saw her first film.

Note that there is a difference between Habitat shops and the Conran Shops. © 870/411-5501. www.habitat.net.

HEAL'S
196 Tottenham Court Rd., W1 (Tube: Goodge St.); 234 King's Rd., SW3 (Tube: Sloane Sq.).

Heal's is the mother of English modern design and the source of Terence Conran's inspiration. It's a furniture and lifestyle department store in the real-people part of London, on Tottenham Court Road not far from Oxford Street. (It takes some degree of purpose to get here.) It offers looks similar to those in other modern housewares stores, but better quality and therefore higher prices. You'll find the squishy sofa of your dreams here (hardly a tourist item) and plenty of yummy bed and tabletop linens. Convenient to the store is a branch of practically everything else as well, so you can see the same looks established by Heal's and then copied at Habitat. The King's Road store is newish; it's across from Chelsea Town Hall. *Tip:* Heal's has great sales. ℂ **207/636-1666.** www.heals.co.uk.

MUJI

41 Carnaby St., W1 (Tube: Oxford Circus); 157 Kensington High St., N8 (Tube: South Kensington); 118 King's Rd., SW3 (Tube: Sloane Sq.); 187 Oxford St., W1 (Tube: Oxford Circus); additional locations around town.

Okay, so Muji is a Japanese company and the subject here is English modern. But this firm has so much become part of the look that I'd be remiss to not include it. Muji is a lifestyle store, and its aesthetic works well with the simplicity of Conran's vision. I shop here for the containers and travel-packing possibilities more than for home furnishings and decor. The look is lean and spare and simple in the best Japanese manner, but there are all sorts of gadgets and gimmicks as well. There's a branch of Muji in every trading area in London, so there are dozens of them. www.muji.co.uk.

RESOURCES: FABRICS & OBJETS D'ART

It's hard to separate the fabric, furniture, and collectible sources from one another. Most often, a fabric showroom will also carry a line of furniture, and a furniture dealer will have an exclusive line of fabrics. Many of the showrooms make individual items out of their fabrics—cosmetics bags, novelty gifts, and such. *Note:* It is illegal to carry paint products on an airplane, so don't even think about it.

ANNA FRENCH
343 King's Rd., SW3 (Tube: Sloane Sq.).

Although Anna French features a lot of lace and lacy looks, her design showroom offers a complete range of all the items necessary to the country-English postmodern look: marbleized wallpapers, faux finishes, swags of lace, fabrics printed with big flowers that aren't cabbage roses. Open to the public. © 207/ 351-1126. www.annafrench.co.uk.

CATH KIDSTON
8 Clarendon Cross, W11 (Tube: Holland Park); additional locations around town.

Kidston does her own prints, in a sort of 1950s style, and her work is bright, clever, and unusual for the United Kingdom. The shop sells assorted items, such as travel kits, made out of her fabrics. But you'll also find wallpaper and fabric by the yard. © 207/221-1400. www.cathkidston.co.uk.

CHELSEA HARBOUR DESIGN CENTRE
108 The Chambers, Chelsea Harbour SW 10 (Tube: Fulham Broadway).

Once a stodgy emporium for the design trade, the Chelsea Harbour Design Centre has been completely refurbished and is now open to retail visitors as well as interior designers and architects. There are more than 70 showrooms (top design sources from around the world have satellite boutiques here), and the Design Café is a great spot for a lunch break. Don't miss the RIBA (Royal Institute of British Architects) bookshop, a wealth of information, specializing in titles on interiors and architecture. Open Monday to Friday 9:30am to 5pm.

COLEFAX & FOWLER
39 Brook St., W1 (Tube: Bond St.); 110 Fulham Rd., SW3 (Tube: South Kensington).

The king of English chic is located, appropriately, near South Molton Street and Old Bond Street, home to all the best designers. Entering the Colefax & Fowler showrooms on Brook Street is like taking a step into an English country home. The building was constructed in 1766 by Sir Jeffrey Wyattville and is clearly being held together with chintz. Inside, the rooms are the size of small sitting rooms, the carpet is worn, and the furnishings are old. This is all part of the mystique. The upstairs houses the most magnificent collection of English chintzes ever to be desired by an Anglophile. Every year, designers bring out a new collection of fabrics and wallpapers more beautiful than the previous year's—assuming you like the look, of course. Anyone may browse and buy. The Jane Churchill collection is featured at the Fulham Road shop. ✆ 207/493-2231. www.colefaxantiques.com.

DESIGNERS GUILD
267–271 and 277 King's Rd., SW3 (Tube: Sloane Sq.).

Tricia Guild has been going for a long time with her Designers Guild, one of the best-known sources in town for all the pieces you need to put together a look. She has prospered because she has been able to change that look and not grow stale; the effect is colorful and stupendous.

If you're tired of the old country-English style, you'll revel in all this energy and excitement. There are two shops, a few doors apart—don't miss either. Even if you aren't going to buy so much as a meter of fabric, come in and absorb all the trends—this is hot. Warehouse sales are advertised annually. Open to the public. ✆ 207/351-5775. www.designersguild.com.

IAN MANKIN
109 Regent's Park Rd., NW1 (Tube: Finchley Central).

Marvelous country textiles in plaids and checks and stripes, but not convenient to the Tube stop (you may want to take a taxi instead). All fabrics here are natural—either 100% cotton or linen, or a mix of the two. ✆ 207/722-0997. www.ianmankin.com.

JANE CHURCHILL
110 Fulham Rd., SW3 (Tube: South Kensington).

A division of Colefax & Fowler, the Jane Churchill lines of fabrics, wallpapers, and trims are English in feeling (it goes with her last name), but international in scope. They're higher in cost than at Laura Ashley, but with a younger look than traditional English chintzes. The style is very packaged and positioned a few rungs up from Laura Ashley. Quite affordable and worth looking at. © 207/244-7427. www.janechurchill.com.

LINLEY
60 Pimlico Rd., SW1 (Tube: Sloane Sq.); 46 Albemarle St., W1(Tube: Green Park).

David Linley, the most talented of the young royals, has recently moved into new digs, in addition to his original flagship store on Pimlico Road. The second Linley shop is in the truly high-rent area of Mayfair, not far from where Granny's palace is located. Linley is famous for contemporary handcrafted wood furniture designs, but also sells some smaller and more affordable items, such as presentation boxes. Don't miss it. © 207/730-7300. www.davidlinley.com.

NICHOLAS HASLAM
12 Holbein Place, SW1 (Tube: Sloane Sq.); 202 Ebury St., SW1 (Tube: Sloane Sq.).

To show you are "in," please refer to this man as "Nicky" and act like you know him and his famous touch: his handmade kilim shoes. His primary showroom, on a small street that intersects Pimlico Road and Sloane Square, is a wonderful collection of every period and style, with preference to none. He recently opened a second store on Ebury Street that focuses more on lifestyle. The truth is that Nicky Haslam is one of London's more sought-after designers, with a very versatile design ability. He will do both small and large jobs, but you must have an appointment to meet with him in person. © 207/730-8623. www.nicholashaslam.com.

NINA CAMPBELL
9 Walton St., SW3 (Tube: South Kensington).

One of the most famous names in London design, Ms. Campbell became well-known to Americans when she stepped in to rescue the Duke and Duchess of York from their American design team. I bought one of her fabric-covered "bulletin boards" (the chic-est bulletin board ever created, I might add) for a wedding present; you can buy a knockoff at any U.S. linen discounter, but the original has a lot of class and is so sophisticated you could faint with pride. © **207/225-1011.** www.nina campbell.com.

OSBORNE & LITTLE
304 King's Rd., SW3 (Tube: Sloane Sq.).

Along with Colefax & Fowler, Osborne & Little reigns as top of the line for The Look. The firm began as antiquarian booksellers, with a sideline of hand-printed wallpapers. However, when Sir Peter Osborne and his brother-in-law Anthony Little won the Council of Industrial Design Award for their first wallpaper collection in 1968, they began a revolution in the interior-design and manufacturing business.

Osborne & Little designs are wonderful because they are always based in history but not limited by it. A charming English botanical print might be reinterpreted in bolder colors. A whole line of wallpapers reflects the paint effects of marbleizing and stippling found in old Italian villas. Because they're now machine produced, the fabrics and wallpapers are even affordable. The showroom is quiet and dignified, just the kind of place where you might like to have high tea. Anyone may browse and buy. © **207/352-1456.** www.osborneandlittle.com.

VALERIE WADE
108 Fulham Rd., SW3 (Tube: South Kensington).

One of those one-woman-with-a-lot-of-style-and-what-an-eye! kinds of shops; Wade is worshiped by locals, by Americans, and even by the French. She sells many items, from carpets to

A Resource for Dogs

Don't miss **Stephanie Hoppen**, 17 Walton St., SW3 (Tube: South Kensington; ℭ 207/589-3678; www.stephaniehoppen. com). This small gallery has portraits of dogs that are just divine; you can also commission a portrait of your family pet. Since it's on the sensational Walton Street, there's no excuse not to stop in, even if you're a cat person.

needlepoint to dishes to just great stuff all put together with a flair we all wish we had. Not too far from Voyage, so do them both on the same day. And yes, our girl Val has pashmina— you will swoon over her color choices. ℭ **207/225-1414.** www. valeriewade.com.

RESOURCES: GARDEN DESIGN

CHELSEA GARDENER
125 Sydney St., King's Rd., SW3 (Tube: Sloane Sq.).

By all means, you must poke into this little enclave of green and park and retail and great stuff—most of the space is taken by the Chelsea Gardener, a nursery and garden shop, but there's a minimall of other stores here, too. The Chelsea Gardener is open daily; it has books on design products as well as plants. This source is actually right off King's Road, hence the unusual address; don't panic—it's right in the heart of things. ℭ **207/352-5656.** www.chelseagardener.com.

COLUMBIA ROAD FLOWER MARKET
Columbia Rd., E2 (Tube: Old St.; or bus no. 26, 48, or 55).

This is a Sunday-only event, and it's over by around 1pm. While there are flowers and plants and greens sold in flats in the street, there's also a big boutique scene—so this isn't a "just gardens" kind of thing. www.columbia-flower-market.freewebspace.com.

MARSTON & LANGINGER
190–192 Ebury St., SW1 (Tube: Sloane Sq.).

Although Marston & Langinger's specialty is bespoke conservatories, they also sell all the necessary things to put in them. Along with an eclectic mix of tableware and linens, you'll find unusual pieces for the garden, from terra-cotta plant containers to a custom line of wire baskets, trays, and specialty gardening tools. © 207/881-5717. www.marston-and-langinger.com.

RK ALLISTON
173 New King's Rd., SW6 (Tube: Parsons Green).

This shop is ideal if you need a gift for the lifestyle gardener who has everything. With an inventory spanning mock-vintage pruning shears to designer wellies, RK Alliston has it all. My favorite gift is the String-in-a-Tin, a retro tin can containing a spool of green twine for £9 ($18). © 207/731-8100. www.rkalliston.com.

RESOURCES: RIBBONS & TRIMS

TEMPTATION ALLEY
361 Portobello Rd., W10 (Tube: Notting Hill Gate).

More than 6,000 trims. © 208/964-2004. www.temptationalley.com.

VV ROULEAUX
102 Marylebone Lane, W1 (Tube: Baker St. or Bond St.);
54 Sloane Sq., at Cliveden Place, SW1 (Tube: Sloane Sq.).

If you're a regular, do note that the company has expanded and now has two stores in London; check out the new flagship on Marylebone Lane.

If you're doing a home-fabrics-and-trimmings spree, or if you're simply a ribbon freak like I am, it's easy enough to get to one of these shops. They have tons of ribbons and trims and swags and things that will make you swoon with their beauty and grace. There's also a large selection of fabric flowers, in velvet, silk, denim, ribbon, and so on. Really special; don't miss it. www.vvrouleaux.com.

Chapter Eight

....

ALTERNATIVE RETAIL

BORN TO RULE

Money and price tags never touch the queen's hands. She asks only certain stores and factories to send 'round goods; these businesses have the royal seal of approval, which is called a "royal warrant." The public can shop these same resources, as their royal warrants are always marked at the door. So if you're hit by the budget crunch and the difficult dollar, you can still have fun just by making a circuit of royal warrant stores to see what the queen buys.

Such stores are allowed to display the royal coat of arms and to use the words "by appointment." Because there is more than one royal family in Europe and there are several members of the Windsor family, you may see several coats of arms on the window of any given shop—appointments from various royals. Note that holding a royal warrant demands total discretion. The warrant holder may not talk about the royals in any way—especially to the press or public—or the warrant holder will lose the warrant. So if you walk into **Turnbull & Asser** and ask what size pj's Prince Charles wears, you'll be met by an icy stare and stony silence.

A warrant is good for 10 years and then must be renewed. If a merchant is dropped, he gets a sort of royal pink slip and has no means of redress. Every year, about 20 to 30 new warrants are issued and the same number of pink slips are passed out. To qualify for a warrant, a business must provide a minimum of 3 years' service to the crown.

There are warrants on everything from royal laundry detergent (Procter & Gamble) to royal china, and there can be several warrants in the same category. For china, Her Majesty has as much trouble getting it down to one pattern as I do—she's got warrants at **Royal Worcester, Spode,** and **Royal Doulton.**

MUSEUM SHOPPING

London museums are excellent and most have very good gift shops that offer a chance to perhaps find a unique souvenir at a reasonable price. Most museums have come up with high-class gifts and reproductions from their collections. The tinny and tatty are out of style.

BRAMAH MUSEUM OF TEA AND COFFEE
40 Southwark St., SE1 (Tube: London Bridge).

You know I could never resist a teapot; this museum traces the history of both tea and coffee and features many novelty teapots, as does the small gift shop. © **207/403-5650.** www.tea andcoffeemuseum.co.uk.

BRITISH MUSEUM
Great Russell St., WC1 (Tube: Tottenham Court Rd., Holborn, Russell Sq., or Goodge St.).

This is a huge museum, it's free, and you can walk to Covent Garden from here if you're strong enough. There are actually four different shops on the premises—the Souvenir and Guide Shop, the Children's Shop, the Bookshop, and the Grenville Shop, where you'll find luxury items including replicas, jewelry, and gifts. If you aren't into kitsch and royal souvenirs, this is the perfect place for unique items. © **207/323-8000.** www.thebritishmuseum.ac.uk.

DESIGN MUSEUM
28 Shad Thames, SE1 (Tube: Tower Hill or London Bridge).

Sure, the museum is neat, and the part of town where it's located (Butler's Wharf) is worth a stop to get a view of the Thames redevelopment—but don't forget the gift shop or the restaurant. Products are featured heavily in the collections, and they are sold, along with postcards and visual arts, in the shop. This entire complex, including the restaurant, is a perfect example of Sir Terence Conran's genius and the new London. © 207/940-8753. www.designmuseum.org.

IMPERIAL WAR MUSEUM
Lambeth Rd., SE1 (Tube: Elephant & Castle or Lambeth North).

If you've got kids (especially boys), they will love this museum and its shop, which sells model airplanes, among other things. Note that you must pay admission if you arrive in the morning, but the museum is free between 4:30 and 6pm. © 207/416-5320. www.iwm.org.uk.

LONDON TRANSPORT MUSEUM
Covent Garden Piazza, WC2 (Tube: Covent Garden).

Although Covent Garden is great on Sunday, this small museum is a treasure any day. Children will love the sensational gift shop, which is also great for adults. There's a lot more here than you would expect; don't miss the thousands of postcards and posters of transport art (drawings that have decorated Tube and train stations since the early part of the century). © 207/379-6344. www.ltmuseum.co.uk.

MADAME TUSSAUDS
Marylebone Rd., NW1 (Tube: Baker St.).

Madame Tussauds is outrageously expensive to visit, and the lines out front can be heavy. But you can quit the scene and walk around to the side of the building, past the planetarium, and gain access to the gift shop. You'll have to knock on the door to be let in, as the tour ends in the shop.

The gift shop itself is rather large, with several rooms. Much of the merchandise is standard London souvenir stuff, but there are some items that are unique to Madame Tussauds. My favorite line is the group of items with the slogan "Some of the people I met in London"—pictures, shirts, and coffee cups of the famous, and infamous, as created in wax. ✆ 870/999-0046. www.madame-tussauds.co.uk.

NATIONAL GALLERY
Trafalgar Sq., WC2 (Tube: Charing Cross or Leicester Sq.).

Cards and calendars are the real finds here, but the posters aren't shabby either. The shop has been moved around the corner and is now free-standing. Although it does great Christmas cards, it also has innovative products based on the most popular works in the museum. For an original and witty gift, spend around £25 ($50) for a Swatch-like watch created from a great masterpiece by someone such as Vincent van Gogh. Where does time Gogh? Hmmm. ✆ 207/747-2885.

NATIONAL PORTRAIT GALLERY
2 St. Martin's Place, WC2 (Tube: Charing Cross).

Not to be confused with the National Gallery (above), the NPG shop is famous for gifts depicting famous faces—Winston Churchill playing cards, Shakespeare chocolates, and itty-bitty Christmas ornament figurines of England's finest, including Catherine of Aragon and Henry VIII. And for the Anglophile who has everything, there's a magnet set of the best of Shakespeare's insults. Guaranteed to liven up your fridge. www.npg.org.uk.

ROYAL ACADEMY OF ARTS
Burlington House, Piccadilly, W1 (Tube: Piccadilly Circus or Green Park).

Because of its tendency to do specialized shows that run for months, the Royal Academy also creates merchandise to tie in with its events—most of these items are made exclusively for the museum. I bought the Charlotte Salomon book during a recent exhibition; the museum told me it was the only store to sell it. © 207/300-8000. www.royalacademy.org.uk.

TATE MODERN
Tate Modern, Bankside, SE1 (Tube: Southwark).

The Tate Modern is the newer kid on the block, even though the block is quite amazing and in an old power plant. The gift shop is large; some of the "modern" line is also sold at Selfridges, although why anyone would buy a coffee mug that just says MODERN on it is beyond me. Maybe that's British wit for you. The postcard selection at the Tate Modern is disappointing.

World traveler: You can walk from the Tate Modern to other points of interest along the river including the restored Globe Theatre. © 207/887-8888. www.tate.org.uk.

TOWER OF LONDON
Tower Hill, EC3 (Tube: Tower Hill or London Bridge).

Just redone, reorganized, and more with-it, the Tower of London shops not only sell basic souvenirs and kitsch, but also make an attempt at reproductions, serious items, and stylish gifts, including costume-jewelry versions of the Crown Jewels. *Note:* The Tower of London is one of several properties managed by the Historic Royal Palaces; each has brought in new merchandise and beefed up the gift shops. © 0870/756-6060. www.hrp.org.uk.

VICTORIA & ALBERT MUSEUM
Cromwell Rd., SW7 (Tube: South Kensington).

You can bury my heart at Wounded Knee or simply in the foyer of the V&A—why these people took the best museum store in the world and tore it down is beyond me. They replaced it with some sorta *moderne* who-ha without as much merchandise and not a crumb of emotion, coziness, or even joy. Although the usual postcards and paper goods are still available, the shop sells jewelry, has some new lines created specifically to beef up the product range, and now even has a few items of clothing. It does mail order as well. Yawn. If they made me queen I can tell you what I'd fix first. © 207/942-2000. www.vam.ac.uk.

TUBE & TRAIN SHOPPING

Retail in train stations is already pretty sophisticated. People like to be able to grab what they need as they dash to and from the train; hence, there are always florists, candy shops, bookstores, and shoe-repair and coffee-bean stores. There are branches of **Knickerbox,** the lingerie chain, in several train stations.

Now then, you really want to know about Chunnel duty-free shopping. I wish I could give an answer that made sense, but I can't because the laws on duty-free have changed. Technically speaking, the Chunnel backs the abolishment of duty-free; there's no duty-free shopping on Chunnel trains and no duty-free shops at the station.

The good news is, there's still plenty of opportunity to part with your last pounds at St. Pancras before you board; it's just not duty-free shopping. There are two new shopping areas within the station: The Arcade, around the perimeter of the building, is a mix of independent and boutique retailers; and The Circle is good for essentials, featuring a **Marks & Spencer** with both clothing and a branch of **Simple Food,** a new concept store from Boots, and a large **WH Smith.** If you want a restaurant meal, you'll find a world-class brasserie and champagne bar, and there's a daily farmers' market to supply the makings of a healthy train picnic.

SOUVENIR SHOPPING

The best place to buy destination-specific souvenirs is from the street vendors who stretch across the "downtown" area— there are quite a few of them on Oxford Street from Marble Arch to Oxford Circus. There's another gaggle at Piccadilly Circus. The vendors seem to have the best prices in town. Much of this same merchandise is sold at Portobello Road Market on Saturdays.

If you're traveling out of season, you can bargain a little bit with the vendors, except at Buckingham Palace, where souvenirs are about the most expensive in town.

Royal commemoratives also make good souvenirs, but be warned that some of these things become collectors' items and are frequently very, very expensive. At the time of a royal event (such as a wedding or a coronation), the commemoratives seem to be a dime a dozen, but once they dry up, they are gone forever and become collectors' items.

If you're buying for an investment, get the best quality you can afford (branded ceramic vs. cheap) and try to pick up something that was created in a limited edition.

Because the Harrods name has become synonymous with London, Harrods souvenirs are also perfectly appropriate gifts. There are scads of them in every price range. Souvenirs are sold both on the street floor and in the lower level of the department store.

STREET MARKET SHOPPING

In London, many market areas are so famous that they have no specific street address. Although it's usually enough to mention the name of the market to a cabbie, ask your concierge whether you may need more in the way of directions. Buses usually service market areas, as does the Tube. There are markets that have everything from clothing and jewelry to books and art; some specialize in antiques. See p. 248 for more on serious antiques fairs, and p. 253 for the antiques supermarkets.

APPLE MARKET
Covent Garden, WC2 (Tube: Covent Garden).

The Apple Market is the official name of the marketplace held under the rooftops of Covent Garden in the courtyard space between the brick lanes of stores. This is a rotating affair that usually houses craftspeople, but antiques are sold only on Mondays to coordinate with the antiques goings-on across the way at the Jubilee Market (see below).

It's easiest to understand what the Apple Market is when you contrast it with the Jubilee Market. Jubilee is often junky; Apple is always classy, and it offers some of the best prices on British crafts.

The courtyard space is filled with vendors who set up little stalls and pin their wares to backdrops; sometimes boxes of loot are under the tables. The market is vetted, so the participants must apply for permission to sell and be granted an official space and day. If they show up on other days—which many do—they set up in stalls other than their regular one.

Many vendors take plastic; some will bargain if you buy a lot. They don't get set up before 10am, and many are still setting up at 11am. They do stay until dark, which is later in summer than in winter. www.uniquecoventgardenmarket.co.uk.

BERMONDSEY MARKET
Corner of Long Lane and Bermondsey St. at Bermondsey Sq., SE1 (Tube: London Bridge or Bermondsey).

This used to be one of my favorite adventures, but the venue's changed so much, I have trouble justifying the taxi fare and time spent en route. Thanks to real estate development, Bermondsey Market has been reduced in size to one small area, and many of the antiques dealers who've exhibited here for years have been forced out. Some have moved to Portobello

Road, some only do the big fairs like Newark, and some have retired or become eBay pros. The building that used to house the indoor stalls is now a condominium and many antiques shops in the area have fallen to the real estate boom. The good news? There's still a Friday market and there are still good deals to be had.

Also known as the New Caledonian Market, Bermondsey is open Friday only, from 5am to 2pm. Go early for the best deals. Take a torch (flashlight) and elbow the dealers who are there to buy it all. The dealers who are buying arrive as early as 5am and leave early, too. The official market opens at 7am, but by this time, the good pieces will have left, only to appear the next day on Portobello Road or in Camden Passage.

I usually go to Bermondsey around 9 or 10am; I am too old to be here before dawn, although I have indeed done it— and many regulars advise it. The market can be cold and nasty in winter, but it's still fun. Dress for the weather. © 207/525-6000. —S.R.L.

CABBAGES AND FROCKS SATURDAY MARKET
St. Marylebone Parish Church, Marylebone High St., W1, opposite the Conran Shop (Tube: Baker St.).

Created by the organizer of the London Designer Fashion Sales, this Saturday market supports new fashion designers, cottage industries, and organic foodstuffs. You'll find retro and vintage clothing mixed in with edgy new design, and handblown glass and jewelry by local artisans. There's children's clothing and ethnic food, as well. © 207/794-1636. www.cabbages andfrocks.co.uk.

CAMDEN PASSAGE
Upper St., Islington, N1 (Tube: Angel).

Like Bermondsey Market, Camden Passage has changed enormously in the past couple of years. Trendy boutiques and retail shops have moved into spaces vacated by antiques dealers, and

Sarah's Antiques Sources, Part 1

—Sarah Lahey

Although my antiques-buying trips take me out of town more often than not, there are several dealers in London who are always worth a look. Below are my favorite sources at Camden Passage.

When I first started my antiques business and realized I needed to buy at decent prices in order to make a profit, I would walk by **Raysil Antiques**, 12 The Mall Antiques Arcade, Camden Passage, gaze at the beautiful items in the window, and wish I could afford to buy it all. Silly me for not stopping in sooner: Not only are these incredible smalls reasonably priced, but the owner will also give discounts for cash, trade, and sometimes just for asking. The shop specializes in picture frames, enamel, and tortoise smalls. Lots of dresser-top sets, perfume bottles, and trinket jars.

Ann & Lou Wax, 49 Camden Passage, is a great source for hallmarked silver—everything from candlesticks to salvers to service for 24. I've purchase several sugar shakers and small trays here. **Kay Leyshon**, 15 Pierrepont Arcade, specializes in cutlery; you'll find a fabulous array ranging from single cheese knives with mother-of-pearl handles to boxed sets. Her prices are competitive and she sells top-quality goods. For beautiful wood boxes—tea caddies, glove boxes, and writing slopes—go to **Christina Tatum**, who is now located at 15 The Mall Antiques Arcade, just as you enter the building from the door closest to the Tube.

(See p. 260 for "Sarah's Antiques Sources, Part 2.")

former antiques collectives have been redesigned for residential use. There are still several antiques stores open every day in Camden Passage, and on Wednesday and Saturday the area becomes more crowded with stalls and stands selling just about everything imaginable.

I think the quality of merchandise in the outdoor stalls has become very junky, but the permanent shops still have a good collection of fine-quality antiques; there are also several vintage-clothing shops. Open Monday, Tuesday, Thursday, and Friday from 10am to 5pm; Wednesday and Saturday from 8am to 4pm. © 207/359-0190. —S.R.L.

JUBILEE MARKET
Covent Garden, WC2 (Tube: Covent Garden).

It's not fair to compare the Jubilee Market to Bermondsey because it's a small-time affair. It's not even fair to compare the Jubilee Market to the Apple Market, a few hundred yards away. It's basically a very touristy, teen-oriented, crass marketplace at the back of Covent Garden. On Mondays, however, all of the dealers (about 25 of 'em) are antiques dealers, and the market is much more fun. It never turns high-end, but it is affordable and very much worth a look. Please note this is a dregs-of-the-dealers market, and there's no telling what can be said to you. I had some anti-Semitic comments shouted at me by a very frightening dealer on one of my last visits. © 207/836-2139.

PICCADILLY MARKET
St. James's Church, 197 Piccadilly, W1 (Tube: Piccadilly Circus).

For 15 years now, the craftsmen and hippies have been meeting in the churchyard right on Piccadilly to sell a less-than-perfect-but-still-fun selection of sweaters, imports, and knickknacks. On Tuesdays, they sell antiques. There are too many imports for me to feel great about this market, but you can't fault either the location or the fun. I've been buying vintage clothing from the dealer in the far-right-hand corner (if you're facing the church from the street); there are Aran sweaters and kilts and other touristy items, as well as the usual incense burners from Nepal. The market is not very big or even very good, but I love it and think it's worth a browse. © 207/734-4511.

PORTOBELLO ROAD MARKET
Portobello Rd., W11 (Tube: Notting Hill Gate).

For me, Saturday in London means Portobello Road; Sunday means Greenwich. That's the way I love my London weekends, no matter what time of the year—even in slight drizzle.

I buy every time I'm in town. Not only antiques, but also dishes, old linens, buttons, reproductions of expensive botanicals that look great when framed, new items such as hand-knit sweaters and cashmere, and more, more, more.

Last trip, I saw some big changes, and heard rumors of more. The Chelsea Galleries has been remodeled and is now home to several new dealers. As you enter the gallery, visit the section on the immediate left—it's full of old friends who no longer exhibit at Bermondsey. My dealer friends report that The Good Fairy arcade is scheduled to close to be redeveloped into luxury flats with retail on the ground floor. Stay tuned.

Here's the skinny: The people with the stands and tables and stalls are there only on Saturday, from 6am to 4pm. The shops behind them are also open on Saturday, but they do not sell the stuff you see in the streets; so don't get your vendors mixed up. If you're a more serious antiques shopper, come back during the week and explore the three or four dozen serious shops (described on p. 259). Note that Fridays are growing in popularity with serious shoppers and dealers. No one at all is open Sunday.

Don't forget to browse the shops on Pembridge Road and Westbourne Grove after you've explored the full range of Portobello Road, and be sure to read chapter 4, "Shopping Neighborhoods," as there's some very exciting retail going on in either side of the market—particularly in Holland Park (p. 100) and in the part of Notting Hill that I call Ledbury Grove (p. 98)—which can lead you right over to Bayswater Road. There's also Golborne Road (p. 100). © 207/229-8354. www.portobello road.co.uk.

SAMPLE SALES

If you subscribe to any of the e-shopping newsletters, you know all about sample sales. What you might not know is that there are usually several in progress in London, most likely on a weekend. Maybe it's because the big stores have big sales only twice a year, or maybe the trend is just catching on, but you can find discounted goods year-round if you try. Your hotel concierge will hopefully have info on current sales events, but you can also check online at www.myfashionlife.com, www.stylebible.com, www.dailycandy.com (London edition, duh), www.billiondollarbabes.com, www.designerfashionsales.co.uk, and www.viewlondon.co.uk. October through March are good months for sales; and of course, that's when you'll get the best value in hotel rates and airfares.

SUPERMARKET SHOPPING

While most of the big British supermarkets are located outside the main tourist areas, they have become an important stop for local fashionistas who snap up great-looking clothes at affordable prices. Supermarkets have even developed their own brands, such as TU at **Sainsbury's** (www.sainsbury.co.uk), George at **ASDA** (www.asda.co.uk), and Florence&Fred at **Tesco** (www.tesco.com). You'll find clothes made from organic cotton at **Whole Foods** (www.wholefoods.com) on Kensington High Street.

DUTY-FREE SHOPPING

Duty-free was abolished for travel between European Union (E.U.) countries but is legal for those of us who are departing the E.U. So if you go from London to Paris, no duty-free; if you go from London to the United States (or Asia), there is duty-free.

The London airports have the best shopping in the world, but it may not be duty-free . . . or if it is, it might not be a bargain.

Some thoughts to keep in mind:

- Know the prices on your favorite scents before you buy in London or in any duty-free shop.
- Keep the airline duty-free prices with you for comparison, as onboard plane prices are often lower than those at airport duty-free shops.
- Look for coupons and promotional deals. The duty-free shop at LHR frequently offers pound-off vouchers or two-for-one promotions if you spend a certain amount.

About the best thing about duty-free in the London airport is the huge selection, including a wide selection of big names, such as Ferragamo and Hermès. The Ferragamo store does not carry my size (alas), but I know several people who swear by its airport bargains.

One last word: Anything you buy at a duty-free price is free only of *British* duty. You pay U.S. duty when you land (see "U.S. Customs & Duties," p. 44).

OUTLET SHOPPING

I am ambivalent in telling you about factory-outlet malls in the area. After all, you came to see London, right? Not an American-style, possibly American-owned outlet village similar to any of dozens in the U.S. On the other hand, with prices as high as they are in London, maybe you do want to get out of Dodge and shop the outlets.

The best outlet mall in the U.K. is **Bicester Village,** in Oxfordshire (www.bicestervillage.com; p. 278). Should you be going to the Dublin area, there is the **Kildare Village,** from the same owners (www.kildarevillage.com).

For an online guide to many of the outlets, try www.chic outletshopping.com.

Chapter Nine

....

ANTIQUES, USED BOOKS & COLLECTIBLES

LONDON, QUEEN OF IT ALL

It isn't possible to write a chapter that completely covers the antiques-and-collectible scene in London. There's just too much of it: the specialty dealers, the collectibles, the books and musical recordings—not to mention the fun you can have every day, even Sunday. This directory, though not complete, should provide enough to satisfy the novice shopper and to give the accomplished shopper (or dealer) a more than adequate overview.

The best thing for an American to remember about shopping for used items in London is that all prices are possible. You cannot get a good price until you know what the going price is; you cannot get a "bargain" until you know exactly what you are buying. Only by studying the finest examples can you decide whether an item is a fake, a copy, a handsome repro, or a deal.

Spend time seeing and learning. Ask a lot of questions.

BOOKING ANTIQUES

The London and Provincial Antique Dealers Association (LAPADA) publishes a paperback book called *Buying Antiques in Britain,* which is filled with advice, tips, resources, and advertising. Most of the ads have pictures. This is an invaluable little guide for those just getting started. You can buy it at antiques markets or through the association at 535 King's Rd., London SW10 (Tube: Sloane Sq.; © 207/823-3511; www. lapada.co.uk).

There are also several collectors' magazines sold on newsstands; these have information on fairs and auctions and editorials about collecting. They usually cost about £2 to £3 ($4–$6) an issue, but you'll enjoy them heartily. Try the *Antique Dealer and Collector's Guide* (www.antiquecollectorsguide. co.uk); *Antique and Collectors' Fayre* (www.luton.gov.uk), a more low-end collectors' magazine; and *Antique Collector* (www.antiquecollector.uk.com), published by the National Magazine Company and our favorite of the bunch. *The Collector,* published by Barrington Publications and often given away in shops, includes maps of London's antiques areas, as well as the usual advertising and lists. The BBC also has its own antiques magazine, price guide, and editorial based on its *Antiques Roadshow* experiences.

Most important to the trade is a tabloid newspaper called *Antiques Trade Gazette,* published each Wednesday. You can buy a single copy at some West End news agents or kiosks, or apply for an American subscription at www.antiquestrade gazette.com. A 1-year subscription mailed to the U.S. is £130 ($260).

Defining Antiques

The U.S. government defines an antique as any object that is 100 years old or older. There is some discussion that this rule may be changed to use the beginning of the 20th century as the new cutoff point. If you are sweating it out, ask before you leave home. If your purchase does not meet this definition, it is merely "used," and you pay duty on it at the regular rate.

ANTIQUES FAIRS

One of the best ways of learning something about the London antiques market is to attend a few antiques fairs. Antiques fairs come in several categories; some of the London ones are *vetted* (a committee certifies that all goods are genuine) and cost several pounds for admission. They may be associated with a charity or fancy-dress ball on opening night. Some fairs are vetted but less formal, and others are just plain old country fairs where anyone can show. By and large, the antiques-fair scene in London is serious, and normally the country shows are held in the country. In the city, it's strictly big time.

Although goods are sold at these fairs, I certainly don't buy them. In fact, I use these big-name fairs merely as an educational device to learn about quality; I cannot begin to afford to buy at these fairs. To be quite honest about it all, I sometimes find the price of admission to such an event more than I can bear—the thought of actually buying an item is almost obscene. On the other hand, CNN has reported that a Georgian table that sold in London for $50,000 some 15 years ago is today worth $150,000. Go figure.

Remember, only you know what's inside your wallet and your living room.

Antiquarian Book Fairs
Conference & Exhibition Centre, Hammersmith Rd., W14 (Tube: Kensington Olympia).

The Olympia Book Fair does not have much to do with furnishings; however, no good library would be complete without a rare book or two in its collection. Collectors and dealers swap stories and collectible items, including book illustrations and prints. www.olympiabookfair.com.

CHELSEA ANTIQUES FAIR
Chelsea Old Town Hall, King's Rd., SW3 (Tube: Sloane Sq.).

This vetted fair is held annually, in September. It has been going on for more than 60 years and will probably continue for another 260. Note that the venue is near several King's Road antiques galleries. Check the website for other Penman fairs in and around London. © 870/350-2442. www.penman-fairs. co.uk.

GROSVENOR HOUSE ART & ANTIQUES FAIR
Grosvenor House Hotel, Park Lane, W1 (Tube: Hyde Park Corner).

One of the best antiques fairs held in London, it's timed each year to run after the Derby (say *Darby*, darling) and before Ascot and Wimbledon. This is "the season," my dears. The top antiques dealers from all over Britain are invited to exhibit their best pieces, and everything except paintings must be more than 100 years old. A committee reviews all items for authenticity. This is one of the top social events of "the season," and watching the crowds is as much fun as examining the antiquities—some are the same vintage. There is a formal preview night before the opening. © 207/399-8100. www.grosvenorfair.co.uk.

INTERNATIONAL CERAMICS FAIR
Park Lane Hotel, Piccadilly, W1 (Tube: Hyde Park Corner or Green Park).

This has become an annual event with a substantial following. The fair usually coincides with the Grosvenor House Antiques Fair (see above) because they complement each other. Some of the antique-glass pieces on exhibit here are so delicate that the technique of getting them from the fair to your home would pose an interesting problem. All forms of ceramics are on exhibit, including some from other countries. © 207/734-5491. www.haughton.com/ceram.

K. M. ANTIQUES FAIRS

Rembrandt Hotel, 21 Thurloe Place, SW7 (Tube: South Kensington); Park Lane Hotel, Piccadilly, W1 (Tube: Hyde Park Corner or Green Park).

This small weekly fair is a great way to spend a couple of hours on Sunday afternoon. There's everything from silver to jewelry to furniture to textiles, all well priced. Along with familiar faces from Portobello Road, Grays Antique Market, and Bermondsey, there are also dealers from other parts of England, most of whom accept credit cards. Goods are mid- to high-quality. Check the website for the weekly location, which alternates between the Rembrandt Hotel and the Park Lane Hotel; the fair hours are 11am to 5pm. ✆ **208/674-8557.** www.kmfairs.com.

LITTLE CHELSEA ANTIQUES FAIR

Chelsea Old Town Hall, King's Rd., SW3 (Tube: Sloane Sq.).

This vetted fair is held twice a year, usually in April and October, with fewer than 100 participating dealers, and should not be confused with the Chelsea Antiques Fair (see above), a bigger and fancier show. ✆ **207/622-9647.**

OLYMPIA FINE ART & ANTIQUES FAIR

Olympia Exhibition Halls (National Hall), Hammersmith Rd., W14 (Tube: Kensington Olympia).

This is an international fair, with several hundred dealers participating. Stands are most often arranged as room sets. The dates of the event—held in winter, spring, and summer—are usually piggybacked with another big fair so that people can plan to attend both. Olympia is usually considered a less expensive fair than some of the other high-end ones, but it is not a jumble sale—it is a vetted event. ✆ **207/370-8234.** www. olympia-antiques.com.

STREET MARKETS

London street markets sell everything from vintage clothing to hand-knit sweaters to jewelry to Tibetan imports. Some specialize in antiques; others have antiques dealers on certain days of the week. See p. 237 for a complete rundown on **Bermondsey Market, Camden Passage, Jubilee Market, Portobello Road,** and the other markets of London.

MONSTER MARKETS

Just about every major British city has markets and fairs. Many are easily reached on BritRail and aren't that far away; Brighton, Lewes, and Bath are three cities that make good day trips for flea market lovers.

There are also some enormous fairs—held mostly for dealers—that are what legends are made of. More than 1,000 dealers convene at these events, so I call them the Monster Markets. The two biggies are Newark and Ardingly. Here are the facts:

- Newark has some 4,000 stands and is the largest market in Europe. Ardingly is a baby, with about half that. However, Ardingly is closer to London.
- These markets are actually for professionals, although anyone can go. There is an entrance charge; single-day admission varies from £5 to £10 ($10–$20), depending on when you go, or you can buy a multiday pass for £20 ($40).
- Markets are held several times a year, but are never in conflict with each other.
- Newark has new days and hours: Thursday from 10am to 6pm, and Friday from 8am to 5pm.
- Ardingly's hours are Tuesday from 10am to 6pm and Wednesday from 8am to 4pm.
- Both fairs are organized by **DMG Antiques Fairs** (© 1636/702-326; www.dmgantiquefairs.com).

Newark Fair Day Trip

—Sarah Lahey

I try to time my buying trips to coincide with the **Newark International Antiques & Collectors Fair,** as this is the biggest and best in the U.K. It attracts dealers from all over the world and has the best prices and inventory—it's the mother lode. God save the queen.

This was a 4-day event for several years, but has now returned to a 2-day format: Thursday and Friday. I always go on Thursday, as many of the dealers will be back in London for Bermondsey on Friday. In fact, some dealers even start packing up by midafternoon on the first day. Thursday is supposed to be VIP trade day, but in reality it's open to anyone willing to pay £20 ($40) to get in.

To get here, it's an easy 1-hour, 15-minute train ride from London's King's Cross Station. A courtesy coach waits at Newark Northgate Station to take you to the fair, about a 10-minute ride away. The driver will give you the departure times for the ride back; these are timed to get you to the station about 10 minutes before the London-bound train arrives. Easy as pie.

Now, I must warn you: Newark is no picnic. If you're looking for a pleasant day in the country shopping for antiques, forget Newark and see my suggestions in chapter 10. Aside from miles to trudge (you can rent a mobility scooter), there are few places to sit and take a break, and the wind may knock you down. Even if it's a beautiful day in London, bundle up in layers, as Newark can be very chilly. The food is generally bad; pack a lunch or head for the homemade doughnut stand near the pavilion buildings at the back of the fairgrounds. And while your bathroom habits are none of my business, I must tell you about the potty facilities, which are often what's called "Turkish style." Or worse.

That said, I love this fair and get a thrill with every bargain I find. I've filled my wheelie cart with tortoise and silver picture frames for £50 ($100), blue-and-white pottery platters for £35 ($70), Tunbridge inlaid writing slopes for £125

($250), brass open-twist candlesticks for £25 ($50), and on and on. The last time I went to Newark, I found the best deals ever. The devalued dollar has prompted dealers to adjust their prices in order to sell to the American trade. Both an ATM and a shipper are on-site; some dealers will accept plastic (though not traveler's checks) for an added surcharge.

Here's how I work it:

- Enter the fairgrounds, where you'll see a row of barracks-like buildings to your right. Make your way through these stalls; then backtrack and do the same with the old stables to the left of the entry.
- Continuing on, head straight down Marrison Way and Presidents Way to the Newark and Cedric Ford Pavilions for more indoor shopping. You'll find other indoor arcades in this area of the fairgrounds as well.
- After that, it's rows and rows and rows of outdoor tents. Some believe the prices are better in the tents; this may be true, but with some exceptions, the quality is lower and this isn't the stuff I buy for resale.

I've also done the Ardingly fair as a day trip. It's a good market; but the courtesy coach runs only on Wednesday, and I like to attend fairs on the first day. I once took a taxi from the station to the fairgrounds and arranged for the driver to pick me up later, but he never showed up. Another dealer took pity on me and gave me a ride, but I wouldn't repeat this experience. There's lots to buy at Ardingly, but once you've done Newark, you'll be spoiled forever.

ANTIQUES & COLLECTIBLES SUPERMARKETS

Antiques supermarkets have been created to give the smaller but established dealers a permanent place to set up and display their wares. These are covered shopping centers for antiques, collectibles, and junk. The fun is figuring out which is which.

The dealers' stalls change often, especially in these hard times; therefore, I'm not really going to point out faves. I suggest that you simply plow through. Don't forget that if you catch a rainy day in London town, an antiques supermarket can keep you busy for hours. The other advantage to shopping at a covered market is that very often other services are offered: There are repair shops at Grays, *bureaux de change* at Antiquarius and Grays, and places to eat at all of them.

ALFIES ANTIQUE MARKET
13–25 Church St., NW8 (Tube: Edgware Rd. or Marylebone).

Alfies is under the same ownership as Grays (see below) and houses 150 stalls. It's a series of blue town houses now joined together higgledy-piggledy, so you weave around a lot when you shop. The market itself is slowly evolving as true antiques are being replaced by pricey 20th-century furniture and lighting. But you can still find treasures; prices are moderate and dealers will deal. Because the location is a tad offbeat, the dealers tend to be a little funkier, so you get high quality and some value. This is perhaps one of the best supermarkets for seeing a lot and feeling that you're getting good value. It's not far from the Landmark Hotel. Open Tuesday through Saturday from 10am to 6pm. ℃ **207/723-6066.** www.alfiesantiques.com.

ANTIQUARIUS
131–141 King's Rd., SW3 (Tube: South Kensington).

Located right on King's Road in Chelsea in the thick of several antiques venues, Antiquarius could be mistaken for a theater from the outside. In actuality, it was constructed in an old snooker-hall building dating way back when. With more than 200 stalls, Antiquarius has gained a reputation for being the place to go for Art Nouveau and Art Deco pieces of every variety, from jewelry to furniture. There's also a very famous dealer (Sue Norman) for blue-and-white porcelain. Now then, I have it from an inside London source that if you're into celebrity spotting, all the big-time stars shop at this market (this is their idea of slumming it), but they never come on weekends. Open Monday through Saturday from 10am to 6pm. ☎ 207/823-3900. www.antiquarius.co.uk.

CHENIL GALLERIES
181–183 King's Rd., SW3 (Tube: Sloane Sq.).

Another one of the Chelsea galleries, this should be combined with your visit to Antiquarius (see above). Chenil Galleries is more of a shopping arcade with a long, thin thrust to the floor pattern and a swell chance to browse good merchandise; it's not intimidating at all. It's known for being a good place for antique medical instruments, as well as 17th- and 18th-century paintings and smaller items. There's a sensational dealer for costume jewelry. Chenil is another celebrity shopping venue. Open Monday through Saturday from 10am to 6pm. ☎ 207/351-5353.

GRAYS ANTIQUE MARKETS
58 Davies St., 1–7 Davies Mews, W1 (Tube: Bond St.).

These two buildings, located on the opposite ends of the same block, house more than 300 antiques stalls containing every variety of item, large and small. Davies Street conveniently intersects South Molton Street at one end and Brook Street at the other, placing it directly in the heart of the big-name-designer section of London.

When you need a break from fashion, it's easy to breeze over to Grays and rest your eyes on some breathtaking antique jewelry, bound to coordinate with any purchase you've made on Bond Street. **Evonne Antiques** (Stand 301) has one of the best selections of silver collectibles in London. Don't miss the river tributary that runs decoratively through the basement of the Davies Mews building. The shops are open Monday through Friday only, from 10am to 6pm. You can grab a bite in the cute cafe on the lowest floor. ☎ 207/629-7034. www.grays antiques.com.

THE OLD CINEMA
160 Chiswick High Rd., Chiswick, W4 (Tube: Turnham Green).

Bond Street to Chiswick High Road is a long way—I think Margaret Thatcher can tell you that—but if you're into a little more funky fun and want furniture, this is a department-store-turned-warehouse. It's open daily, with tons of stuff. Yes, you can get here on the Tube—exit the station and turn left, get to the next road, turn left again, and there it is.

There's a second warehouse at 157 Tower Bridge Rd., SE1 (Tube: Tower Bridge). You could combine it with a trip to Bermondsey Market (although Bermondsey is open only on Fri). © 208/995-4166. www.theoldcinema.co.uk.

ANTIQUES NEIGHBORHOODS

The best thing about antiques neighborhoods is that the good shops stay for a long while, and they attract other shops. High rents plague London, but these neighborhoods are nuggets where you can just wander and gawk.

Church Street/Marylebone (NW8)

This antiques area, on the way to **Alfies Antique Market** (see above), is fun and pretty much affordable. It's open Tuesday through Saturday from 10am to 6pm. Aside from Alfies, there's the **Gallery of Antique Costume & Textiles** (2 Church St.), as well as **Beverley** (no. 32), **Andrew Nebbett Antiques** (nos. 35–37), **Cristobal** (no. 26), **Bloch & Angell Antiques** (no. 22), and **Susie Cooper Ceramics** (no. 18). This is a kind of funky neighborhood where you can wear casual clothes and not have to worry about the posh, but be sure to also wander over to Marylebone High Street, the latest new yuppie area for chic (Tube: Edgware or Marylebone).

Covent Garden (WC2)

The neighborhoods surrounding Covent Garden, from Charing Cross to the Strand and over to Leicester Square, are known as important haunts for those interested in antique books, used books, stamps, records, and also ephemera. There are some famous antiques stores sprinkled in here, and many vintage-clothing shops, but it's mostly a paper-goods neighborhood.

But wait: On Mondays, there are two markets at Covent Garden—**Apple Market** and **Jubilee Market** (about 100 yards away from Apple Market). At the Apple Market, the stalls, which are normally devoted to craftspeople, are taken over by rather high-end antiques dealers. The Jubilee Market is more open—many price ranges are available, and there's more room for bargaining and fun. You may also find local publications about other markets and fairs at some of the dealers at Jubilee. I'm not talking hoity-toity antiques here, but you can have fun anyway. (Tube: Covent Garden.)

Fulham Road (SW3)

This is another way to get to the upper King's Road area, then the Fulham Road area, and then over toward Brompton Cross, depending on which way you want to walk. Look at a map!

There's a lot of stuff in the Fulham area between the Gloucester Road Tube stop and Brompton Cross, but within a special block or two of Fulham Road, you'll find either an antiques shop or a decorator showroom behind every door. Look in at **Today's Interiors** (no. 122), **Peter Lipitch** (no. 120), **Michael Foster** (no. 118), **Christophe Gollut** (no. 116), and **Colefax & Fowler** (no. 110). If you keep walking you'll hit Michelin House, which is where the **Conran Shop** (no. 81) has made history. At the other end of Fulham, check out **Judy Greenwood Antiques** (nos. 657–659) for elegant yet affordable continental furniture (Tube: Fulham Broadway or South Kensington).

Kensington Church Street (W8)

Shoppers, please note that few of these stores are open all day—if at all—on Saturday, so despite the fact that you're a stone's throw from Portobello Road, Saturday is not really the day to combine these neighborhoods.

Of course, a lot of serious Portobello Road dealers are open during the week—without the stalls and stands of the Saturday market—and you can combine the two neighborhoods that way. The best way to do so is to exit the Kensington High Street Tube, cross the street at the light, and head slightly to your right before you zig up Kensington Church Street.

A zillion shops and a small gallery line Kensington Church Street. Many of the stores are the small fancy kind that make you nervous to even press your nose to the glass. The closer you get to Notting Hill Gate (at the top of the hill you are climbing), the funkier the stores get.

The month of June can be tricky for shopping this area, as most of the good stores exhibit at the important shows and close up shop.

Oliver Sutton (34 Kensington Church St.) sells only Staffordshire figurines; peering through the window may suffice, as you can see quite a selection from the street. At no. 58, **Antiques Centre** is a small gallery with very serious dealers in their tiny glass cubbyholes. **Jonathan Horne** (no. 66) is another famous dealer for pottery, tiles, and ceramics—also very serious. **Simon Spero** (no. 109) has more pottery, and **Jeanette Hayhurst** (no. 32A) is a glass specialist. For a slight change of pottery pace, pop in at **New Century** (no. 69), a gallery that sells new art pottery that is hoped will become collectible. Don't miss three little dealers in a row along Peel Street, which have Kensington Church Street addresses (it's a corner junction)—among them is **Hope & Glory** (no. 131A), specializing in royal porcelain memorabilia. (Tube: Kensington High St. or Notting Hill Gate.)

Portobello Road (W11)

I just love this Saturday market event (described on p. 242). But don't think that it's just a flea market scene or that Saturday is the only day. Saturday is the main event, but during the week, especially on Friday, the regular shops are open without the Saturday circus atmosphere. And yep, there is a ton to see, even on a weekday. *Warning:* A few arcade galleries open Friday from noon to 4pm as well as Saturday, but are not otherwise open; there's also some vintage-clothing action on Sunday.

There are a few antiques markets here, with many stalls and dealers, as well as some free-standing shops on Portobello Road and on Westbourne Grove. Get here via Pembridge Road to check out a few more shops (especially strong for vintage clothing) or by walking up the hill via Kensington Church Street, where there are a few more dealers (see above). Note a change in postal codes; this is nothing to be alarmed about.

Without the Saturday circus, the main action on Portobello Road is the number of galleries packed with dealers. These are often called arcades. Check out **Chelsea Galleries** (nos. 67–73), **Van** (no. 105), **Admiral Vernon Antique Market** (nos. 141–149), and **Lipka's Arcade** (284 Westbourne Grove). (Tube: Notting Hill Gate or Kensington High St.)

King's Road (SW3)

For upscale shoppers, the better part of King's Road is the middle 200 to 300 range. There are several antiques malls here, as well as lots of showrooms. In terms of visual stimulation and the possibility of affording something nice, this neighborhood may offer the best combination of the right things. Other areas are cheaper, but this one has a trendiness that can't be ignored, even in antiques.

Whatever you do, check out **Steinberg & Tolkien** (193 King's Rd.), extraordinary dealers in vintage clothing, costume

Sarah's Antiques Sources, Part 2

—Sarah Lahey

My London antiques-buying trips are usually more outside of London than inside, as I find great bargains in the country—and besides, getting out of town is half the fun. There are, however, several dealers in town who always have good stock and fair prices. Some of them also sell at Newark and other fairs. Below are my favorite Portobello Road sources.

My antiques clients sometimes call me the "tortoise lady" because I always have lots of silver and shell frames, boxes, and decorative knickknacks. **Michael Goldstone & Klaus Schilling,** Chelsea Galleries, 67 Portobello Rd., is a good source for high-quality tortoiseshell goods at reasonable prices. Also check out **Chanticleer Antiques** in the Admiral Vernon Arcade, 141–149 Portobello Rd. Inventory can be hit-or-miss, but stop by and you might luck out. (By the way, it's okay to bring these items back into the U.S. as long as they're over 100 years old. And you'll pay no duty on vetted antiques.)

Along with my "tortoise" identity, I'm also known at the local shows as the "box lady." I've loved and collected English tea caddies, writing slopes, jewelry and glove boxes, and many others for years; in fact, it was my growing stash of boxes that convinced me I should start an antiques business. I'd guess that over half of my inventory comes from **M. J. Barham,** 83 Portobello Rd. The small shop is packed sky-high with the most gorgeous boxes you'll ever see—all in perfect condition and all reasonably priced, beginning at around £125 ($250) for simple tea caddies and going up to £300 ($600) or more for a large writing slope. You'll also find a good selection of inkwells, candlesticks, and barware. This is my favorite shop on Portobello Road.

Judy Fox Antiques, 81 Portobello Rd., has beautiful high-end furnishings, most of it too ornate and expensive for my taste; however, I come here to buy Judy's incredible picture frames. She takes old Victorian (and earlier) frames, refurbishes them, and adds silk moire fabric to make the most elegant frames in town. Very expensive, but trade discounts are offered. This shop is one of the few on Portobello Road that keeps regular hours during the week.

Abras Gallery, 292 Westbourne Grove, off Portobello Road, doesn't sell antiques, but I'm including it in this section as my best source for new hallmarked silver frames. It stocks hundreds of choices in all shapes and sizes. You can choose from velvet or wood backs, plain or ornate frames, large or small. I always try to keep several on hand—they make great christening or wedding gifts. All are in stock, and quantity discounts are given to all customers. (See p. 240 for "Sarah's Antiques Sources, Part 1.")

jewelry, and the like, with two floors of space and drool-over pieces, including old Chanel and tons o' Pucci. The owner is American. (Tube: Fulham Broadway or Sloane Sq.)

Lower Sloane (SW3)

I call the area including Pimlico Road, Ebury Road, and Lower Sloane Street simply Lower Sloane. It is an extension of Sloane Street, after you pass Sloane Square. Most of the dealers here are fancy, as is the clientele, but everyone is a tad more approachable than the high-end, don't-touch crowd. There are a lot of showrooms here, as well as antiques shops. If you're on Sloane Street, instead of turning to the right to get to King's Road, walk straight and follow Lower Sloane Street to Pimlico Road. Convenient for cutting back to King's Road and Chelsea antiques shops. (Tube: Sloane Sq.)

Mayfair & Mount Street (W1)

This is the most expensive part of London; the prices in the antiques shops reflect the rents and the unwritten law that objects displayed in windows must be dripping with ormolu. New Bond Street is the main source, but don't forget side streets such as Conduit Street, Old Bond Street, Vigo Street, and Jermyn Street. Mayfair is also headquarters for several auction houses, decorating firms, and big-time dealers. If you're just looking, make sure you're dressed to kill. If you're serious, you should probably have an appointment or a letter of introduction or both.

If you like a fancy but good market, browse **Grays Antique Markets** (p. 255). If you like hoity with your toity, don't miss **Mallett & Son** (141 New Bond St.), **S. J. Phillips Ltd.** (139 New Bond St.), or **Wartski** (14 Grafton St.).

Mount Street begins, appropriately enough, with an **American Express** office (no. 89), where you will undoubtedly have to go for more cash. As a shopping destination, Mount Street is easy to miss because it's set back a little bit. It's sort of a 2-block job, stretching from behind the Dorchester right to Berkeley Square, a sneeze from Bond Street. Here you'll find a group of excellent antiques shops; my favorite on this street is **Stair & Co.** (no. 14). Then pass the Connaught to connect to more of Mount Street and **Blairman and Sons** (no. 119).

Tower Bridge (SE1)

Hidden in the shadows of the imposing Tower Bridge, there's a small enclave of informal (some are pretty grungy) antiques shops that cater mostly to locals and dealers. *Important note:* Do not get Tower Bridge and London Bridge mixed up or you will be in the wrong place.

The focus is on furniture, but there are accessories and smalls as well, so dress down and go with a sense of adventure. Begin at the two-story former warehouse of tin box manufacturer Wyatt & Co., which has been transformed into **Tower Bridge Antiques** (71 Tanner St.); it's now full of furniture in all shapes, sizes, and conditions, but you'll also find lights, mirrors, and great paintings. On down Tower Bridge Road, don't miss **Capital Antiques** (168a Tower Bridge Rd.) and **Europa House Antiques** (160 Tower Bridge Rd.), both of which have furniture and smalls.

This truly is an area of contrasts. As you leave the shabby side streets and return to the riverside, you'll be rewarded for your sleuthing efforts with a choice of lunch spots including **Butler's Wharf Chop House** in the Butler's Wharf building, 36D Shad Thames, and **The Blue Bird Café** in the Design Museum, also on Shad Thames.

World traveler: Borough Market (a Sat-only affair) is located between London Bridge and Tower Bridge, closer to Tower Bridge. See p. 145.

ANTIQUARIAN BOOKS, MAPS & AUTOGRAPHS

If you collect first editions or antiquarian books, or even if you're just seeking a title that's currently out of print, flip this way.

The West End

BERNARD QUARITCH LTD.
5–8 Lower John St., Golden Sq., W1 (Tube: Piccadilly Circus).

In October 1847, Bernard Quaritch came to London, determined to become a bookseller. He succeeded, attracting along the way clients such as prime ministers William Gladstone and Benjamin Disraeli, publishing Edward FitzGerald's *The Rubáiyát of Omar Khayyám,* and being eulogized by the *Times* as "the greatest bookseller who ever lived."

Quaritch Ltd. has attained an international reputation. Boasting perhaps the largest stock of antiquarian books in London and 32 experts in fields as diverse as Arabic, bibliography, and psychiatry, Quaritch maintains an atmosphere that is quiet yet not formal. The firm attends auctions on the Continent (sometimes bidding for the British Museum) and assembles collections that can run the gamut from Tibet and Henry James to rigging and shipbuilding.

Because of its size, Quaritch is able to airfreight its own crate of books to New York once a week; the contents are then sent separately to clients via UPS, bypassing the post office and possibly careless (and financially damaging) handling. ☎ 207/734-2983. www.quaritch.com.

G. HEYWOOD HILL LTD.
10 Curzon St., W1 (Tube: Green Park).

If Maggs (see below) is a showplace for books and autographs of the illustrious, nearby G. Heywood Hill represents the cramped, Dickensian bookshop most visitors associate with literary London. For 50 years, Heywood has been a beacon to authors, librarians, and collectors around the world.

The shop's limited space is packed to the rafters—yet this is probably the only bookseller in London that will refuse to sell books that don't meet its Olympian standards. Antiquarian books pay the bills, but Heywood also stocks contemporary titles on a variety of subjects merely to satisfy its clients' needs. The shop specializes in books on design, architecture, gardening, and the allied decorative arts. There's also an extensive collection of biographies and a subspecialty in literary criticism.

Heywood's bookishness has attracted many writers as steady customers, including Evelyn Waugh, Anthony Powell, Nancy Mitford (who worked here during World War II), and other Waughs, Mitfords, and Sitwells for several generations. The shop's family feeling, as well as its terrifically high standards, often ensures it first crack at extensive private libraries when they become available.

The location is right around the corner from the Park Lane and Connaught hotels, off Berkeley Square. ☎ 207/629-0647. www.heywoodhill.com.

JONATHAN POTTER LTD.
125 New Bond St., W1 (Tube: Bond St.).

I got a letter from William Latey asking that Jonathan Potter, a gallery specializing in antique maps, be included in these pages. This firm is 25 years old, as opposed to 120 like some of the other sources, but exhibits regularly in the United States. In addition to maps, it stocks atlases, antique globes, and books on cartography. It is a member of BADA (that's British Antique Dealers' Association). ℘ **207/491-3520.** www.jpmaps.co.uk.

MAGGS BROS. LTD.
50 Berkeley Sq., W1 (Tube: Green Park).

Although it had been rumored for years that the Maggs mansion, built in 1740, was haunted, no ghosts were spotted during World War II, when fire-watch rules required at least one Maggs employee to sleep on the premises each night. Of course, the house next door was completely destroyed, and the one across Berkeley Square suffered heavy damage—but there are no ghosts.

Such eccentricities are allowed any bookseller with an enormous collection of travel books, militaria, maps, illuminated manuscripts, autographs, and Orientalia. Maggs's travel section alone would fill the ordinary bookstore with its first-edition, on-the-spot reminiscences by the likes of Stanley, Livingstone, Robert F. Scott, and Admiral Byrd. Ten specialists attend auctions around the world on a regular basis. Maggs also boasts a sizable autograph collection. ℘ **207/493-7160.** www.maggs.com.

SOTHERAN'S OF SACKVILLE STREET
2–5 Sackville St., Piccadilly, W1 (Tube: Piccadilly Circus).

Sotheran's has been selling books since 1761 in York and has been established in London since 1815. Charles Dickens was a regular customer, and when he died, Sotheran's sold his library. The firm also purchased a number of volumes from Winston Churchill's library and was the agent for the sale of Sir Isaac Newton's library to Cambridge.

The firm specializes in ornithology and natural science. The atmosphere is neat, formal, and as silent as a library. A lower floor is given over exclusively to antiquarian prints and maps, drawings by book illustrators such as Kate Greenaway and Arthur Rackham, sporting prints, and military and naval subjects. Sotheran's offers search services; hand-binds serial publications, such as the Bills and Acts of Parliament; restores books; and also maintains subscriptions to overseas periodicals for its customers. ✆ 207/439-6151. www.sotherans.co.uk.

Charing Cross Road

Visitors searching for 84 Charing Cross Rd. will be disappointed to find a record store, not the bookshop that inspired Helene Hanff's bestseller; nevertheless, the long street is filled with other equally engaging book emporiums, all of which are open Monday through Saturday from around 9am to 6pm.

    Cecil Court, a block-long street between Charing Cross Road and St. Martin's Lane, has some charming secondhand bookshops. Most are open Monday through Saturday from 9:30am to 6pm. Start with **Tindley & Chapman,** 4 Cecil Court, WC2 (Tube: Leicester Sq.; ✆ 207/240-2161).

    Long Acre, the "Main Street" of Covent Garden, is also lined with bookstores on both sides of the road; it is a block from Cecil Court.

FOYLES
113–119 Charing Cross Rd., WC2 (Tube: Leicester Sq.).

There's a small antiquarian library here within London's largest bookstore. There's also a branch in Selfridges on Oxford. See p. 130 for more details on Foyles. ✆ 207/437-5660. www.foyles. co.uk.

FRANCIS EDWARDS
13 Great Newport St., Charing Cross Rd., WC2 (Tube: Leicester Sq.).

Francis Edwards is the leading antiquarian bookseller on the street. It carries natural history and militaria. Open Monday through Friday from 9am to 5pm. ✆ 207/240-7279. www. francisedwards.co.uk.

STANFORDS
12–14 Long Acre, WC2 (Tube: Covent Garden).

This firm, founded in 1853 by Edward Stanford, is a mecca for maps, charts, atlases, and travel books. A particular specialty is guides for mountain climbers, skiers, and other outdoor types. Open Monday through Friday from 9am to 5:30pm, Saturday from 10am to 4pm. © 207/836-1321. www.stanfords.co.uk.

COLLECTIBLES

Shopping for the real thing in London is a tricky business. Remember:

- England is indeed a nation of shopkeepers.
- Many of the shops they keep are crammed with collectibles.
- Some of these collectibles are as real as St. George's flagon or that grand old American collectible, the Brooklyn Bridge.

Coins & Medals

Collectors' note: In addition to the Spink publication (described below), there are also periodicals called *Coin News* and *Medal News* and a book, *Coin Yearbook,* all published by Token Publishers. www.tokenpublishing.com.

B. A. SEABY LTD.
136 Regent St., W1 (Tube: Bond St.).

Early coins bearing the likenesses of royalty from Corinth, Phoenicia, and Rome rub shoulders with tradesmen's tokens issued by coopers in Dover and fishmongers in Margate; each is presented with care, panache, and the necessary historical background. The firm is deep in antiquarian coins, and that interest has led to sidelines such as collections of jewelry and copperplate from ancient Greece, Rome, and Jerusalem. Seaby publishes the bimonthly *Coin & Medal Bulletin,* which is likely to contain scholarly pieces related to archaeological finds, as well as price lists of coins. Open Monday through Friday from 9:30am to 5pm.

SPINK
69 Southampton Row, Bloomsbury, WC1 (Tube: Russell Sq. or Holborn).

If you've yearned for those glitzy costume jewelry medals, you'll all-out faint and go stark raving mad with delight when you see the original medals that inspired the current fad. Why was a man always so dashing in his uniform? Because of his medals, of course. And, chances are, they came from Spink. Spink has tremendous stock in Orientalia, paperweights, and Greek and Roman coins, as well as an ample supply of early English hammered coins in gold and silver and milled pieces dating back to the late 1600s; however, as Hamleys is to toys, so Spink is to medals. Along with sheer size, Spink offers an expertise born of creating decorations for Great Britain and 65 other countries. The company also issues the monthly *Spink Numismatic Circular,* which includes large sections on medals, orders, and decorations. Open Monday through Friday from 9:30am to 5:30pm. © 207/563-4000. www.spink.com.

Scientific Instruments

Collectors' note: Collectors of scientific instruments should be aware of two specialty publications: *Rittenhouse Journal of the American Scientific Instrument Enterprise,* published by David and Yola Coffeen and Raymond V. Giordano, and *Bulletin of the Scientific Instrument Society,* published by the Scientific Instrument Society.

TREVOR PHILIP & SONS LTD.
75A Jermyn St., SW1 (Tube: Piccadilly Circus or Green Park).

Philip & Sons carries gyroscopes, English drafting instruments, sundials, stethoscopes, and a selection of books about scientific instruments. The shop also sells miniature instruments, such as pocket botanical microscopes, pocket globes, and exquisite orreries—small clockwork representations of the solar system. Open Monday through Friday from 10am to 6pm. © 207/930-2954. www.trevorphilip.com.

Stamps

The Strand—and offshoots such as King Street and Cecil Court—is a magnet for philatelists in London. All the shops are in the Strand area, although we label some as in Charing Cross Road/Covent Garden; this is the same neighborhood and is an easy walk (Tube: Charing Cross).

Collectors' and shoppers' note: Most of these shops are open Monday through Friday from 10am to 5pm (Gibbons opens at 9am) and the same hours Saturday, except for Gibbons, 9:30am to 5:30pm on Saturdays; however, some merchants may have odd hours, or close to exhibit at a show, so it's a good idea to call.

There are several periodicals for stamp collectors, including *Stamp News*. Collectors should also keep in mind the large auction houses: **Phillips** (p. 214) has a postage-stamp auction nearly every Thursday, and **Christie's** (p. 214) recently offered a collection that included proofs and essays from Bradbury, Wilkinson & Co., which has printed British stamps and bank notes for nearly 150 years.

STAMP-CENTRE
79 The Strand, WC2 (Tube: Charing Cross).

Three dealers operate as Stamp-Centre and deal in Commonwealth material. Even though Gibbons has a larger stock in this area, these dealers often come up with particular items from India or Australia that the big kid on the block doesn't stock. Moreover, Stamp-Centre isn't pricey and is particularly patient with younger collectors. If you've gone to the trouble to seek the neighborhood, don't blow it now—you must stop in here. ✆ 207/836-2341. www.stamp-centre.co.uk.

STANLEY GIBBONS LTD.
399 The Strand, WC2 (Tube: Charing Cross).

Stanley Gibbons has the largest collection of British Empire stamp material in the world, as well as the most complete selection of stamp accessories—albums, tweezers, and perforation gauges—and its own well-researched catalogs.

Gibbons also sells extraordinary philatelic material. We were once shown an issued but unused full block of 12 of the Twopenny Blue with the original gum. Brilliantly colored and lettered "SG-TL" in the lower left- and right-hand corners (to prevent counterfeiting), this museum-quality piece was offered at a mere £12,000 ($24,000).

Such lofty material is viewed in private, secure surroundings on the second floor. On a more mundane level—the ground floor—Gibbons stocks a few topics such as birds and the royal family, and has specialists in first-day covers, plate blocks, precancels, overprints, color variations, and so on. The firm gave up the coin and medal business several years ago but now carries a full selection of postcards and pertinent literature.

Gibbons is impossibly famous and therefore impossibly crowded—you may get less service, and it may not have what you are looking for. Don't be afraid to wander around the neighborhood and try the competition. Smaller and lesser-known dealers may be more fun. ✆ 207/836-8444.

Also try:

CHRISTIE'S
8 King St., SW1 (Tube: Green Park).
✆ 207/839-9060. www.christies.com.

HARMERS
111 Power Rd., Chiswick, W4 (Tube: Gunnersbury).
✆ 208/747-6100. www.harmers.com.

SOTHEBY'S
34–35 New Bond St., W1 (Tube: Bond St.).
✆ 207/293-5000. www.sothebys.com.

SPINK
69 Southampton Row, Bloomsbury, WC1 (Tube: Russell Sq.
or Holborn).
✆ 207/563-4000. www.spink.com.

Dolls & Toys

Parents and grandparents, please note: This section, in keeping with this chapter's theme, covers only collectible dolls and
toys. ***Collectors' note:*** *Antique Toy World* covers these collectibles on a monthly basis.

LONDON TOY AND MODEL MUSEUM
23 Craven Hill Rd., W2 (Tube: Paddington).

In a case devoted to dolls based on the royal family, a German-
made Princess Elizabeth doll from 1932 sits next to a Princess
Anne doll made in 1953. This royal rite of passage from child
to queen is nearly overshadowed by other dolls at the museum—
poured-wax dolls; bisque (china) dolls; a wax-headed Quaker
lady in her original costume from 1840; and a Topsy Turvy doll,
which can be either white or black, depending on the owner's
fancy. In addition to dolls, the museum has 25,000 Matchbox
and Corgi miniature cars, several working rocking horses, a collection of Paddington bears, an entire room of toy trains, and
a display of toy soldiers from Pierce Carlson.

The latest addition (requiring a separate admission fee) is
the Baywest exhibit, a computer-controlled model of 1,000
houses, 50,000 lights, a railway system, and a helicopter. There
are also two smaller, coin-operated versions by the same

designer—a snow scene and a small town at twilight. Open Tuesday through Saturday from 10am to 5:30pm, Sunday from 11am to 5pm. Admission is £4.95 ($9.90) for adults, £2.95 ($5.90) for children. © 207/706-8000.

POLLOCK'S TOY MUSEUM
1 Scala St., at Whitfield St., W1 (Tube: Goodge St.).

Nearly 100 years ago, Robert Louis Stevenson wrote, "If you love art, folly, or the bright eyes of children, speed to Pollock's." Thousands still do—and find a treasure island of toys housed in two adjoining buildings overflowing with dolls, teddy bears, tin toys, puppets, and folk toys from Europe, India, Africa, China, and Japan.

Exhibits of mechanical toys and construction sets fill the lower floor of Pollock's Toy Museum; the second story has exhibits of the paper "toy theaters" and cutout actors and actresses that have fired the imagination of British children for generations. Museum hours are Monday through Saturday from 10am to 5pm. Admission is £3 ($6) for adults, £1.50 ($3) for children. © 207/636-3452. www.pollockstoymuseum.com.

In addition to the museum, there's **Pollock's Toyshop,** 44 The Market, Covent Garden, WC2 (Tube: Covent Garden; © 207/379-7866; www.pollocks-coventgarden.co.uk), set up when the original was destroyed in the Blitz. The shop sells theaters and dolls; open Monday through Saturday from 10am to 8pm.

Comic Books

Ten years ago, there were small comic-book departments in some of the better bookstores. Now, according to the comic cognoscenti, there are more than 40 comic book specialty stores in Great Britain and a baker's dozen in London, each with a slightly different appeal.

FORBIDDEN PLANET
179 Shaftesbury Ave., WC2 (Tube: Tottenham Court Rd.).

You are about to enter three strange worlds, one inhabited by aliens, a second in which fantasy princes and monsters reign supreme, and yet a third where comic book characters rule—but that's not all. At Forbidden Planet, you'll also find videotapes of all James Bond movies, trading cards from the original *Batman* movie, and the complete works of Al Capp *(Li'l Abner)*. It's a comic-aholic's dream. Where else would you find the unauthorized biography of *Superman* baddie Lex Luthor? The stock is vast, with some 10,000 different titles available. (Parents dragging kids should be aware that some items are decidedly not for family consumption, such as *The Adventures of Johnny Condom.*)

Although the emphasis is on new comic heroes, Dick Tracy, Superman, and Little Lulu are represented, as is, believe it or not, cowboy hero Tom Mix, who died 40 years before current comic collectors were born. The shop also has a limited stock of back issues and offers fantasy masks, an incredibly complete assortment of science fiction books and videos, and toys, such as miniature versions of the original *Starship Enterprise.* © 207/420-3666. www.forbiddenplanet.com.

GOSH!
39 Great Russell St., WC1 (Tube: Holborn or Tottenham Court Rd.).

Across from the British Museum on Great Russell Street is Gosh!, which dispensed with signs during the *Batman* craze and just hung an image of the Caped Crusader to attract passersby. Gosh! has a serene atmosphere very much in tune with museumgoers. An employee confided, "We're dependent on the museum trade." As a result, you'll find, along with comics, complete histories of faded favorites, such as *Captain Easy* and *Wash Tubbs* in eight volumes, plus scholarly histories of cartoon strips and comic books. Open daily from 10am to 6pm (until 7pm Thurs–Fri). © 207/636-1011. www.goshlondon.com.

THE TINTIN SHOP
34 Floral St., WC2 (Tube: Covent Garden).

If you know Thomson from Thompson and could pick the evil Rastapopoulos out of a police lineup, you'll be in heaven at this all-Tintin shop near Covent Garden. Tintin turned 60 recently, and his exploits have charmed children all over the world in more than 50 languages—including Esperanto. The shop features all 22 Tintin adventures and other merchandise, including drawing pads and posters (both unframed and framed). There's even a wool Tintin sweater if you're feeling expansive. If your kids have not yet discovered Tintin, now's the time. ℂ 207/836-1131. www.thetintinshop.uk.com.

Cigarette Cards

Just as baseball cards became wildly popular in the United States beginning in 1981, so cigarette cards have become highly collectible in England. Sets that used to sell for £3 ($6) in 1986 are now fetching £17 ($34).

You might expect that cigarette-card dealers would be proliferating; just the reverse is true. With more cards being held by collectors (and investors), the number of sets that used to turn over at flea markets and in antiques stores specializing in ephemera has decreased. One of the best shops specializing in cards is the following.

MURRAY CARDS LTD.
51 Watford Way, Hendon Central, NW4 (Tube: Hendon Central).

Murray has become the mecca for cigarette-card collectors around the world. Since 1967, the company has published the only annual price catalog in the field. Murray has also been active reprinting valuable old sets (clearly marked REPRINT) and publishing its own checklists and books; a recent one, *Half Time*, covers English football (soccer) cards.

Murray's shop is served by the Hendon Central stop on the Northern Line. If you've got any idea at all of becoming serious about cigarette cards, the trip to Hendon is an absolute must. To save time for all concerned, come equipped with a list of the sets you want and their manufacturers' names. © 208/202-5688. www.murraycards.com.

CDs & Records for Collectors

If the impersonality and sheer size of **HMV** and **Virgin** have gotten you down, consider the following specialty sources for new and used CDs, LPs, and rare 78s. Otherwise, turn to p. 137 for the address of the megastore near you.

JAZZ & CLASSICAL SPECIALTY SHOPS

LES ALDRICH
98 Fortis Green Rd., N10 (Bus: 43 or 134).

This shop has the largest stock list of classical music in London. There's also a special children's classical section where you'll find sheet music for budding musicians. In addition to classical, there's some pop (of the Norah Jones variety), and a good jazz section that continues to grow each year. © 208/883-5631.

RAY'S JAZZ SHOP
Foyles, 113–119 Charing Cross Rd., WC2 (Tube: Tottenham Court Rd.).

Foyles gave Ray's Jazz a new home when skyrocketing rents forced the jazz institution to close its doors on Shaftesbury Avenue. Wallow here in all things jazz: LPs, CDs, books, and magazines. The staff is very helpful and more knowledgeable than the employees in most megastores' jazz departments. © 207/440-3205. www.foyles.co.uk.

SECONDHAND RECORDS

If the record you're looking for can't be found by browsing the specialty stores, there are always secondhand shops; however, such stores are almost as used as the merchandise they sell. They're generally dirty, dusty, and jumbled up. (We like that in bookstores, but hate it in record stores.)

INTOXICA!
231 Portobello Rd. (Tube: Ladbroke Grove).

This shop stocks all vinyl, and the bulk of the inventory is 1960s. The upstairs houses some discs from the '50s and soundtracks from the '60s and '70s, while you'll find R&B, blues, soul, and rock 'n' roll on the downstairs shelves. Leopard prints and voodoo figures make the record-buying experience memorable. ✆ 207/229-8010.

More secondhand:

CHEAPO CHEAPO RECORDS
53 Rupert St., W1 (Tube: Piccadilly Circus).
✆ 207/437-8272.

MINUS ZERO RECORDS/STANK OUT COLLECTORS RECORDS
2 Blenheim Crescent, W11 (Tube: Ladbroke Grove or Notting Hill Gate).
✆ 207/229-5424.

ON THE BEAT
22 Hanway St., W1 (Tube: Tottenham Court Rd.).
✆ 207/637-8934.

Chapter Ten

....

LONDON DAY TRIPS

By now, you know how expensive London has become since the dollar has plummeted, and you also know that things tend to cost less outside the greater London area. Do you feel a waltz coming on? Perhaps a day trip?

Although locals grumble and mumble about train service, London has many rail stations and an extensive network that can get you just about anywhere outside of the city for a day trip. And yes, technically, you could even make it to Edinburgh and back.

Depending on your interests, you can easily ride the rails to greater deals, be they name-brand designer duds or antiques and collectibles. It just takes time, patience, and a little bit of know-how.

If you're planning 1 or 2 days out, it's probably cheaper to buy tickets at the station on an as-you-go basis, but if you're planning a number of day trips, or traveling to faraway places, consider buying a BritRail pass. Like the Eurail Pass, it's available in many combinations and prices, so go online and decide what makes the most sense for you and your group. Railpass.com almost always has a deal. I just found BritRail passes discounted 20% for travel between November and March, and a savings of 50% if you buy three or more BritRail Party Passes, good for a minimum of three people traveling together.

BICESTER: OUTLETS 'R' US

I feel very mixed about sending you to a factory-outlet village when you may have only a few days in London, so I'll just give you some information and let you decide for yourself. I have been to Bicester (say *Bista*) but not McArthurGlen's Great Western, in Swindon. Below are the basics on Bicester Village.

BICESTER VILLAGE
50 Pringle Dr., Bicester, Oxfordshire.

This center is co-owned by an American firm and looks like other American factory-outlet villages. Tenants include Aquascutum, Burberry, Cath Kidston, Dior, DKNY, Molton Brown, Polo Ralph Lauren, and Racing Green. There are more than 60 outlets, the usual food court, a kiddie play area, and so on.

Bicester is about a 70-minute drive from London; parking is free. You can also get here by train or tour bus. Chiltern Railways operates daily service from London's Marylebone Station to Bicester North Station; ask for a through ticket to Bicester Village that includes bus travel to and from Bicester North Station. Open Monday, Tuesday, Wednesday, and Sunday from 10am to 6pm; Thursday, Friday, and Saturday 10am to 7pm. © 1869/323-200. www.bicestervillage.com.

LEWES

—Sarah Lahey

I actually discovered Lewes (say *Louis*) by accident. I had planned a day trip to Brighton and the Lanes antiques district, so I took an early train, figuring I would have time to see the pavilion, buy antiques, and arrange for shipping if necessary. I grabbed a taxi at the Brighton station and told the driver to take me to the antiques neighborhood; I even had a map with the Lanes highlighted.

London Day Trips

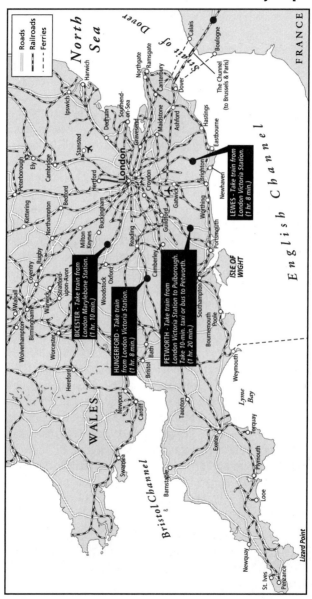

BICESTER - Take train from London Marylebone Station. (1 hr. 10 min.)

HUNGERFORD - Take train from London Victoria Station. (1 hr. 8 min.)

PETWORTH - Take train from London Victoria Station to Pulborough. Take 10-min. taxi or bus to Petworth. (1 hr. 20 min.)

LEWES - Take train from London Victoria Station. (1 hr. 8 min.)

Well, let's just say that the Lanes isn't the antique mecca it used to be, as many of the shops have been forced out by high rents and real estate development. One of the few remaining dealers suggested I go to nearby Lewes, so I went back to the Brighton train station; 15 minutes later, I was in Lewes.

Located in East Sussex, Lewes is a medieval town with narrow streets and twisting lanes, all unchanged by time. Now a major antiques center, it boasts three auction houses and more than enough antiques shops and collectives for a full day's shopping. Yes, it's charming, but the real attraction is the bargains. Oh, how I love Lewes. I've surely found the Loehmann's of English antiques.

The rents must be much lower here, as I continue to find prices too good to be true and find more to buy than I can possibly haul home. Note that I buy smalls, which is mostly what you'll find in Lewes. There's also furniture, but it's neither high-end nor museum-quality. Most of it is not really old; you'll find junk in the mix as well. I found some tables and chests dating back to the late 1800s, but there's a lot of early-20th-century stuff. If you're looking for "important" furniture, skip Lewes and head to Petworth (see below).

Trains run from London's Victoria Station to Lewes every half-hour; travel time is 1 hour and 8 minutes. As you exit the train station in Lewes, walk up the hill on Station Street. (Don't worry, this is your cardio for the day; the rest is all downhill.)

Your first stop will be **Church Hill Antiques,** 6 Station St., © 1273/474-842, on the right. This collective has more than 60 dealers and features an excellent selection of Staffordshire—I found beautiful pairs of dogs in excellent condition for under $450, many less than $200, and yes, that's *dollars!* You'll see lots of porcelain, blue-and-white pottery, paintings, tabletop, and some furniture. If I had been filling a container on my last trip, I would have bought a bamboo-and-lacquer desk for $900 that would easily have sold in the U.S. for more than $3,000.

Leaving Church Hill, turn right and continue up the hill to High Street. If you're out of cash already, there's an ATM about a half-block to your left, along with the post office. Turn right on High Street and begin walking downhill, past the War Memorial.

The **Lewes Flea Market,** © **127/348-0328,** is a large collective, just off High Street on Market Street. On my last visit, I saw a pair of Windsor twin beds for £25 ($50) each, as well as an 18th-century landscape oil painting in its original gold leaf frame, signed by an unknown artist, for £45 ($90). There was a bamboo letter rack for £8 ($16) on a bargain table at the entrance. As with most dealers, you'll get a 10% discount if you ask politely.

Robson's, 22A High St., © **1273/480-654,** is a good spot for lunch. The menu features sandwiches, jacket potatoes, and salads, and you can sit in front of a big bay window and gaze out at a perfect English garden.

Refueled and rested, you should continue down High Street through the pedestrian mall and over the bridge. You're now on Cliffe High Street, where you'll want to browse the **Lewes Antiques Centre,** 20 Cliffe High St. (© **1273/476-148**). I saw lots of bamboo here, including a set of nesting tables for £25 ($50) and a corner display unit for £35 ($70).

Across the street is **Fur Feathers 'n' Fins,** © **1273/473-970,** 41 Cliffe High St., a one-stop pet shop, dog grooming, and antiques store. What a kick! There's lots of kitchen and garden stuff in the basement here.

The **Emporium Antiques Centre,** 42 Cliffe High St., © **1273/486-866,** is also on this end of town.

By now you're probably exhausted, so backtrack to the bridge and take a left on Railway Lane, cut diagonally through the car park, and wind your way back to the train station, which you'll see ahead on the left. There are a couple of places to buy snacks on Cliffe High Street, including a **Marks & Spencer** food hall.

Sunday in the Car Park with George

I've already told you about the Lanes in Brighton and why you should go to Lewes to buy antiques instead; what I didn't mention is that both towns have Sunday car-boot sales and flea markets and, yes, you can do both on the same day.

The **Lewes Car Boot Sale** is held from 6am to 2pm every Sunday year-round in the lot opposite the bus station (behind Waitrose). This is about a 10-minute walk from the train station. There's lots of junk for sale but there are also treasures. It's here that the shop owners come to buy stock, so if you can catch an early train (snooze en route), you can claim the booty and cut out the middleman.

When you've loaded your wheelie tote in Lewes, head back to the station and take the next train to Brighton. It's a 15-minute ride, trains come every 15 to 20 minutes, and it will set you back £3.15 ($6.30).

Brighton's eclectic boot sale and flea market is held in the car park of the train station—how convenient is that? There's bric-a-brac along with antiques and treasures; mingled with broken CD players and odd shoes, you can find ornate gilt mirrors, chandeliers, and Asian statues. Official hours are 9am to 2pm, but insiders report that the dealers start arriving around 5am.

Trains to Lewes and Brighton run every half-hour from London's Victoria Station. www.nationalrail.co.uk.

HUNGERFORD

—*Sarah Lahey*

I think of Hungerford as "Antiques 101." It makes a great day trip for beginners: You can browse the shops, have lunch in a fabulous old inn, and be back in London in time for tea. Yet there's lots to buy.

The goods are of better quality than in Lewes, with decent variety. It's never crowded, either; in fact, I always visit on a weekday and I'm often the only client in the shop.

Much smaller than Lewes, Hungerford has boasted art and antiques shops for centuries. Today, there are two antiques centers, general antiques shops, and several specialists. Although Hungerford's street plan was laid out in the 12th century with winding lanes, the majority of the shops are on two main roads, Charnham Street and Bridge Street/High Street.

Trains run from London's Victoria Station to Hungerford every half-hour; travel time is 1 hour and 8 minutes. Once in Hungerford, follow the redbrick pathway from the station; after about a block or so, you'll come to High Street.

Turn left and you'll be at **Roger King Antiques**, 111 High St. (☎ **1488/682-256;** www.kingantiques.co.uk). Be sure to say hello to Coco, the resident chocolate Lab, as you enter the shop. Roger has one of the oldest established dealerships in town with some of the fanciest stuff—and, of course, the highest prices. You'll find mostly 19th-century furniture, with lots of tables, chair sets, and chests of drawers. There are a few smalls, but furniture is why you visit this shop.

Just up the street to the left is **Below Stairs of Hungerford,** 103 High St. (☎ **1488/682-317;** www.belowstairs.co.uk), a shop with multiple showrooms and courtyard displays of 19th- and early-20th-century antique lighting, hardware and fittings, ironworks, and furniture. You'll also find kitchen antiques and garden items, most of which won't fit in the overhead. Still, there's plenty of unique stuff to bring home, such as loo pulls for £50 ($100) and up, doorknobs, cabinet pulls, and unusual lighting fixtures. If you're offended by taxidermy, don't look up.

Cross High Street here and walk down to the **Hungerford Arcade,** 26 High St. (☎ **1488/683-701**), where you'll find 80 stalls and over 6,000 square feet of antiques. Many of the kiosks are behind locked glass, but the staff will be happy to take out as many items as you'd like to see. I bought a fabulous crystal-and-silver sugar shaker here for about half of what I'd pay at the London Silver Vaults. And there was a good selection of copper lusterware pitchers and mugs priced from £20 ($40) on up; these sell for over £100 ($200) in the hoity-toity shops in San Francisco.

Leaving the arcade, turn left and head down the hill and over the bridge to two specialty dealers: **MJM Antiques,** 13 Bridge St. (© 1488/684-905; www.oldguns.co.uk), and **Styles Silver,** 12 Bridge St. (© 1488/683-922; www.styles-silver.co.uk). Mike Mancy, of MJM, has the shop of my husband's dreams: guns and swords. I did see a small ladies' piece with an ivory butt, but most of his stuff is for the guys—dueling sets, pistols, and more. His wares are sold solely as collectors' items and are not warranted for shooting. Next door is Styles, one of very few shops outside London specializing in silver. This family-run business has great gift items for weddings and christenings, including a nice assortment of frames and napkin rings. You can also order online. I think the prices are high, but the selection is very good.

Across the street are two very fancy and pricey furniture shops, **Turpin's Antiques,** 17 Bridge St. (© 1488/681-886), and the **Old Malthouse,** 15 Bridge St. (© 1488/682-209). Both sell 18th- and 19th-century furniture. If you like the more formal walnut pieces as opposed to country oak, check out these shops.

Continue on down Bridge Street and you'll come to a T junction at Charnham Street. My favorite collective is just around the corner to the right: **Great Grooms Antique Centre,** Riverside House, 1 Charnham St. (© 1488/682-314; www.great grooms.co.uk). This beautiful Georgian three-story building is packed with antiques from 50 dealers. All are displayed in room settings—you'll probably want to move in. I've bought wooden tea caddies here for about £100 ($200), and last time, I saw an incredible George III knife box for £500 ($1,000). Wish I'd bought it, as I saw a similar one at Jackson Square in San Francisco for $3,800. You'll want to check your bags as you enter; space here is tight.

For lunch, take a left out of Great Grooms, cross Bridge Street, and walk right into **The Bear**, 41 Charnham St., a three-star hotel and pub built back in 1464 and once owned by Henry VIII. You can sit at an antique table by an open fire in the restaurant. Order at the bar; they will bring your food to you. If you need a potty break, go into the hotel and up the stairs.

PETWORTH

....

—Sarah Lahey

If Hungerford is a beginner's seminar, you'll receive AP and honors credit for shopping Petworth, which was voted the "Best Antiques Town in the U.K." at the British Antiques and Collectibles Awards.

Petworth is a beautiful medieval town filled with good buys. It's also quite small. You can walk around in 20 minutes, yet it's home to nearly 40 antiques shops and centers. Of the towns I visit, Petworth has the highest-quality goods with the best all-around selection.

Most shops specialize in 18th- and 19th-century furniture, which makes for competitive pricing. But, yes, there's still plenty to buy that will fit in your suitcase. The prices are lower here than in the Cotswolds and its one-stop shopping.

At first, I was hesitant to go to Petworth by train, as its station was turned into a country inn years ago and I feared a difficult journey. Not so. I now shop Petworth all the time.

Take the train from London's Victoria Station to Pulborough; travel time is 1 hour and 8 minutes. After a scenic ride through the West Sussex countryside, you'll arrive at the Pulborough station, where you can grab a taxi to Petworth, about a 10-minute ride away. **Silverline (© 1798/874-321)** has a taxi office in the train station; it's a good idea to call ahead and reserve before leaving London, as this guarantees a waiting cab. I used to arrange for my taxi driver to pick me up in

Petworth for the return trip, but now I take the no. 1 bus from Market Square, which goes straight to the Pulborough station. *Tip:* Don't try to book a return taxi between the hours of 2 and 4pm, as all the drivers will be taking children home from country schools.

Upon arrival in town, ask the driver to drop you off in Market Square, which is the center of Petworth. All of the shops and collectives are an easy walk, circling the square on small side streets and lanes. Maps and antiques guides are available in all stores, so pick one up as you begin exploring.

My first stop is always **Richard Gardner Antiques,** right on Market Square (© **1798/343-411;** www.richardgardner antiques.co.uk). When you enter his shop, you'll think you're in a museum and wonder why I've sent you to such a pricey store. The answer? Because it's no doubt the best display of English antiques I've seen anywhere, anytime. These are "important" pieces, including artwork, furniture, and accessories. I'm still dreaming about the silver-and-tortoise music box in the shape of a *coble* (small boat). Richard will welcome you, answer your questions, and encourage you to browse. His prices are very high; but the goods are top-notch, and he's won awards for best dealer in the U.K.

You've now done the museum bit and it's time to get serious about bargains. There are lots of great deals out there, especially on furniture.

Petworth Antique Centre & Market, on East Street (© **1798/343-178;** www.petworthantiquecentre.co.uk), has more than 30 dealers, each with its own specialty. You'll see a lot of kitchen, tabletop, and decorative items, as well as furniture. There's also lots of copper ware for kitchen and fireplace. This is not a high-end collective.

At **Lantiques,** on Middle Street (© **1798/344-020;** www. lantiques.com), you'll find country French farm tables, garden and kitchen accessories, and the like, most with the shabbychic distressed look.

As the oldest shop in town, **Tudor Rose** (© **1798/343-621;** www.tudor-rose-antiques.co.uk) is an antique all on its own—

not to mention the ever-changing goodies that are displayed inside. This antiques center was built in the 16th century and today houses more than a dozen dealers over two floors. They also have one of the best websites—it's updated daily so you can check out the great buys before you visit.

For lunch, try the **Bay Tree Bakery,** in Golden Square (© **1798/342-260**). Along with fabulous sweets, it serves sandwiches, pasties, and soup. This is also a good spot for a latte or ice-cream break.

Size Conversion Chart

....

Women's Clothing

American	8	10	12	14	16	18
Continental	38	40	42	44	46	48
British	10	12	14	16	18	20

Women's Shoes

American	5	6	7	8	9	10
Continental	36	37	38	39	40	41
British	4	5	6	7	8	9

Children's Clothing

American	3	4	5	6	6X
Continental	98	104	110	116	122
British	18	20	22	24	26

Children's Shoes

American	8	9	10	11	12	13	1	2	3
Continental	24	25	27	28	29	30	32	33	34
British	7	8	9	10	11	12	13	1	2

Men's Suits

American	34	36	38	40	42	44	46	48
Continental	44	46	48	50	52	54	56	58
British	34	36	38	40	42	44	46	48

Men's Shirts

American	$14\frac{1}{2}$	15	$15\frac{1}{2}$	16	$16\frac{1}{2}$	17	$17\frac{1}{2}$	18
Continental	37	38	39	41	42	43	44	45
British	$14\frac{1}{2}$	15	$15\frac{1}{2}$	16	$16\frac{1}{2}$	17	$17\frac{1}{2}$	18

Men's Shoes

American	7	8	9	10	11	12	13
Continental	$39\frac{1}{2}$	41	42	43	$44\frac{1}{2}$	46	47
British	6	7	8	9	10	11	12

INDEX

Explore over 3,500 destinations.

TOKYO — 7766 miles
LONDON — 3818 miles
TORONTO — 4682 miles
SYDNEY — 5087 miles
NEW YORK — 4947 miles
LOS ANGELES — 2556 miles
HONG KONG — 5638 miles

Frommers.com makes it easy.

Find a destination. ✓ Book a trip. ✓ Get hot travel deals.
Buy a guidebook. ✓ Enter to win vacations. ✓ Listen to podcasts.
Check out the latest travel news. ✓ Share trip photos and memories.
And much more.

Frommers.com

FROMMER'S® COMPLETE TRAVEL GUIDES

FROMMER'S® DAY BY DAY GUIDES

PAULINE FROMMER'S GUIDES: SEE MORE. SPEND LESS.

FROMMER'S® PORTABLE GUIDES

Acapulco, Ixtapa & Zihuatanejo
Amsterdam
Aruba, Bonaire & Curacao
Australia's Great Barrier Reef
Bahamas
Big Island of Hawaii
Boston
California Wine Country
Cancún
Cayman Islands
Charleston
Chicago
Dominican Republic

Florence
Las Vegas
Las Vegas for Non-Gamblers
London
Maui
Nantucket & Martha's Vineyard
New Orleans
New York City
Paris
Portland
Puerto Rico
Puerto Vallarta, Manzanillo & Guadalajara

Rio de Janeiro
San Diego
San Francisco
Savannah
St. Martin, Sint Maarten, Anguila & St. Bart's
Turks & Caicos
Vancouver
Venice
Virgin Islands
Washington, D.C.
Whistler

FROMMER'S® CRUISE GUIDES

Alaska Cruises & Ports of Call

Cruises & Ports of Call

European Cruises & Ports of Call

FROMMER'S® NATIONAL PARK GUIDES

Algonquin Provincial Park
Banff & Jasper
Grand Canyon

National Parks of the American West
Rocky Mountain
Yellowstone & Grand Teton

Yosemite and Sequoia & Kings Canyon
Zion & Bryce Canyon

FROMMER'S® WITH KIDS GUIDES

Chicago
Hawaii
Las Vegas
London

National Parks
New York City
San Francisco

Toronto
Walt Disney World® & Orlando
Washington, D.C.

FROMMER'S® PHRASEFINDER DICTIONARY GUIDES

Chinese
French

German
Italian

Japanese
Spanish

SUZY GERSHMAN'S BORN TO SHOP GUIDES

France
Hong Kong, Shanghai & Beijing
Italy

London
New York
Paris

San Francisco
Where to Buy the Best of Everything.

FROMMER'S® BEST-LOVED DRIVING TOURS

Britain
California
France
Germany

Ireland
Italy
New England
Northern Italy

Scotland
Spain
Tuscany & Umbria

THE UNOFFICIAL GUIDES®

Adventure Travel in Alaska
Beyond Disney
California with Kids
Central Italy
Chicago
Cruises
Disneyland®
England
Hawaii

Ireland
Las Vegas
London
Maui
Mexico's Best Beach Resorts
Mini Mickey
New Orleans
New York City
Paris

San Francisco
South Florida including Miami & the Keys
Walt Disney World®
Walt Disney World® for Grown-ups
Walt Disney World® with Kids
Washington, D.C.

SPECIAL-INTEREST TITLES

Athens Past & Present
Best Places to Raise Your Family
Cities Ranked & Rated
500 Places to Take Your Kids Before They Grow Up
Frommer's Best Day Trips from London
Frommer's Best RV & Tent Campgrounds in the U.S.A.

Frommer's Exploring America by RV
Frommer's NYC Free & Dirt Cheap
Frommer's Road Atlas Europe
Frommer's Road Atlas Ireland
Retirement Places Rated